C. W. Linen
Mrs. W. H. Denning
Jno. Be Veil

<hr>

Easter Monday, April
14, 1873.

E. B. Coolidge
E. J. Blount
B. N. Huntington

<hr>

Easter Monday, April
17, 1875.

Fanny Waterman

<hr>

Tuesday apl. 3. 1877

Mrs. P. W. Huntington
Mrs. F. W. Case
E. H. Dunn
Mrs. T. Comstock

<hr>

Easter Monday, 1888.

T. M. Lindsay
R. H. Platt
A. H. Smythe (see 1870)
W. H. Albery   Easter 1890
George Hardy
W. A. Walden
Mrs. W. H. Miller (by

<hr>

Easter

Fran

Elizabeth J. Newman

Amelia L. Ambos
Fanny P. Fullerton
Lucretia M. Phelps — by Bessie Smith
Ella White —
Mrs. Francis Collins.
Frank C. Hubbard by
Mrs. H. C. Hubbard.
Mrs. G. F. Wheeler
Annette S. Jones
Matie & Geo. Jones
Mrs. W. A. Henderson —
Mrs. Geo. U. Gleason.
Mrs. H. M. Hubbard
Mrs. Wm P Savage
Mrs. J. H. Harn
Mrs. M. B. Montfreny.

C. J. Hardy   } by
A. C. Cady   } Geo. Hardy
C. L. Crawford   } by proxy
H. P. Allen.

Mark M. Denig   } by W. O. Henderson
Frank J. Failing   } by Starling B. Wilcox
Anne M. Starling   } Wm. Hann.

18 June 2006

BE IT REMEMBERED

+ Barbara C. Harris

+ Jane Helms Dixon

+ Gevalyn Wolf

+ Marylleadelia G. McLeod

+ Laura Ynna Levien

+ Carolyn M. Callaghan

+ Catherine M. Waynick

+ Gayle Elizabeth Harris

+ Chilton R. Knudsen

Katharine Jefferts Schori

+ Carolyn T. Irish

+ Catherine S. Roskam

BE IT REMEMBERED

The Story *of*
Trinity Episcopal Church
on Capitol Square

Columbus, Ohio

Lisa M. Klein

by Lisa M. Klein

ORANGE FRAZER PRESS
Wilmington, Ohio

ISBN: 1-882203-26-7

Published by Trinity Episcopal Church in cooperation with Orange Frazer Press.

Additional copies of *Be It Remembered* may be ordered directly from:

Trinity Episcopal Church   or   Orange Frazer Press
125 East Broad Street   P.O. Box 214
Columbus, OH 43215   Wilmington, OH 45177
614.221.5351   1.800.852.9332
                                     www.orangefrazer.com

Designed by Danielle Chen
Printed in Canada

Library of Congress Cataloging-in-Publication Data

Klein, Lisa M., 1958-
    Be it remembered : the story of Trinity Episcopal Church on Capitol Square, Columbus, Ohio / by Lisa M. Klein.
        p. cm.
    Includes biliographical references.
    ISBN 1-882203-26-7
    1. Trinity Episcopal Church (Columbus, Ohio)--History. 2. Ohio--Columbus--Church history. I. Title.

    BX5980.C6769k54 2003
    283'.77157--dc22
                                                              2003057972

Front cover: The choir poses with the choirmaster and rector on the steps of Trinity in 1889. (By permission of the Ohio Historical Society)

Back cover: The front entrance to Trinity Episcopal Church

Endsheets: A record of membership signatures from the annual meetings.

FOREWORD by the Rector

You hold in your hands a labor of love. The project Lisa Klein presents began in the exuberant hours of memory—at a dinner where women and men reflected on the ways Trinity Episcopal Church nourished them for ordained ministry and professions as religious educators in the years following World War II. In some respects, the story of this old parish church—one of America's first beyond the mountains that defined the Middle West from the East, and the only one set from its beginnings until today on Ohio's Capitol Square—is not so unique. Trust in God and a collective purpose of redemption, hope and compassion in the city describe many congregations across our nation. You now hold a specific portrait of *one* congregation in *one* capital and university city as it has reflected Christian life in America for nearly 200 years.

But as you read this story, I hope you will feel the thrill of something reminiscent of a courtship. I pray the drama of human affections, selfless service, renewed faith and imaginative leadership for the common good will catch you, and you will fall in love with the house of prayer for all people at the corner of Third and Broad.

A generation ago, acclaimed poet and Ohio native James Wright (a graduate of Kenyon College, an Episcopalian institution founded, as was Trinity, by Bishop Philander Chase) wrote these lines on the transforming power of love:

> And lovers, flicking on the lights, turn to behold each lovely other.
> Let them remember fair delights.

Now you, through this history, "turn to behold" a rich tale of faithful people in a growing, changing metropolitan community. And as you fall more deeply in love with Trinity, remembering her "fair delights" and assaying her hurts and struggles through the years, may you be enlightened "to behold each lovely other" through this work.

The people of Trinity Church, Capitol Square can be most grateful to fellow parishioner Lisa Klein for the end product of her thorough and insightful exploration into Trinity's history. I believe this book will be rewarding to many in our parish community and the city of Columbus thanks to Lisa's discerning labors and beauty of expression. Many others in the life of Trinity Church and in the city have aided in the presentation of this book, and I join Lisa in thanking them.

To God be all praise and glory.

Richard A. Burnett, Rector
Easter 2003

Acknowledgements

"Be it remembered" begins the founding document of Trinity Episcopal Church, enjoining us to perpetual acts of remembrance. This history would not be complete without a record of the many people who have contributed to the work.

The Reverend Richard Burnett lent his intellectual and pastoral gifts to the project, and his support has been unstinting. Dick joins me in thanking parishioners Julia Johnson, Bill Dargusch, Julie Newhall Morrow, Richard H. Oman, and Bill Davidson, who served as a team responsible for bringing this book to publication. I am especially grateful to Bill Dargusch for his invitation to write this book and to Julie Newhall Morrow for her editorial skills. The wardens and vestry of Trinity, especially Brad Sturm, deserve special mention for their willingness to fund the research for this project. Bill Form and Joan Huber conducted the parish survey in 2000, analyzed the results, and mentored this amateur sociologist. John Stoddard, former parish historian, demonstrated careful stewardship of Trinity's archives. Stuart Hobbs generously read an early draft of the manuscript and Peter Williams did so twice; his faith in the work has been a source of great encouragement.

The Ohio Humanities Council supported the early stages of research, including a 2001 conference on writing congregational history, and the Historical Society of the Episcopal Church provided funds for photographs. Their support is greatly appreciated.

For assistance with research and photographs, I thank staff members of the Ohio Historical Society Research Division, the Columbus Metropolitan Library, the Archives of the Diocese of Ohio, and the Grandview Heights Public Library; Georgeann Reuter of the Kelton House Museum and Garden; and Andy Murphy and Jim Hunter of the Columbus *Dispatch*. I am grateful to Doug Rose for his pictures of the church interior, and I thank Thomas Brunk, David Platt, Robert Griffith, Ann Chauncey, Sally Larrimer, Betsey Kausch and others who loaned or located scarce photographs. The patient Robert Groh of Slide Services International scanned most of the images in this book. Marcy Hawley and the staff of Orange Frazer Press deserve praise for their professionalism and fine taste in designing a book I hope many will treasure and enjoy. For all the effort and care put into this book by many hands and minds, in the end, I take responsibility for any errors that remain in it.

I reserve special regard and deep gratitude for all those who shared their stories with me in interviews, phone conversations, and correspondence. They are Eloise Allison, Clara Anderson, Jim Bills, Jim Bliek, Bill Brettmann, Richard Burnett, Jack Chester, Bill Dargusch, Bill Davidson, John Deinhardt, Lori Dhiraprasiddhi, Kitty

Morton Epler, Sherm Everett, Bill Form, Anne Gast, Joel Gibson, Doris Graham, Bob Hansel, Wilbur Held, John M. Hines, Joan Huber, Margaret Kay, Sally Larrimer, Claudia Lauer, Elizabeth Lilly, Polly Lindemann, Jim Miner, Rocky and Molly Morris, Betty Nichols, Dick and Jane Oman, Janetta Orris, Bill Osborne, Gordon Price, Ellen Rose, Donn and Bobbie Schneider, Jerry Sellman, Marilyn Sesler, Rufus and Peggy Short, John and Barbara Stoddard, Peter Strimer, Joan and Fred Taylor, Walter Taylor, Betty Varney, and Kevin Wines. Their diverse experiences and insights have enriched this book and its author immeasurably.

During this journey, my family has sustained me in ways beyond words. Thanks to my husband, Robert Reed, and my sons, David and Adam, for reminding me daily of God's blessings.

This book is dedicated to the congregation of Trinity Episcopal Church, which is one in faith with its founders in the past and its descendents in the future.

Lisa M. Klein
May 2003

Hymn 609

Where cross the crowded ways of life,
Where sound the cries of race and clan,
Above the noise of selfish strife,
We hear thy voice, O Son of Man.

O Master, from the mountain side,
Make haste to heal these hearts of pain;
Among these restless throngs abide,
O tread the city's streets again;

Till all the world shall learn thy love,
And follow where thy feet have trod;
Till glorious from thy heaven above,
Shall come the city of our God.

Words: Frank Mason North (1850–1935)
The Hymnal 1982 c. Church Pension Fund
Used by permission

In Gratitude

The publication of this history was supported by friends and
members of Trinity Episcopal Church, who are hereby
gratefully acknowledged:

Eloise M. Allison

The Rev. Richard & Katharine Burnett

Chester Family Fund

William D. & Maureen M. Dargusch

William R. & Anne E. Davidson

John B. Deinhardt

Harold T. & Phyllis T. Duryee

James L. & Ida L. C. Ginter

Fordham & Susanne Huffman

Julia F. Johnson

William Form & Joan Huber

Richard F. & Wendy L. Hillis

Robert H. & Anne K. Jeffrey

J. Jeffrey McNealey

S. Noel & Anne H. Melvin

Frank R. & Molly R. Morris

Richard H. & Jane W. Oman

Bradley E. & Kay A. Sturm

Fred & Joan Taylor

Table *of* Contents

Trinity Episcopal Church in its late 20th-century urban environment

INTRODUCTION

by Lisa M. Klein

A photograph of the downtown Columbus skyline no longer shows Trinity Episcopal Church, which was the tallest building in the residential neighborhood where it was built in 1869. But it is there, a historic landmark at the corner of Third and Broad Streets, nestled now among high-rise banks. Trinity has been a presence on Capitol Square since 1833, when the congregation built a pillared Greek Revival church at the corner of Broad Street and Pearl Alley, a few steps from the very center of the new city.

The present Trinity Church predates the city's first skyscraper, the eleven-story Wyandotte Building that faces the Palace Theatre. The church is older than the venerable Great Southern Theatre and the former post office at Third and State Streets, now law offices. Many historic city buildings, among them the bustling central market and city hall, have gone the way of the wrecking ball, but Trinity still stands. The railroad depot where Trinity's first mission was established is now the site of a convention center. But Trinity Church endures. The sounds of horses' hoofbeats, iron cartwheels on brick, clanking streetcars, and klaxon car horns are heard no more, but Trinity's chimes ring out over the modern downtown din with the same tones as in 1911.

Even older than its historic building is the congregation that first gathered in 1817. It had already seen three generations when the present church was opened for worship after the Civil War. Although most of those who ever worshipped at Trinity are long dead, their names remain in yellowed record books, on memorial windows and plaques throughout the church, and on stones and monuments dotting Greenlawn Cemetery. Despite the fact of individual death, the congregation is continuous and alive, for the Holy Spirit calls Trinity to be forever new and eternally faithful to her unfolding mission at the corner of Third and Broad Streets.

Trinity's central location has been a defining feature of its history, shaping the character and experience of the congregation, its worship and its public works. While the church's external appearance has altered little, its urban context has changed dramatically. At first, stately homes were Trinity's neighbors. Today, steel and glass icons of the secular world tower over its sandstone walls. From its crenelated tower housing the chimes to its smooth marble altar, the building embodies traditions and beliefs that many consider irrelevant in a post-Christian age. But the church's neo-Gothic design has shaped the congregation and its preference for traditional forms of worship.[1] People are still drawn to Trinity because of its location and its architecture, two constant features of the church in a changing environment.

The sight of the Ohio Statehouse has always greeted worshippers exiting Trinity into the world. But for most people who have made up Trinity's congregation, churchgoing has had little to do with politics. Those in the pulpit and in the pews have been active in struggles for social justice—fighting to end slavery and local poverty, advocating women's suffrage and civil rights. Merely by virtue of its presence on Capitol Square, Trinity is a reminder to secular powers of their deeper moral obligations to society.

As one of the oldest congregations in Columbus, Trinity's history is entwined with that of the changing city. Citizens prominent in government, business, and industry were founders and leaders of Trinity. The tenor of life in the growing capital shaped their experience as much as any theology. Conversely, they brought their Protestant values to bear upon business, politics, and charitable institutions in the city. Over time, the congregation grew more middle-class and Trinity became a metropolitan church, drawing members throughout the city. Trinity resisted the flight to the suburbs and, despite declines in membership, remained committed to its identity as a downtown church with a mission to its increasingly needy urban neighborhood.

Throughout its history, the congregation has been home to all sorts and conditions of men and women, from governors to grocers, state senators to street people, all saints and all sinners, all touched both by greed and by God. Thus Trinity fulfills the words from Isaiah imprinted above the church's red doors: "An house of prayer for all people."

The Congregation and Social Change

According to James P. Wind, "congregational behavior is one of the oldest and most enduring forms of human activity."[2] Even in today's predominantly secular society, people still gather to relate to the holy, express their collective world view, and act on their shared hopes and beliefs. Congregations are like earthen vessels, bearing the biblical heritage.[3] In congregations, individuals find their identity and place in a tradition. At the same time, they give form and life to tradition.[4]

A congregation is not a place set apart from the world, but participates in it, shaping people for public life.[5] Its history is an important thread in the larger tapestry

The congregation in the 1950s.

of social history; it is part of a story told beyond the church walls. Knowing its place in sacred tradition and in secular society can help a congregation better understand itself and live into its mission. Trinity's commitment to its urban neighborhood, for example, is rooted in the social gospel movement of the late nineteenth century and is the result of many conscious decisions to remain on the corner of Third and Broad Streets.

Throughout its changing history, Trinity has exemplified different models of congregational life. At first Trinity was literally a family, with most of its members linked by kinship or business ties. As the congregation grew, it came to be a pillar church that attracted elite citizens and demonstrated a sense of responsibility for the entire community.[6] Trinity retained this status for more then a century, counting political and civic leaders as members, organizing social services, hosting public lectures, and giving homeless people refuge in the church. With the rise of the nuclear family during the 1950s, Trinity embodied the "family" model with parish programs creating a loyal and close-knit congregation.

Today many are nostalgic for the preeminence Trinity enjoyed in the past. Now, Trinity no longer provides city wide leadership. It is primarily a house of worship offering rituals—Sunday worship, marriage, and baptism—that give meaning to people's lives. For many in the Sunday congregation, downtown is less significant as a defining area of mission than as the location of the beloved historical church in which they take pride.

The choir leads the procession on Easter Sunday, 2003.

Change is a key theme of all history, as is its companion, continuity. Change is constant, even in religious institutions that seek to preserve unchanging truth. A congregation is organic and ever changing, its members baptized and buried, welcomed and wished well as they depart. A history of Trinity's congregation explores the question: How do people of faith, who believe in eternal life and truth, structure their common life in the world bound by time, imperfection, and uncertainty?

The Issue of Authority

*L*eadership is a vital theme of Trinity's story, as it was in the development of the Episcopal Church in America. Most settlers in the American colonies were Puritans who were hostile to the Church of England. The Anglicans who settled in the American colonies were mostly wealthy landowners and members of the ruling class. A disproportionate number of America's founders were Anglicans: George Washington, Alexander Hamilton, James Madison, James Monroe, Patrick Henry, and more than two-thirds of the signers of the Declaration of Independence.

In the colonial Anglican church, parish vestries composed of aristocratic landowners were all-powerful. Priests and deacons were scarce, and civic leaders managed church affairs. There were no bishops in colonial America, for they were resented as agents of the Crown. The frontier was also ill suited to the dignified

Overlooked by Harold Broome, a new member signs the articles of association, a ritual of the annual meeting since Trinity's inception in 1817.

lifestyle of a bishop. More importantly, a candidate for ordination had to undertake a treacherous and expensive sea voyage to England and back. Not until 1786 did England's Parliament allow its bishops to consecrate American bishops without requiring the oath of loyalty. Thus, from the beginning, the Anglican church in America confronted issues of authority.

When the Protestant Episcopal Church in America formed following the Revolution, one issue was the role of bishops. Bishop Samuel Seabury of Connecticut held out for absolute episcopal authority and wanted to deny the laity any role in church government. Bishop William White of Pennsylvania denied that the episcopate was divinely ordained and sought to limit the power of bishops. A compromise was achieved, and the church's constitution provided for a House of Bishops and a House of Deputies with an equal number of clerical and lay delegates elected by the diocese. The new church reflected the republican ideals of the new nation. Each diocese makes its own constitution and laws, though it may not contravene those passed by General Convention. At the same time, changes in the constitutions or canons of the national church must be approved by the dioceses. Authority in the church is dispersed rather than centralized.[7]

The church's framers rejected a strictly hierarchical model of authority in favor of a delicate balance of power between bishops, clergy, and laity. At Trinity leadership has been shared, not always equally, between clergy and laypeople. For the pioneers who founded Trinity, local control was important, but a bishop was a practical asset for organizing and legitimizing churches. Over the course of the nineteenth century, the authority of priests and bishops increased, and the congregation of Trinity gradually came to accept the new order.[8] The tie between rector and congregation was seen as binding, like the mystical marriage of Christ and the church. Such perfection, however, was understandably difficult to come by, and the average Trinity rector spent seven years with the congregation before greener pastures beckoned.

While spiritual authority resided in the rector, matters of governance were the domain of influential vestrymen and wealthy members of the congregation. In the last fifty years, the lay movement has encouraged greater sharing of authority among ordained and lay Episcopalians. While there were always those who joined or left the congregation because of the minister or in response to conflict, the congregation survived because of the deeper bonds that tied members to Trinity: years of experience and common history, financial obligation, a sense of ownership, and shared faith.

Grassroots History and Congregational Memory

ost church histories take the great-men-and-their-deeds approach, featuring shepherds ably leading their flocks. A rector is, of course, a necessary and vital member of the congregation, for what is a body without a head? But conversely, what is a head without all the members of the body? A grassroots history focuses on the activities and attitudes of ordinary people, including women, who are often overlooked by traditional history.[9] The stories of people, both in the pulpit and in the pews, collectively make up the history of Trinity Episcopal Church. All who have habitually prayed in this house and worked toward its mission in the world are part of its history.

Traditional sources viewed with a fresh eye are the foundation of congregational history. Minutes of vestry meetings not only convey dry business, but also disclose moments of unexpected drama in the accounts of communal decision-making. Journals of the annual diocesan conventions indicate how issues in national church life played out at the local level. Parish statistics enable one to trace growth and decline in membership.[10] Baptism, confirmation, marriage, and death records show how a congregation once closely tied by kinship grew into a metropolitan church whose members had many ties beyond the church. Census records combined with parish records yield important demographic evidence about the congregation.[11] Collections of papers, letters, and journals in the Ohio Historical Society enable one to reconstruct the world in which members of the congregation lived, worked, and prayed in the nineteenth century.

So often the lines of Trinity's story depend upon what material has survived. A batch of letters makes it possible to tell how Trinity ousted a high-church rector in 1842 and in 1889 called a minister who persuaded the congregation to make sweeping changes. Newsletters convey a vital sense of parish life, but these were not consistently published or preserved. Vestry minutes are missing for several years. Lists of members are rare before the days of annual directories. The archives contain few records of parish organizations and regrettably fewer copies of sermons preached to the congregation. Photographs are abundant for some years and nonexistent for others. Reconstructing the past with only piecemeal evidence is like trying to imagine a completed jigsaw puzzle when dozens of pieces are missing.

Researching the twentieth century offers new opportunities and challenges. Scrapbooks of newspaper clippings show the church's public face. Interviews with members of the congregation disclose a more personal side, and the two images do not always coincide. Oral evidence, while precious, is not infallible, for individual

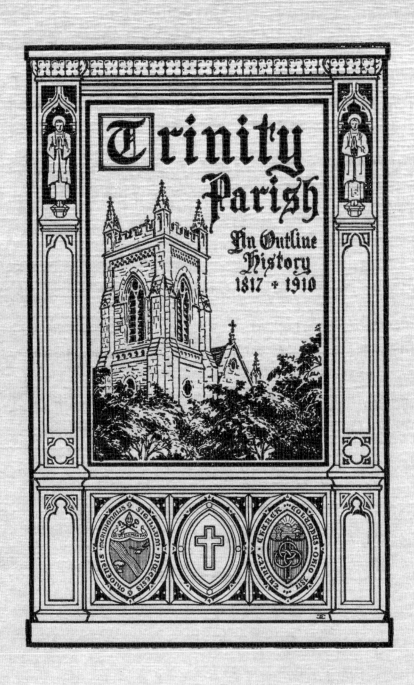

Trinity Parish

An Outline History
1817 ✦ 1910

memory colors events by reflecting upon them. The challenge is to compose a story that is faithful to the experience of individuals, yet representative of the congregation's life as a whole. It should not ignore conflict in the interests of promoting progress, growth, and godliness—traditional themes of church histories. In the end, however, history can never be objective, complete, or definitive. Writing history is an act of interpretation, not a claim to absolute truth.

What is true, however, for individuals, churches, and nations is that memory is crucial to identity. Without memory, a person would not know her name, recognize a tree or be able to eat. Likewise the church, in the words of William Palmer Ladd, "must have a memory. It cannot live, much less progress, except in the light of history…Only Christian history can give life to Christian faith."[12] Ladd voices the paradoxical truth of history—that understanding the past is what enables wise action in the present and vision for the future. As Henry Ford put it even more plainly, "The farther you look back, the farther you can see ahead."[13]

Trinity's founders realized the importance of memory when they first held "divine service" in May of 1817. The Rev. Philander Chase drafted a document (reprinted here on p. 2), that begins "Be it remembered," a command for those assembled to recall when and where they first met, and for what purpose: "to build up churches to the glory of God and the good of human souls."

Episcopal worship is an act of remembrance. In sharing the Eucharist, the congregation recalls and reenacts the meal Christ shared with his disciples and the subsequent sacrifice of Christ's own body and blood for the salvation of all. History is likewise an act of remembrance, albeit an incomplete and faulty one. A good parish history can extend and complement liturgical acts of remembrance by reminding the congregation that its faith is not reinvented with each new era but deeply rooted in the experiences of those who have, in common and over the ages, remembered Christ's sacrifice. A grassroots congregational history, then, tells human stories that complement the sacred story. It gives the faithful many solid shoulders to stand on, expanding their view of the past and their vision for the future.

This 1910 booklet contains photographs of Trinity's early rectors, bishops, laymen, and buildings.

A Note on Citations

In the interest of readability, endnotes have been kept to a minimum. Unless otherwise noted, accounts of parish business have been drawn from vestry minutes; in important cases, dates of meetings are given. After the 1950s most parish news is distilled from the newsletter, the Chimes, *and cited only when a quotation is used. Material from diocesan convention journals is referred to by year within the text, unless a quotation is used. The many local histories that cover people and events of the nineteenth century contain much overlapping material; only in unique cases are these works cited individually. Archival material and man-uscripts are cited for the benefit of readers interested in primary sources and their location. Newspaper articles are cited when the source and date are available; some who assem-bled scrapbooks did not date items. A list of interviewees is given in the acknowledgements. Other notes are used to credit specific individuals, scholars, or unique works.*

The index has been prepared with the general reader in mind. With few exceptions, material from the notes is not indexed.

Notes

1. My thinking about church buildings has been influenced by Peter Williams and his work, especially *Houses of God: Region, Religion & Architecture in the United States* (Urbana and Chicago: University of Illinois Press, 1997), xiv.

2. James P. Wind, *Places of Worship: Exploring Their History* (Walnut Creek, CA: AltaMira Press, 1997), 103. In chapter 8 (101-117), Wind makes a strong case for congregational history as an important adjunct to social history and the study of religion.

3. Wind, *Places of Worship*, preface; James P. Wind and James W. Lewis, *American Congregations, Vol II: New Perspectives in the Study of Congregations* (Chicago: University of Chicago Press, 1994), introduction, esp.6.

4. This paraphrases Dorothy C. Bass, "Congregations and the Bearing of Tradition," 169-91 in James P. Wind and James W. Lewis, eds., *American Congregations*, vol. 2 (Chicago: University of Chicago Press, 1994).

5. Martin Marty, "Public and Private: Congregation as Meeting Place," in Wind and Lewis, *American Congregations*, vol. ii, 162.

6. The description of a "pillar church" comes from Carl S. Dudley and Sally A. Johnson, "Congregational Self-Images for Social Ministry," 104-121 in Carl S. Dudley, Jackson W. Carroll, James P. Wind, eds., *Carriers of Faith: Lessons from Congregational Studies* (Louisville, KY: Westminster/John Knox Press, 1991), 112-13. In Penny Edgell Becker's terminology, this would be a "leader congregation." She also identifies "house of worship" and "family" models that apply to Trinity. See *Congregations in Conflict: Cultural Models of Local Religious Life* (Cambridge University Press, 1999).

7. On the establishment of the Church in America, see John E. Booty, *The Church in History* (New York: Seabury Press, 1979, 64-5; 71-3).

8. For a historical overview, see Jay P. Dolan, "Patterns of Leadership in the Congregation," Wind and Lewis, 225-256, esp. 231-239.

9. See David E. Kyvig and Myron A. Marty, *Nearby History: Exploring the Past Around You* (Nashville: American Association for State and Local History), 1982. An excellent collection of essays in *The Pursuit of Local History: Readings on Theory and Practice*, ed. Carol Kammen (Walnut Creek, CA: Altamira Press, 1996). Fine examples of congregational history that is richly situated as social history include Rima Lunin Schultz, *The Church and the City: A Social History of 150 Years at Saint James, Chicago* (Chicago: The Cathedral of Saint James, 1986) and Deborah Mathias Gough, *Christ Church, Philadelphia: The Nation's Church in a Changing City* (Philadelphia: University of Pennsylvania Press, 1995).

[10] The number of communicants reported to the diocese was the official determinant, but the actual size of the congregation (including children) might have been much larger. Before the 1970s, to be a communicant, one had to be a baptized and confirmed adult. In the nineteenth century, many adults did not undergo confirmation but still considered themselves members. See Gough's note, p. 204. Membership figures could be inaccurate due to poor record-keeping and the high mobility of families and individuals.

[11] United States Bureau of the Census publications and schedules (on microfilm) are available at the Ohio Historical Society, the State Library of Ohio, and the Columbus Metropolitan Library. As the congregation and Ohio's population grew, tracing members in census records becomes unwieldy and impractical. Moreover, census records after 1930 are sealed for 70 years.

[12] William Palmer Ladd, *Prayer Book Interleaves* (1942), p. 3.

[13] Cited by David E. Kyvig and Myron A. Marty, "Nearby History: Connecting Particulars and Universals," in Kammen, ed., *Pursuit of Local History*, p. 109.

This plaque on the north face of Trinity's exterior informs passers-by on Broad Street.

Chapter 1

FOUNDERS *of* TRINITY

It was 1817 in Ohio's new capital town of Columbus. Most of the area was a swamp. There was a spring where Spring Street would later run and an Indian burial site on what would become Mound Street. On the ten-acre public square, amidst amber waves of wheat and corn, stood a small Capitol building. Several hundred people lived in the vicinity of Capitol Square, compared to the few thousand in bustling Franklinton, across the Scioto River. Throughout Ohio, families were sleeping more securely, for fears of Indian raids had been mostly put to rest by the treaties ending the War of 1812. More people were coming to Columbus every day, drawn by new opportunities in business and government. They made their way along Broad and High Streets, mere rutted roads but expansive, as their names suggest, at 120 feet and 100 feet wide respectively.

The arrival of a missionary in frontier Columbus was a rare event. The news traveled only as fast as a man on horseback through backwoods and rough trails to the houses surrounding the square. In May of 1817, at least thirty men crowded into the High Street house of storekeeper Lincoln Goodale to see and hear the Rev. Philander Chase, the itinerant priest from the east. Among those who gathered at the house were Philo Olmstead, son of a Revolutionary War veteran who worked as a newspaperman; Matthew Matthews, the town's first postman; Orris Parish, one of its first lawyers; and Cyrus Fay, a merchant. John Kilbourne, kinsman of Worthington founder James Kilbourne was there, along with Abram McDowell, a captain in the Franklin Dragoons and a government clerk. Both Olmstead and McDowell would later serve Columbus as mayor. Many of the young men there were unmarried, but others surely brought their wives and children.

Monuments in Greenlawn Cemetery mark the burial sites of Trinity's founders and earliest parishioners.

Some of those who came were merely curious. Others believed that God's inerrant providence brought them to that spot. All listened with reverence as Chase intoned the service from the Book of Common Prayer and preached to them. Some had not been able to worship together since emigrating to Ohio. Chase, at six feet four inches, was an imposing presence, and no doubt persuasive. He had prepared a standard statement that thirty of the men present signed, bringing Trinity Episcopal Church into existence. This was their declaration:

We, the subscribers, deeply impressed with the truth and importance of the Christian religion, and earnestly desirous of promoting its holy influences in the hearts and lives of ourselves and our neighbors, do hereby associate ourselves together by the name, style, and title of the Parish of Trinity Church, in Columbus, State of Ohio, in communion with the Protestant Episcopal Church in the United States of America.

The men adopted a constitution and elected among themselves wardens and vestrymen. Chase then moved on, founding in the same month St. Peter's in Delaware and Christ Church in Cincinnati, where he made his appeal from the pulpit of the Presbyterian meeting house.[1] Upon his return, he became rector of Trinity and St. Peter's, as well

First page of vestry minutes showing the organization of Trinity Church in 1817. This is the copy of a prior document, whose location is unknown.

as St. John's, a circuit that was nearly fifty miles on horseback. He baptized Joel Buttles and his infant daughter, Evelina, and George Williams, his wife Rebecca, and their seven children in October of 1817. Williams served briefly on the vestry before the family, like many restless pioneers, resumed its journey. Chase, on the move from Worthington to Delaware to Columbus, did his work for the love of God alone, for he received no salary.

Trinity's congregation sprang up at an intersection that was significant both geographically and politically. To the north of Columbus, the Western Reserve area was largely settled by New England emigrants. To the south lived mostly those who had come across the Ohio river. According to one local historian, "the clash of southern Ohio Jeffersonianism and New England values was inevitable," and it continued as late as the Civil War.[2] This theme of conflict and compromise carried over into religion, as immigrants from the north and east, most with high church practices, and those with low church customs from the south converged in the area. The influence of Baptists and Methodists pressed up from the Appalachian region, making the churches, like the city, a point of convergence for differing peoples.

The founders and early families who joined Trinity made it a kind of melting pot for its time. Despite their shared Anglo-Saxon roots, their regional customs and economic means differed, sometimes greatly. Many came from Connecticut, including Philo Olmstead, Joel Buttles, and John Kilbourne. From Kentucky and Virginia arrived the southern Episcopalians and some Presbyterians who joined Trinity by marriage or conversion, most notably some members of William Neil's family.

Many of Trinity's founders were among the small town's prominent citizens, related by circumstance and often by marriage. Others were not so well-connected or prominent. Men of the gentry and laborers, educated lawyers and common men, all came together to form Trinity Episcopal Church. Though the former became the leaders, the latter were not excluded from fellowship. A kind of bond must have united them: the experience of emigration, whether west from Connecticut or north from Kentucky, the struggle to forge a living on the frontier, fears of Indian raids, the desire to create new towns and churches like those they had left.

A missionary priest like Chase was an important catalyst and leader, but it was laymen, ordinary citizens of a still-young democracy, who formed vestries, conducted worship services, and supported the fledgling parish. Their wives formed prayer groups, taught Sunday school, sewed clothing for the poor, and raised devout children. These men and women, drawn together by social need and spiritual desires, shaped the early history of Trinity Episcopal Church.

The Reverend
Philander Chase
(1775–1852),
first rector of
Trinity from
1817–1819.
Later elected
bishop of Ohio,
Chase founded
Trinity and
several other
Ohio parishes as
well as Kenyon
College in
Gambier, Ohio.

Philander Chase

The Rev. Philander Chase was a man of almost limitless energy, strong-willed and irascible and confident of his mission, even under unimaginable adversity. His authoritarian nature made him an able bishop, but it was also the source of many conflicts with lay leaders and other clergymen.

Chase was born in 1775, the fifteenth child of Dudley and Alice Chase. His father and grandfather were deacons in the Congregational Church. While he was attending Dartmouth, young Chase found a Book of Common Prayer, a rare book in those days. The book was instrumental to his conversion and his desire to enter the ministry. There was no Episcopal seminary in the United States at that time, but through persistence and self-study, he was ordained a priest in 1799. So persuasive was Chase's personality, it was said that he converted even his own parents to the Episcopal faith.[3]

Before coming to Ohio, Chase logged many miles as a missionary in New York, among the Oneida and Mohawk Indians, and in Louisiana. Enroute to New Orleans, he lost all of his possessions in a shipwreck. In New Orleans he organized the first Protestant church in Louisiana. After six years Chase returned to Connecticut as rector of Christ Church in Hartford. In 1817 Chase left this comfortable society for the Ohio frontier, where he felt called to be a missionary. There he encountered another missionary, Roger Searle, formerly of Plymouth, Connecticut, and they began plans to form an Episcopal diocese in Ohio.

That Chase ended up living in Worthington and founding Trinity was the result of the workings of divine providence and human machination. In Worthington the Rev. James Kilbourne was intent upon establishing the Episcopal Church in Ohio. Kilbourne was deacon of St. John's, the first Episcopal parish west of the Alleghenies. He was also the boss of Worthington: founder of the town, leader of the emigrants who settled there, merchant, mill builder, newspaper publisher, and congressman. When he heard of Searle's presence in Ohio, Kilbourne hired a man to ride 130 miles on horseback to bring him to Worthington. He then sent Searle to the General Convention in New York with instructions to plead for the organization of an Ohio diocese and for missionaries to counter the corruptions being planted by Methodist preachers.[4] Meanwhile Chase was also summoned to Worthington and invited to remain as rector.

A controversial figure, James Kilbourne (1770–1850), was deacon of St. John's in Worthington, the first Episcopal parish west of the Alleghenies. Many of Kilbourne's kin and associates settled in Columbus and founded Trinity.

Kilbourne rightly judged that Chase's presence would be a powerful impetus for the organization of the Episcopal Church in Ohio. The first convention of the diocese was held at Lincoln Goodale's house in January, 1818, with two clergymen in attendance (Chase and Searle) and nine lay delegates, including Trinity's Joel Buttles and Benjamin Gardiner. A second convention was held in Worthington that summer, and Chase was elected bishop.

Besides missionary zeal, personal matters may have affected Chase's decision to settle in Worthington. In 1796 Chase married the 16-year-old Mary Fay, whose family had emigrated to Ohio. Her brother Cyrus Fay lived in Worthington. Chase purchased five lots and a 150-acre farm in Worthington and brought Mary and their infant son Dudley to live there. He wrote to his son George, who was being schooled in Connecticut, "I have told your uncle Cyrus Fay that if he will take care of me till he gets into business, I will reward him." Apparently Chase depended for a time upon his brother-in-law's family. Perhaps it was Cyrus Fay who persuaded James Kilbourne to offer

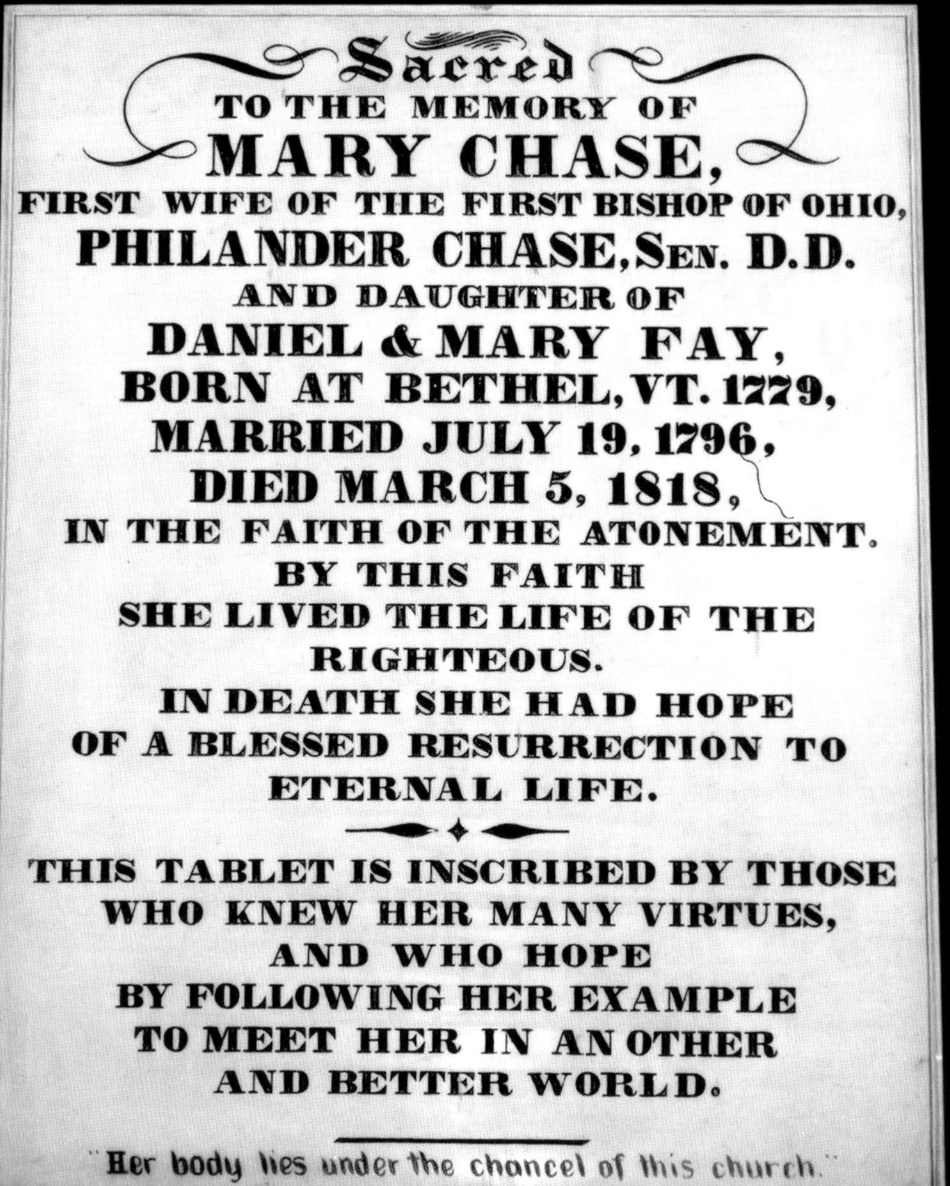

Sacred

TO THE MEMORY OF

MARY CHASE,

FIRST WIFE OF THE FIRST BISHOP OF OHIO,

PHILANDER CHASE, Sen. D.D.

AND DAUGHTER OF

DANIEL & MARY FAY,

BORN AT BETHEL, VT. 1779,

MARRIED JULY 19, 1796,

DIED MARCH 5, 1818,

IN THE FAITH OF THE ATONEMENT.
BY THIS FAITH
SHE LIVED THE LIFE OF THE
RIGHTEOUS.
IN DEATH SHE HAD HOPE
OF A BLESSED RESURRECTION TO
ETERNAL LIFE.

THIS TABLET IS INSCRIBED BY THOSE
WHO KNEW HER MANY VIRTUES,
AND WHO HOPE
BY FOLLOWING HER EXAMPLE
TO MEET HER IN AN OTHER
AND BETTER WORLD.

"Her body lies under the chancel of this church."

Tablet in St. John's Episcopal Church in Worthington,
commemorating Bishop Chase's first wife,
who is buried beneath the chancel.

the post of rector to Chase, not Searle. Fay may have brought together the group that met at Lincoln Goodale's house in May of 1817. Certainly the family connection between Philander Chase and the Fays was a vital circumstance in the establishment of Trinity.

Sadly Chase's wife Mary died barely a year after their arrival in Ohio. The story of her funeral, related by Whiting Griswold, gives some insight into Chase's character and firm faith. Though he was "almost inconsolable" with grief, Chase officiated at her burial, there being no other clergyman available.

> *When the sympathizing friends of the departed had collected at the house around the coffin he was in an adjoining room in great agony.... He walked with his friend to the corpse, wept for a moment and imprinting a last kiss upon the pale and life-less clay audibly bade it* "farewell for a little while." *The lid having been screwed upon the coffin he himself performed the services at the house; walked to the Church where he read the usual service and preached a funeral sermon. At the grave also he read the burial service and all this was done with his usual composure.... His voice never once failed while the whole congregation was in tears and the choir was so much affected that they several times faltered in singing....*[5]

Chase married a woman named Sophia May Ingraham after returning from his consecration in Philadelphia in 1819. Despite having a helpmeet, his punishing schedule only worsened and he did not thrive financially.

As bishop on the rugged Ohio frontier, Chase knew none of the comforts attending that exalted position, not even a salary. Besides farming, he took the job of principal of Worthington Academy to supplement his income. Nearly penniless in the winter of 1820-21, Chase was forced to discharge his hired man and to thresh grain, haul wood, feed livestock, and build fires himself, in addition to tending his three parishes and the diocese. He began to question whether God was punishing him for past errors.

One of Chase's greatest achievements was the founding of Kenyon College. Recognizing the need to educate young men for the ministry, Chase opened a seminary in Worthington with one pupil in 1824. His plans to build a permanent college, however, ensnared him in church politics. His opponents, eastern high churchmen, accused Chase of trying to install "primitive Methodists and Ranters" in Ohio pulpits. Attempting to raise money, Chase fumed in frustration, "If the Son of God had stayed in heaven till he was duly patronized, the world would have had no Saviour."[6] Finally, Chase found favor with Lord Gambier, Lord Kenyon, and other evangelical English churchmen, who donated rich sums to found Kenyon College, set in the wilderness near Gambier, Ohio.

Chase's triumph soon turned bitter. The faculty of Kenyon College cried out that he was a tyrant. At the 1831 convention Chase resigned the presidency of Kenyon and the office of bishop, though this move was not permitted by the canons. He retired to Michigan but emerged in 1835 to become Bishop of Illinois and founder of Jubilee College near Peoria. He was tireless in his work of preaching, teaching, and presiding until his death in 1852 from injuries sustained in a riding accident. He was 77.

Chase placed his stamp on the infant Episcopal Church in southern Ohio, giving it a foundation at once evangelical and traditional. At Trinity, the presence of this experienced, scholarly, and pious man compelled people to join the growing group of worshippers at Lincoln Goodale's. It is likely, however, that many in the congregation were relieved by his departure. Chase's Connecticut parishioners had found him sometimes more zealous than prudent. There was mutual bitterness by 1822 when Chase left St. John's, Worthington, and charges of tyranny caused him to resign from Kenyon. Even if his authoritarian manner was unpopular, his leadership would prove hard to equal.

Early Lay Leaders of Trinity: the Kilbourne Connection

Ordained Episcopal clergy were few and far between on the Ohio frontier. Once Chase became bishop, he was able to visit Trinity only three or four Sundays a year, when he performed baptisms and confirmations. Not until 1829 did Trinity have a resident rector. Lay readers led the congregation and the vestry met and conducted elections without a clergyman present. Even while Chase was rector and in the long interval between his departure and the arrival of a new rector, lay leaders sustained and directed the church.

When religious people tell their history, conventions of their faith guide them. Thus churches spring up like fig trees planted by a divine gardener, then spread like shoots on a vine. Often more mundane events and conflicts are excluded from the story. One factor that must be acknowledged in the founding of Trinity is the misconduct of James Kilbourne. In 1820 Kilbourne was brought before the diocese for trial, though the specific charges were not recorded. Based on the canonical grounds for trying a clergyman, however, Kilbourne's offenses would have had to include neglecting his clerical duties, immoral conduct (perhaps related to questionable business practices), or disregarding church doctrine and liturgical practices. This last error would have been intolerable to Bishop Chase as it would threaten the integrity and purity of the church.[7] Kilbourne's conduct had caused many in his congregation to become dissatisfied and leave the church. Some even became Methodists.

Ultimately Kilbourne was not brought to trial. Because he was a man of great influence and known to be "possessed of a revengeful disposition," it was feared that a trial would injure the infant church.[8] Instead Kilbourne was persuaded to give up his license as deacon. He also had to listen as Bishop Chase preached a stern sermon at the 1821 convention, condemning ignorant and unholy ministers. His relationship with St. John's irreparably broken, he departed complaining of "viper-like hissing of envy and toad-like croakings of malice and atheism."[9]

James Kilbourne's troubles with his Worthington congregation affected the early growth of Trinity. Many residents were abandoning Worthington for opportunities in the new state capital, Columbus. Joel Buttles, Cyrus Fay, Matthew Matthews, and Demas Adams, all sons-in-law of James Kilbourne, settled in Columbus and signed Trinity's articles of association. John Kilbourne, his kinsman and publisher of the popular *Ohio Gazetteer,* joined Trinity, as did Alfred Upson, James Kilbourne's hired man. Austin Goodrich, member of a Worthington family that had fallen on hard times, signed the articles. Possibly these men sought a livelihood in Columbus and organized as Trinity Church in part to escape Kilbourne's control over their lives and what they perceived as his immoral behavior or heterodox beliefs.

Still James Kilbourne remained central to the kinship networks of Trinity's early members. Matthew Matthews, a founder of Trinity who became an important lay leader of the congregation, was a merchant who dealt with James Kilbourne and married his daughter Lucy in 1813. When Kilbourne was elected to Congress, he secured his son-in-law's appointment as postmaster. After a year Matthews resigned the position to become manager of Worthington Manufacturing Company, a James Kilbourne conglomerate. When Kilbourne's business collapsed around 1819, Matthews moved to Columbus and went into business with Joel Buttles. Joel Buttles married Lauretta Barnes, the daughter of Cynthia Goodale Barnes, sister of Lincoln Goodale and then wife of James Kilbourne. Hence Joel Buttles was related by marriage to both Goodale and Kilbourne and in a position to benefit greatly from the association. He was step-brother-in-law to Matthew Matthews, and when Matthews resigned the office of postmaster, Buttles appealed to Kilbourne, his step-father-in-law, and was granted the position.[10]

The growing numbers of Episcopalian laymen who settled in Columbus created the opportunity for mission and the need for a church. Given Kilbourne's unpopularity, they turned to Cyrus Fay's brother-in-law, Philander Chase, to organize them. The men who assembled at Lincoln Goodale's home and signed the instru-

Who was this man, Lincoln Goodale, who lent his home for meetings of the fledgling congregation of Trinity? Goodale's life epitomized the excitement and danger of frontier Ohio. In 1792, when he was ten, Goodale's father, a former officer in the Revolutionary War, mysteriously disappeared, apparently a victim of Indians. His brother, Nathan, was also taken captive by Indians. Goodale studied medicine and when he moved to Franklinton at the age of 23 he opened the first pharmacy. As the keeper of a general store, he dealt with Indians, settlers, and traders, taking furs, skins, venison, maple sugar, baskets, and cranberries in exchange for powder and lead, tobacco, knives, cloth, and whisky. Goodale was one of the first volunteers in the War of 1812, after which he returned to Columbus and continued to prosper.

Goodale never formally joined Trinity church, but he was a pew holder, befitting his own status in the community and the growing respectability of Trinity Church. He also supported First Presbyterian Church and was noted for his general benevolence. In 1851 he dedicated 40 acres of virgin beech, maple, and oak to the city. Today that land is still known as Goodale Park. During the Civil War, Goodale Park became Camp Jackson, and the woods resounded with shots and shouts of men drilling for war. Goodale protested this use of his parkland, and the camp was moved west and renamed Camp Chase.[11] An anti-slavery activist, Goodale helped to purchase the freedom of a family of 48 slaves and return them on a ship to Liberia. He was also instrumental in freeing a black man named Mitchell from prison. For more than 20 years, he employed a colored man named Joseph Harris, whom he considered a part of his own family and who was respected by many in the community.

In 1864, when Goodale was nearly 82, he received a Christmas letter from the Rev. Julius Grammar, former rector of Trinity, who wrote: "I often think of my pleasant visits to your home and your warm hospitality....You have lived long among them, helped the city by your business enterprises and public charities and I am sure it is the wish of all that know you in the church, and in the state that your life may be spared many years…"[12] Almost a half-century after hosting the congregation of Trinity, Lincoln Goodale was still a friend of Trinity, and his home was still a center of hospitality for its leaders.

Lincoln Goodale
(1782–1868)

ment that brought Trinity Church into being were already a kind of clan. Their families depended on each other as neighbors scratching out a living on the frontier. They intermarried and formed business partnerships, combining their talents and energies and prospering together. Their relationships and commitments would be intensified, complicated, and tested by this new partnership as an Episcopal congregation.

The Deceptions of Benjamin Gardiner

The case of Benjamin Gardiner, one of Trinity's early leaders, is a sober reminder that sinners as well as saints have done God's work in the world. Around the year 1812 Gardiner came to Columbus and obtained a position as quarter master with the army, stationed at Franklinton. He cultivated relationships with the town's up-and-coming citizens, succeeding Lucas Sullivant as president of the Franklin Bank in 1818. In 1820 he made a respectable marriage to Betsy Frazer. Membership in fraternal organizations, the Masons and Knights Templar, cemented his business and social ties with James Kilbourne, Lincoln Goodale, and Joel Buttles. His association with these men probably led him to the gathering at Goodale's house, where he was one of the 30 men who founded Trinity. Gardiner was appointed the first warden, along with lawyer Orris Parish. Through 1821 he functioned as warden or convention delegate, sometimes both.

Gardiner also enjoyed the esteem of Philander Chase. He accompanied Chase to Cincinnati for the founding of Christ Church. On that occasion Chase wrote to Roger Searle, "I am in company with Capt. Gardiner one of our Wardens at Columbus living in Franklinton. One of the best and most agreeable men I ever knew."[13] So highly did Chase regard the man that in 1819 he appointed Gardiner Trinity's first lay reader. Lay readers were authorized to lead divine service and read appropriate sermons to the people. Such an appointment placed on these men the responsibility of being exemplary models of lay leadership, morality, and spirituality. Indeed Gardiner was considered "grave and dignified in his appearance and manners" with a "high reputation in the church and society generally."[14]

Around 1822 Benjamin Gardiner suddenly disappeared. It was later discovered that his real name was Barzillai Gannett, and that he had left his wife and family in Massachusetts in 1812. As Barzillai Gannet he had graduated from Harvard and studied theology. He was active in local government, was elected to the Massachusetts state legislature, and served in Congress from 1809–1812. When his past caught up with him, he fled Columbus to avoid prosecution for bigamy and was never heard from again. He died in New York City in 1832.[15]

The community and the congregation were dismayed to be betrayed by a man they had esteemed as a model of godliness and good citizenship. How exactly did Gardiner/Gannett rationalize his life of adultery and deception while regularly intoning the services from the Book of Common Prayer and reading Scripture before the congregation? Perhaps he considered his position at Trinity a sign of status like his office in the Knights Templar. No doubt some mysterious motive drove him to abandon first one family, then another.

Lay Leaders and the Growth of Trinity

Once Benjamin Gardiner disappeared, shrouded in scandal, Matthew Matthews was appointed to fill the position of lay reader. He was an outstanding choice to repair any damage to Trinity's reputation, and he became a recognized leader of the congregation. As Bishop Chase observed at the convention of 1826, "in Columbus the zeal of the Parish has been enkindled by the piety of their excellent Lay Reader, Mr. M. Matthews; and their number is increasing and their union strengthened." Matthews continued as lay reader, convention delegate, and warden until he moved to Iowa in 1839 after his wife's death.

Another lay reader who took his parochial responsibilities quite seriously was Cyrus Fay. Fay was appointed lay reader in the same year, 1819, that Gardiner was commissioned. Throughout his tenure as lay reader and vestryman, Fay was deeply involved in decisions, some of them controversial, that shaped Trinity's course. Given his family relationship to Chase, he must have felt a proprietary and personal stake in the congregation he helped to found. (His descendant Robert Fay would serve as Trinity's rector from 1945–1959.)

Trinity grew slowly at first, for it had no regular clergyman and no church building. Services were held in private homes, which limited the size of the congregation and its openness to the public. Once he was appointed lay reader, Matthews held services in his home and read from a selection of sermons. When his neighbors began to attend and the congregation grew too large for the Matthews's house, they met at the schoolhouse of Cyrus Parker on the corner of Fourth and Chapel Streets. When they outgrew that space, the

Letter dated November 7, 1825 and signed by Bishop Chase appointing Matthew Matthews as lay reader.

By the Grace of God thro' Jesus Christ our Lord, I do hereby appoint our Well beloved Brother in the Lord, Matthew Matthews— Lay Reader within and for the Parish of Trinity Church Columbus, he conforming to the Rubricks and rules of the Church and to the orders of his bishop, and until another be appointed in his stead.

Philander Chase

Bishop of the Prot. Epis. Church in the Diocese of Ohio

Columbus Nov. 7th A 1825

Lutherans allowed them to use their church on South Third Street, for their small congregation occupied it only one Sunday a month. There the diocesan convention was held in 1826 and the Sunday school was formed in 1827.

The small size of the congregation in the 1820s suggests that few of the founders remained as members or brought their families into the church. Parish records are spotty at best; in 1822 there were ten communicants, in 1825 six child baptisms. In 1826 Trinity reported to the diocesan convention that it had 14 families, 12 communicants, and six child baptisms. St. John's in Worthington and St. Peter's in Delaware had 35 and 20 families respectively. Cincinnati, which was a prosperous city of 8000-9000 inhabitants in 1817, boasted the largest congregation in the diocese, Christ Church, with 85 families, 71 communicants, and 21 baptisms that year.

Also affecting the establishment of Trinity was the priority and prominence of First Presbyterian Church. Founded by Lucas Sullivant in 1806 with 13 members, it was within ten years a large and thriving congregation located at Third and Spring Streets. Betsey Deshler, whose son William G. Deshler would become a prominent banker and member of Trinity, wrote in 1818 that "the Presbyterian congregation of the place is very large. Almost every respectable family of the town belongs to the meeting."[16] It was the religious home of the Sullivant family, founders of Franklinton, and brothers William and Robert Neil, landowners and stagecoach magnates. The Rev. James D. Hoge, reputed to be the most eminent Presbyterian clergyman west of the Alleghenies, headed the congregation for over fifty years. At the time of Trinity's founding, First Presbyterian had moved from a log cabin to a building at the corner of Front and Town Streets that had seating for 400 people. Pews rented for as much as $40 per year.[17] In this frontier town First Presbyterian Church stood for civilization, piety, and respectability.

Presbyterians, however, were a stern, severe group, preaching a grim Calvinist theology of predestination. The Episcopal Church offered an alternative to Puritanism, emphasizing free will, reasonableness, practical godliness, and a sacramental ministry. Episcopalians allowed yuletide celebrations, which were rare among Protestant denominations until after the Civil War. They tolerated dancing and the use of alcohol. Membership in fraternal organizations was allowed, and many of Trinity's men were active in the Masons and Knights Templar. The appearance of the Episcopal Church in Ohio was welcomed by settlers such as the Kilbourne and Buttles families, who had pulled up roots from Anglican congregations in Connecticut, Virginia, and elsewhere. Not only its more moderate theology, but also its reputation as the church of the wealthy and educated elite, attracted many of those respectable families who, until Trinity's founding, associated with the Presbyterian Church. One of these was Hannah (Mrs. William) Neil, who was one

Hannah Neil, who was confirmed by Bishop Chase in 1830, was known for her philanthropy. Her husband, William Neil, earned his fortune in the stagecoach business. The Neil family kept a tavern and inn, the Neil House, and held a front-row pew at Trinity.

of the 14 persons confirmed by Bishop Chase in 1830, the first recorded confirmations at Trinity.

The only other established congregation in town in 1817 was the Methodists, who worshipped in a hewed log church on Town Street. Methodists had formally separated from the Anglicans in 1784 and set out to evangelize the common people. While the Episcopalians and Presbyterians required an educated clergy committed to preaching and catechetical instruction, Methodists ministers were often uneducated. Everyone recognized the figure of the Methodist circuit rider in black cape and hat, his saddlebags bulging with Bibles. Isolated frontier dwellers hungry for social contact gathered at their camp meetings. Periodic religious revivals swept hundreds of new members into their fold.[18]

Believe me truly yours,

Joel Buttles

The life of Joel Buttles is an archetypal pioneer success story.[19] Levi Buttles was one of the proprietors of the Scioto company, the group of stockholders led by James Kilbourne who settled Worthington. The Buttles family arrived in the winter of 1804, and the following year Levi died, leaving his wife and seven children. Joel, the eldest, contributed to the family's upkeep by working the family's farm and hunting. He also taught school for a paltry fee and boarded at his pupils' homes.

Joel Buttles (1787–1850) kept a diary from 1835 until his death. The diary reveals much about the character of a man who was a key player in Trinity's early history and that of Columbus. An educated man and a religious seeker who also nourished worldly ambitions, Buttles is the spiritual ancestor of every Trinity man and woman.

When he set out to make a living in earnest he had a good rifle, $340 worth of property from his father's estate, and the resolution to become rich.[20]

In 1813 when Buttles moved to Columbus, it was a town of some 300 inhabitants growing in the shadows of bustling Franklinton. In 1835 the population had grown to 5000. By 1850, the year of Buttles's death, the city had 17,851 inhabitants. This phenomenal growth was due to the canals that linked the Great Lakes to Ohio's rivers and cities. Both the canals and the east-west National Road boosted trade and immigration. The railway boom was just beginning. As the city grew so did Buttles's fortune. He was a judicious businessman and investor with enterprises ranging from store-keeping to printing to pork-packing. He lived in a fine home on Capitol Square, the city's premier residential area. He was the president of City Bank, Columbus's most respected bank, from 1845 until his death. Like most of his class Buttles favored the Whig party, while the Democrats were the party of commoners and immigrants. Buttles had every reason to be satisfied that he had achieved his youthful goal of being rich. Yet he was plagued by worries about politics, his wayward children, and the health of his body and soul.

Family sufferings, common in those frontier days, tested Buttles's faith and consumed his fortunes. In 1829 three of his youngest children "dropped away by some sudden, fatal, sweeping malady. It would seem as though it was the hand of God that chastened" but, he wrote, he was too proud to heed God's warning.[21] By 1835 his wife, Lauretta Barnes, had borne him ten children. In November of 1845 his youngest daughter Helen, only ten years old, died. A grieving Buttles recounted in his diary how he slept with her and held her soothingly while she babbled in a feverish dementia throughout the night. In the morning as he lifted her head from the pillow to give her medicine, he discovered that "the spirit of the dear little cherub had flown…I trust to a better world."[22] Buttles's living children also caused him worry, especially the dissipated lifestyle and spending habits of his son Albert, who graduated from Yale in 1842.

A great deal of the wealth Buttles accumulated was spent on his large and extended family. Besides his own children, Buttles raised a nephew who eventually joined him in business, and he took in a widowed niece and her infant. He also housed his sister, Mrs. Bristol, and her children after her husband died and left them impoverished. He educated his servants, in particular an immigrant German boy, Henry Weilerts, and a black girl, Mary Shepherd. Buttles gave land to a Milwaukee cousin and his family who could not thrive on their own.

Joel Buttles was continually amazed by his own longevity, and in his lifetime he made a strong mark on Trinity. His legacy at Trinity ended with his grandson George Hardy, who served on the vestry until his death in 1922. Hardy and his wife left no children.

The Spiritual Journey of
Buttles and Bailhache

*G*iven the choices available to Ohio settlers, what led them to join the Episcopal Church? John Bailhache came to Columbus in 1828 as the state printer and served on Trinity's vestry from 1834–1837. The tragic loss of all of their children drove him and his wife westward to escape their grief. In his auto-biography, Bailhache explained that he joined the Episcopal Church when it was organized in Ohio, "in full persuasion that its doctrines are at least as conformable to the Holy Scripture as those of any other Christian denomination; while its incomparable liturgy affords the best guaranty that mere human wisdom can provide against any material departure from 'the faith once delivered unto the Saints.'"

While favoring Episcopal liturgy, Bailhache declared that he could join in fellowship with "all whose lives show that they fear God, and love their neighbor," regardless of doctrine.[23]

Joel Buttles, by contrast, admitted that circumstances, more than religious sentiment, brought him to the Episcopal Church.[24] The circumstances were compelling. His 1814 marriage brought him into the families of Lincoln Goodale and James Kilbourne. His publishing interests further linked him with the Kilbournes and with Philo Olmstead, who had taken over both the *Western Intelligencer* and its offspring, the *Columbus Gazette,* from Buttles. He was in business with Matthew Matthews. Thus his relationships with other men who founded Trinity made his association with the new Episcopal congregation natural and inevitable. He and his infant daughter Eveline were the first baptisms at Trinity, on October 5, 1817.

Through the years the web that bound him to the congregation became even more tightly woven: his brother, also active in the church, married a daughter of James Kilbourne. His sister married a relative of Olmstead. Another sister married Dr. Peleg Sisson of Trinity; their daughter married Thomas Sparrow, an attorney who served on Trinity's vestry. Buttles's daughter Eveline married Thomas Gwynne, from an "old" Columbus family who held a pew at Trinity. His son Albert married Elizabeth Ridgway, daughter of a prominent Trinity family active also in business and politics. Several family members served on the vestry at Trinity. After Joel Buttles's death, his daughter Sarah married Charles J. Hardy in 1853. Though she and her newborn child died in 1864, her husband and four surviving children remained members of Trinity for many years. Another daughter married an attorney, the son of banker (and Trinity member) John W. Andrews, in 1859.

If the 30-year-old Buttles felt the spirit calling him to this new congregation in 1817, he did not record it. His dealings were businesslike. He was immediately elected vestryman, convention delegate, and secretary, and he occupied some office at Trinity almost without interruption throughout his life. He was generous in his support, though sometimes in conflict with the vestry over financial matters. By 1839 Buttles rented nine of the 46 Trinity pews that were claimed, and he was related to at least four other pew-holding families. Conflicts were inevitable within a congregation so tightly woven of one's family, neighbors, and business associates. Yet over the years, marriages, baptisms, and funerals served to strengthen social ties between members, so that it could truly be said that the congregation of Trinity Church was Joel Buttles' extended family.

Despite his strong ties to the congregation, Buttles did not always remain in his Trinity pew, content to be counted among the city's prominent families. Like Bailhache he was tolerant and willing to associate with clergy and congregations of many stripes: Presbyterian, Congregational, Unitarian, and even Baptist, known for their emotional preaching and revivals. "How much it is to be regretted that the different denominations as such entertain so little charity for each other," Buttles commented in his diary.[25]

When a wave of religious revivalism swept the country in the early 1840s, Buttles was carried along. He began attending other churches when an unpopular, high-church rector took the helm at Trinity in 1841. At the Baptist church he was impressed by the preacher's point that one's "ten thousand dollars…is not yours, it is God's, and he has only permitted you to obtain it to use to some useful end for a little while."[26] As a wealthy merchant himself, Buttles was often moved by sermons about wealth. As he aged he determined to attend more closely to the state of his own soul. Year after year he was amazed to find himself still alive and among the oldest people he knew. He reasoned that God was "still sparing the barren tree till he shall…at length yield some fruit."[27] At age 58 he wrote, "It seems impossible that I have lived so long. Why what good have I done?…I wish I could say that I had laid up a better treasure in Heaven instead so much upon earth."[28]

During his hiatus from Trinity, Buttles also had contact with the radical Millerites, who argued from biblical prophecies that the world would end in 1843. One zealous convert to Millerism regaled Buttles and the customers at his store with visions of the coming apocalypse, the world wrapped in flame, and the dead leaving their graves. Adding to the fervor was the appearance of a comet in 1843 and an unusual number of earthquakes and tornadoes. Though Buttles was not persuaded, he nonetheless heeded the message of preparedness and wrote in his journal: "There can nothing be lost in being always ready. But Oh! how far short of being ready…do I always find myself."[29]

Though Buttles retained his formal association with Trinity Church, he found his true spiritual home among the Methodists, an irony that did not escape him. Finding the Episcopal Church too "formal" and "lukewarm," he felt drawn to the sincerity and emotionalism of the Methodists. Daily he attended Methodist prayer meetings, struggling to overcome his elitism in the interest of saving his soul.

> *I have been trying to divest myself of pride so as to be able to join them in their exercises. It is hard to do.... I cannot pray with as much earnestness as I want to do for a change of heart and pardon of my sins. I go into their crowded meetings and am surrounded by a different class of society from those with whom I am accustomed to move for their congregations are mostly made up of those which the world call the middle class, if they are even that. They all look upon me as though I was out of place.... I would have gone and humbled myself with a parcel of apprentices and boys and women who were all seeking salvation in an agony of prayer and penitence. I was even anxious that some of their leaders, who I know had me in their thoughts, would come to me and ask me forward. I should have gone readily, willingly.... But I intend to try again and again. And I pray God to strengthen, support me in the endeavor. Satan is managing me, I know, and hanging on to my skirts to keep me back.*[30]

One can easily picture the well-dressed Buttles, stiff and awkward among the throng of "apprentices, boys, and women" unashamedly seeking salvation. Spiritual isolation and social ostracism combined to increase his sense of sin and helplessness. For all his desire to experience salvation as the Methodists did, he lacked any sort of social connection to facilitate his entry into their midst.

Despite his dissatisfactions and his seeking, Buttles remained a member of Trinity until his death. Given the strength of his social connections there, he could no more depart the congregation than he could sever the ties with his own flesh and blood family. He admitted that what kept him involved at Trinity, despite his inclination to join the Methodists, was his wife. Lauretta Barnes Buttles was a devoted member who attended every service and made her husband accompany her. She was among those staunch church women overlooked by history. We glimpse her momentarily as she and the Buttles family, minus the ailing Joel, celebrate Independence Day in 1845. Buttles described his family departing in carriages for a Sunday school outing in the woods, probably Goodale Park, taking with them cakes Mrs. Buttles had baked for the entire class. Though her husband was a feature on the public face of Trinity, Mrs. Buttles was one of those strong links supporting the church from within.

The formation of an Episcopal congregation in town, however small its beginnings, affected the social alignment of citizens. No longer was the Presbyterian Church the only respectable place of worship. The successive appearance of Roman Catholics, Lutherans, Baptists, and Congregationalists on the Columbus scene further altered the landscape. As the case of Joel Buttles illustrates, religious affiliation was more than a matter of spiritual inclination. It was a choice affected by one's background, circumstances, and social and familial networks. But it was far from determined by these. Matthew Matthews founded Trinity, led it for years, and moved on. Joel Buttles, though bound to Trinity, freely pursued his religion beyond its doors. It was the pioneer way, to journey from distant places to new destinations, both geographically and spiritually.

Notes

[1] Mary Ann Denison Cummins, *St. Peter's Church, Delaware, OH: The First Hundred Years: A Collection of Documents and Genealogical Data* (Bowie, MD: Heritage Books, 1993), 5. See J. Wesley Morris, *Christ Church Cincinnati 1817-1967.* (Cincinnati: Episcopal Society of Christ Church, 1967).

[2] Betty Garrett, *Columbus: America's Crossroads* (Tulsa, OK: Heritage Press, 1980).

[3] For the facts of Chase's life and career, see Wallace J. Baker, *Bishops of Ohio 1819-1968* (Protestant Episcopal Church, Diocese of Ohio, 1968); Rev. Arthur Chace, "Second and Third Reunions of the Chase-Chace Family Association," (1903), excerpt rpt. as "Two Pioneer Bishops," *The Interchange* (Diocese of Southern Ohio: October, 2000), 6-7; Philander Chase, *Bishop Chase's Reminiscences: An Autobiography* (2 vols.) Boston 1848; Evelyn A. Cummings, "The Beginnings of the Church in Ohio and Kenyon College," *Historical Magazine of the Protestant Episcopal Church,* "The Church in Ohio" Issue. Vol. 6 (1937); and George Franklin Smythe, *A History of the Diocese of Ohio Until the Year 1918* (Cleveland, 1931).

[4] James Kilbourne, Letter to General Convention of Protestant Episcopal Church in New York. May 1817. In "Records of Parishes and their Locations in Ohio." Ms. fols. 27-29. Cleveland, Archives of the Diocese of Ohio.

[5] Whiting Griswold, "The Early Church in Ohio." Ms. Cleveland, Archives of the Diocese of Ohio, fol. 9-10.

[6] Chase, *Reminiscences,* I, 473.

[7] On Kilbourne's problems with the church, see Goodwin Berquist and Paul C. Bowers, Jr., *The New Eden: James Kilbourne and the Development of Ohio.* (Lanham, MD: University Press of America, 1983), 177-83; 218-19. The Griswold ms. sheds some light as well. An excellent study of Kilbourne is included in Virginia E. and Robert W. McCormick, *New Englanders on the Ohio Frontier: Migration and Settlement of Worthington, Ohio.* (Kent, Ohio: Kent State University Press, 1998).

[8] Griswold ms., fol. 12.

[9] Salomon, Richard G. "St. John's Worthington and the Beginnings of the Episcopal Church in Ohio," *The Ohio Historical Quarterly* 64 (1955): 55-76, p. 71.

[10] Emma Jones, *A State in the Making: Correspondence of the late James Kilbourne* (Columbus: Tibbetts Printing, 1913), 34-5.

[11] Weisenburger, "Columbus During the Civil War" *Publications of the Ohio Civil War Centennial Commission* 12 (Columbus: Ohio State University Press, 1963), 16.

[12] Emma Jones, *A State in the Making,* 107.

[13] Philander Chase, Letter to Roger Searle, May 22, 1817, in "Records of Parishes and the Locations in Ohio." Ms. fol. 36-37. Cleveland, Archives of the Diocese of Ohio.

[14] William Alexander Taylor, *Centennial History of Columbus and Franklin County* (Chicago and Columbus: S. J. Clarke Publishing Co., 1909), 67.

[15] *Biographical Directory of the United States Congress 1774-1989.* (United States Government Printing Office, 1989), 507.

[16] Cited by Weisenburger, " A Brief History of the Presbytery of Columbus," 1959 (no pagination).

[17] James Ingraham, *A History of Central Presbyterian Church, Columbus, Ohio* (Columbus: Central Presbyterian Church), 3.

[18] On Methodism see David L. Holmes, *A Brief History of the Episcopal Church* (Valley Forge, PA: Trinity Press International, 1993), 46-7, 66-7; Sydney E. Ahlstrom, *A Religious History of the American People* (New Haven: Yale University Press, 1972), 436-9.

[19] The Diary of Joel Buttles and related family papers are housed at the Ohio Historical Society (Vol 1206; VFM 4586; MSS 951; VFM 1620). The Diary, formerly in the possession of Trinity Church, was given to OHS in 1990; a typed transcript was made by members of the church in 1991, and this version was used as the primary source, with the original used for verification. Biographical sketches of Buttles can be found in Alfred E. Lee, *The history of the City of Columbus* (New York: Munsell and Co., 1892) I, 56; 857-859 and other city histories; McCormick's studies of Worthington history and Cole's history of early Columbus and a series of articles (based on the diary) by Ben Hayes, published in the *Columbus Citizen Journal* May 1-5, 1967.

[20] Diary, January 26, 1846.

[21] Diary, February 1, 1935.

[22] Diary, November 8, 1845.

[23] John Bailhache, "Brief Sketch of the Life and Editorial Career of John Bailhache of Alton, Illinois," 1855. Ohio Historical Society, Bailhache Papers, VFM 1110. Typescript of original manuscript in the possession of the American Antiquarian Society.

[24] Diary of Joel Buttles, February 1, 1845.

[25] Ibid., November 29, 1841.

[26] Ibid., April 14, 1843.

[27] Ibid., February 1, 1843.

[28] Ibid., February 1, 1845.

[29] Ibid., January 5, 1843.

[30] Ibid., January 19, 1843.

Chapter 2

EVANGELICAL ROOTS *of* OLD TRINITY

During the decade of the 1830s Trinity carved its niche in the city's landscape, erecting a new church on Broad Street that was an instant landmark. Close by ran the busy National Road, an important east-west thoroughfare that brought jobs, new markets for goods, and immigrants to the city. Trinity's congregation was growing under the regular ministry of a well-loved rector, the Rev. William Preston. Ohio was becoming a bastion of evangelical Episcopalianism, and Trinity exemplified that strength with its pioneering Sunday school programs and low church forms of worship. For a brief time, however, Trinity was a stage for dramatic controversies within the Episcopal Church. The short and troubled tenure of the Rev. Charles Fox, a rector with high-church sentiments, brought conflicts over worship directly into the life of the congregation and occasioned a crisis of leadership.

Trinity's New Church and Civic Idealism

Trinity welcomed its second rector, William Preston, to the pulpit on Easter Sunday, 1829. At that time Trinity reported a membership of only 15 families. The year after his arrival Preston reported "a revival of religion," with fervent preaching, prayer, and testimonials. The results were 14 baptisms and 21 new families. No doubt the regular presence of the rector and the promise of spiritual leadership did much to attract members.

The Rev. William Preston, a fervent evangelical and low churchman. Born around 1801, he was rector of Trinity from 1829–1841 and 1850–1855. He and his wife Caroline had three children.

The next step was for Trinity to erect its own church. This was a dream shared by all the founders, several of whom remained and worked to make it a reality. In September of 1830 a building committee was organized. An act of the state legislature, dated February 11, 1832, incorporated Trinity as a parish, enabling it to hold property. Trinity then purchased a lot on the north side of Broad Street between High and Third Streets for $1000. Terms called for the property to be paid for within six months, with interest. The estimated cost of the new church was nearly $11,000. The lion's share, a sum of $7,400, was financed by Joel Buttles and his business partner, Matthew Matthews.

The first Trinity Episcopal Church, erected in 1833 and torn down to make room for the construction of Peter Hayden's modern office building. The Hayden-Clinton Bank Building, dating from 1869 (later the State Savings Bank), and the present Trinity Church are the oldest buildings on Capitol Square.

Buttles had occasion to regret his large financial stake in the new building, for settling this debt would cause him to fall out with the church on a number of occasions. Phineas B. Wilcox, a prominent lawyer who arrived from Connecticut in 1821, invested $1,300 in the new building.

Trinity's architect and stonemason was, like many in the congregation, a self-made man, but unfortunately also a self-destructive one. Charles Romanoff Prczrminisky was a Polish émigré, a scholar, musician, and mapmaker who became a Professor of Mathematics at Kenyon. He left Ohio after a failed romance and was shot to death in Memphis.[1] Before meeting this tragic end, he built Trinity's first church in the style of a Greek temple. Made of limestone with a plastered exterior, it was graced by fluted Ionic columns flanking the steps. Greek Revival was a popular architectural style at the time for churches and public buildings, in part because it expressed the young republic's faith in the ideals of Greek democracy. There are

The mansion of Alfred Kelley, completed in 1838 and torn down in 1960.
It was constructed, like Trinity church, in the popular Greek Revival style.

no descriptions of the interior, but most likely it resembled other early nineteenth-century churches, with a small chancel set against the wall and dominated by a large central pulpit with a small communion table. In the nave were box pews entered from the side.[2]

Just a few years after Trinity Church was completed, Alfred Kelley, a wealthy member of the congregation and the embodiment of civic virtue, built a grand home in the Greek Revival style. Kelley's mansion on East Broad Street was perfectly symmetrical, with Greek columns on all four sides and a two-story Ionic portico. Though Kelley did much of the work himself, his house cost more to build than did Trinity Church.[3] On Sundays he and his family would sally forth in their carriage from their Greek-style mansion to their Greek-style church, where they occupied a prominent pew next to the altar.

Alfred Kelley was proof that wealth and power came to those who were faithful, dutiful, and enterprising. A native of Connecticut, he married Mary Seymour Welles in 1817, the year Trinity was founded. She bore him eleven children, six of whom were still living at the time of Kelley's death in 1859. Kelley was criticized in the Connecticut press as "the proudest nabob in the West" for his opulent house and lifestyle, but the *Ohio State Journal*, a Whig paper, defended him as "a man of plain dress and manners…[who] treats all classes of society with familiarity [and] lives in plain style."[4]

In keeping with the spirit of the Greek-inspired architectural models in which he lived and worshipped, Kelley had a keen sense of civic duty. He served 43 years in the Ohio legislature and was responsible for laws abolishing imprisonment for debtors and reforming the banks. He financed and oversaw the building of the canal that linked Columbus to Circleville. Then he risked bankruptcy to retire the debt Ohio incurred in building the canal, pledging his own house and grounds as surety. The gamble succeeded and Kelly kept his house while preserving the state's credit. It was Kelley who transformed the flat Statehouse square into sloped, park-like grounds ringed with stately elms. He lived, worked, and worshipped in spaces that he shaped to reflect his belief in the ideals of democracy and progress.

Kelley's all-consuming public work left little time for service to Trinity. He was never elected to the vestry, though he supported the church and was called upon when the church needed his financial wizardry. The women of his family, however, were active at Trinity.[5]

Building a church in the style of a classical temple was a statement of faith in progress and a resolute attempt to civilize what was still a rough frontier town. In 1830 Columbus streets were studded with tree stumps that damaged carriage wheels. Broad and High Streets were corduroy roads built of flat-sided logs, but they still turned to muck and mire in the rain. The year Trinity was completed, a

Alfred Kelley (1789–1859) and his wife, Mary Seymour Welles Kelley. They were married in 1817 and came to Columbus in 1830. Six of Kelley's eleven children outlived him.

Alfred Kelley's eldest daughter Maria kept a diary in which she recalled her wedding, on October 18, 1837, to James Bates, a young lawyer. Bates had come to Columbus on a canal boat in 1835 with nothing more than $10 in his pocket and a good education. Two years later he married this daughter of the wealthy financier and canal-builder, a woman with a lively and independent spirit.

Maria's account of the wedding reveals much about the Kelley family dynamics and the personality of Trinity's rector, William Preston. The wedding was held at the bride's home, as was customary. The nineteen-year-old bride wore a dark green travelling dress with a linen cambric collar. As she dressed, she considered her hopes and fears:

How I wished, yet feared to look forward and see if the love of either of us would grow cold; if he to whom I was to bind myself for weal or woe, would prove kind and faithful and true, and would be to me a compensation for the dear parents and sister I was about in a measure to forsake. Hope, of course, predominated, but enough of fear would steal in to sober me considerably.

Gathering her composure she descended to the dining room for the brief rehearsal prior to the wedding. One of her concerns surfaced in a conversation with the minister:

'Oh, Mr. Preston,' said I, in a half joke, 'don't make me promise to obey.' He smiled and turning to Mr. B. asked what he said about it. He replied that he did not care if that part was left out. Says my father, 'Oh, make her obey—make her obey,' and so we all laughed and said no more.

No doubt to everyone's surprise, Preston omitted the wife's promise to obey, and Maria repeated the same vows as her husband.[6] Preston, no hostage to convention, deferred to the young couple in a manner that must have raised many eyebrows among the assembled guests.

Maria Kelley Bates bore three daughters and a son and remained a lifelong member of Trinity. James Bates, a Republican, became a highly respected judge. They had been married for almost fifty years when Maria died suddenly. Her husband wrote of the shock of his wife's death: "I had never associated her in my mind with death. She was always strong and healthy, and I never thought of her except as young." He never recovered from the loss, dying a few years later.[7]

recurring and deadly cholera epidemic ravaged the city. Still there were signs of progress. In 1834 Columbus was formally declared a city. Between 1830 and 1840 the population of Columbus more than doubled. Many of the new arrivals were German immigrants. The public square, no longer a grain field, was enclosed by posts, and legislators were considering building a larger Statehouse. Institutions were being built for the deaf, the blind, and the mentally ill. In 1834 the penitentiary was built at a cost of $93,370. That same year, Trinity was completed at a cost of about $10,000.

In 1834 Ohio's bishop, the Rt. Rev. Charles P. McIlvaine, dedicated Trinity's new church. In his address to the convention that year, he praised the building as "a very tasteful ornament to the town." He proclaimed that

> *The history of the Church in Columbus, from its feeble origin to its present prosperous condition, should greatly encourage its pastor. It is a city set on a hill, and I trust it will ever be more and more a habitation of holiness.*

In contrast to the bishop's enthusiasm was Preston's cautious assessment of the spiritual state of his congregation. He was encouraged by Trinity's prospects, but he deplored "the state of indifference and lukewarmness prevailing among them." A few years later he was still unsatisfied. "We greatly need the reviving influence of the Holy Spirit," he told his bishop, "to quicken and invigorate the Christian and to convert the impenitent sinner." Preston's manner of speaking was characteristic of evangelical clergy.

Preston was worried that the congregation's growth was slow, despite the impressive new church, which could be expected to draw many new members. In 1836 there were 65 communicants. By 1840 the number reached 106. By comparison, First Presbyterian Church boasted 326 communicants in 1839, almost ten percent of the city's population, and Second Presbyterian was newly formed.[8] Meanwhile Trinity's new building was already in need of major repairs. In 1840 a pew tax was levied for the purpose of whitewashing the church's interior, installing a new furnace, repairing the steps, and fixing timbers in the steeple. Trinity needed more members to ease the church's financial burdens, which fell again and again on the same shoulders.

Lay Governance

While the congregation was still small, most of its adult males were involved in governance. As the congregation grew, a core group of men was repeatedly elected to the vestry, sometimes by only a handful of voters, and Trinity's lay leadership resembled an oligarchy led by Joel Buttles, Cyrus Fay, and their relatives.

The vestry oversaw the temporal affairs of the church, including caring for its property, keeping order during the service, and calling and supporting a minister. They met at members' homes, offices, or places of business, seldom in the church itself. Raising money was a constant struggle. The usual method was for the vestry to solicit pledges, or subscriptions, for the support of the rector or capital improvement projects. This method was not conducive to financial security, for people often defaulted on their pledges. Someone dissatisfied with the rector would simply stop contributing and the vestry would have to make up any shortfall in the rector's

Phineas B. Wilcox (1798–1863), a Yale-educated lawyer, came to Columbus in 1821, joined Trinity, and became one of its prominent lay leaders.

salary, sometimes out of their own pockets. A vestry-man, therefore, had to be a man of some means.

The vestry was elected by licensed voters of the parish at the annual meeting, which was held on Easter Monday. To be a licensed voter of the parish, one had to own or rent a pew and sign the articles of association, the official record of membership. In 1836 there were about 30 licensed voters, two-thirds of whom were present at the meeting. Eleven voters were current or former wardens and vestrymen, among them Joel Buttles, Cyrus Fay, John C. Broderick, and Matthew Matthews. Three women who were pew-holding com-municants were present: Eliza Gregory, Mary Ellis, and Temperance Backus, widow of a lawyer and mill owner. Though qualified, they probably did not vote because of their sex. Another voter was Arora Buttles, younger brother of Joel. A skilled bricklayer, he was married to yet another daughter of James Kilbourne. Philip Reed, who eventually prospered as a saddler, and Charles Scott held pews near the back of the church but were never elected to the vestry. Samuel McClelland, born in Nova Scotia, was a recent arrival in Ohio by way of Connecticut. Though a member of Trinity for the next forty years, he never held office. These were the voters who gathered in the year 1836.

Voter participation could be low, suggesting a lack of competition for vestry positions. In 1840 there were not enough voters present at the annual meeting, so the incumbent vestry continued another year. On other occasions, lacking a quorum, the meeting was adjourned while additional voters were rounded up. In 1856 the bylaws were amended to define a quorum, formerly a majority of qualified voters, as ten voters. In 1857 only ten of more than two dozen voters were present, and they elected seven amongst themselves as wardens and vestry.

Apparently the adult parishioners who did not vote or hold office were satisfied that their interests were being represented by the vestry and wardens. Yet when a crisis of leadership occurred in 1841 and the desperate congregation acted on its own, it was clear that they lacked confidence in their elected vestry as well as their rector.

Bishop McIlvaine and the
Evangelical Movement

Shortly after Trinity welcomed Preston as rector, the diocese elected Bishop Charles P. McIlvaine to fill the vacancy left by Chase's sudden resignation. McIlvaine was consecrated and began his service as bishop in 1832. In contrast to Chase's rugged, even aggressive temperament, McIlvaine was quiet, scholarly, and prone to melancholy. While Chase had the pioneer's impulse, McIlvaine was reluctant to leave the refined society of New York City for a diocese on the frontier. Wrote McIlvaine in his diary, "My heart does not thirst for a bishopric. Its honour I could willingly forego, its responsibility I am not sufficient to bear. Its duties are unspeakably holier than any spirit I could bring to them."[9] But called to Ohio, he came, and he served and led the diocese for 41 years. Together Bishop McIlvaine and William Preston set Trinity firmly on an evangelical course, though not without some resistance from more traditional members of the congregation.

Bishop McIlvaine was a standard-bearer of the emerging evangelical movement, whose adherents by and large embraced low church practices. High churchmen put great stock in the laws and institutions of the church. They precisely followed the rubrics, the instructions in the Book of Common Prayer for the conduct of services. They believed the sacraments of the church to be the only means to salvation. Evangelicals, on the other hand, deemphasized sacrament and ritual, for they believed that a conversion experience was necessary to salvation. (McIlvaine had undergone a conversion.) While not ignoring the rubrics, they allowed extemporaneous prayer and preaching, which were low church practices. High churchmen, more than low churchmen, insisted on the importance and authority of bishops. (McIlvaine, however, came to relish his authority as a bishop, and he could also be a stickler for the rules.) Evangelicals tended to be active in social reform movements such as abolition and temperance. High churchmen, on the other hand, insisted on the strict separation of church and state, neglecting social issues to preserve the purity of the church.[10]

These distinctions are important to understanding Trinity's place on the wide spectrum of the Episcopal Church in the nineteenth century. The rector William Preston spoke like a true evangelical. Joel Buttles, like many evangelicals, sought emotional experience and longed for conversion. He felt alienated by the high church contingent at Trinity, which included Matthew Matthews, his business partner. Being the only Episcopal church in town, however,

The Rt. Rev. Charles Pettit McIlvaine, bishop of Ohio from 1832–1873, a staunch evangelical churchman, author of several theological works and collections of sermons.

Trinity accommodated both high church and low church adherents.

Bishop McIlvaine fought in the vanguard against the errors he saw creeping into the church as a result of the Oxford movement, so named for its origin among Oxford University scholars in England. Its proponents were often persecuted by evangelical church leaders, who saw their attempts to reintroduce Catholic elements into worship and theology as a profound threat to Protestantism. The fears of evangelicals were only heightened by the fact that thousands of European Catholics, especially the Irish, were immigrating to cities like Columbus. This "constant tide of popery" personally worried McIlvaine.[11]

McIlvaine's weapons were his published sermons and theological works in which he defined and defended Protestant orthodoxy. His greatest work, *Oxford Divinity Compared with that of the Romish and Anglican Churches*, was published in 1840. To the clergymen of his diocese, McIlvaine preached the doctrine of justification by faith, commanding them to reject the Catholic error that salvation was contingent upon good works. They in turn were to preach this central doctrine of the Reformation to their congregations.[12] McIlvaine saw it as his duty to educate the clergy of his diocese on such matters as the importance of infant baptism. He exhorted them to preach the Gospel of Christ crucified, to ask always, "What is the testimony of Jesus?" upon any subject; only then could their preaching justly be considered evangelical. He also published sermons and theological discourses in the United States and in England, evangelizing as far as his printed word would reach.[13]

Under McIlvaine's leadership, the diocese underwent a shift in the evangelical direction. Before 1825 there was not a single low churchman in Ohio, according to an early historian of the diocese. However, more evangelical clergymen were being ordained, among them William Preston. By 1839 there was a strong evangelical majority at the diocesan convention, though not all the evangelicals were low churchmen. Under McIlvaine the Ohio diocese saw phenomenal growth. In 1832 there were only 17 clergymen in Ohio, including the bishop, and only six consecrated churches. Within three years there were 46 clergymen, 24 new parishes had sprung up, and the number of churches had more than quadrupled. One of these was Trinity's newly completed Greek revival church.

The Evolution of Sunday School

*T*he education of children was a cornerstone of evangelical Episcopalianism, for it was the means of increasing the ranks of church members. Trinity's Sunday school was founded by Isaac N. Whiting, another of James

How did the evangelical movement affect everyday life of Trinity's members? In his diocesan pastoral letter of 1848, Bishop McIlvaine urged his flock to live with piety in a world given to pleasures. Though dancing, racing, theatre-going, and fashionable dressing were not intrinsically evil, "the spirit that goes after these things and the spirit of earnest love to Christ and his Gospel cannot dwell together in any community." He reminded his listeners that the baptismal promise called them to renounce the "vain pomp and glory of the world."

McIlvaine's teachings were more honored in the breach, especially among the wealthy for whom parties and drinking were the *sine-qua-non* of social and political life in Columbus. Attorney Orris Parish, a founder and the first warden of Trinity, was a regular customer at the Eagle Coffee House, a tavern across from the Statehouse on High Street. He could rouse the house with his singing. Henry Stanbery, who briefly served on the vestry in the 1840s and was attorney general from 1846-51, also frequented the Eagle. The coffee house was notorious for the gambling that occurred in broad daylight, the "most prominent men and ablest statesman with white fixed faces bent over the green cloth."[14] As the Eagle was a kind of Whig headquarters, no doubt many colleagues of Stanbery and Parish who were also members of Trinity patronized the place as well.

Trinity's musical offerings to the community were an attempt to raise the moral and cultural tone of Columbus society. On February 24, 1843, a concert at Trinity featured Baron DeFleur in an oratorio of sacred music accompanied by Trinity's choir. Joel Buttles attended and found the church full and the performance pleasing. Most of the program was original music never before performed, including pieces by DeFleur and anthems by Trinity's own choir director, Mr. Ward.

As the center of government, Columbus offered its visitors and resident politicians a constant round of parties. One of the grandest events ever was the festive opening of the new Statehouse in 1859. Frederick J. Fay, son of Trinity founder Cyrus Fay, regretted that he had not paid the $5 to attend. He watched as thousands of men and women thronged the entrance, some waiting for hours to get in. The fashionable hoop skirts of the ladies were crushed by the crowd. The inns being full, many people had nowhere to stay so they danced all night.[15]

Joel Buttles was inclined to agree with Bishop McIlvaine and often avoided parties, for he suffered after even a small amount of drinking. But he nonetheless followed local custom by hosting a party for 300 people in January of 1847. It lasted until 1:30 a.m. and was a success, though Buttles worried that the dancing by some young people would occasion gossip. In January of 1848 Trinity member Fanny Platt, wife of William Platt, noted the "gay times since Christmas—more fashionable ladies from abroad and more large parties than I have known…before." The practice continued into the next generation, with her daughter Fanny in 1864 being invited to three parties in one week of January and riding out to deliver 100 invitations to her own party.[16] Fanny and her mother, though devout members of Trinity, apparently did not feel that partygoing and piety were incompatible.

Kilbourne's sons-in-law. A bookseller and publisher of works of law, theology, and history, he was considered a very strict Episcopalian. In 1826 while Whiting was still a student at Kenyon College in Worthington, he established a school with 170 students at St. John's Episcopal Church. He was invited to do the same at Trinity, and on March 4, 1827, Trinity's Sunday school opened with 17 teachers and 139 students. By 1830 the school had grown to 203 students. Most were children of non-members. The superintendent was Cyrus Parker, an experienced teacher in whose schoolhouse the congregation worshipped.

Parker reported in 1830 that some of the students were "seeking out the spiritual meaning of what they are taught." The school was serving its evangelical purpose, for some of the teachers had also been baptized and some confirmed.[17]

Isaac N. Whiting (1799–1880), founder of Trinity's Sunday school in 1827. He came west to study for the Episcopal ministry with Chase, but changed his plans due to poor health, becoming a publisher and bookstore owner. Whiting lived in a stone house on South Third Street facing Capitol Square.

Originally Sunday schools such as Trinity's served as charitable institutions offering reading and writing to all children. In the days before public schooling, few parents could afford even the modest stipend of a schoolmaster, as Joel Buttles, once a struggling teacher, knew well. The campaign to educate all citizens was perhaps the earliest reform movement, motivated by a belief that the extension of knowledge would eliminate human misery.[18] Protestant churches such as Trinity were the first to address this need, both within their congregations and in the wider community. Trinity members Orris Parish and Dr. Peleg Sisson were leaders of a group that met at the Presbyterian church in 1826 to organize public schools. Not until 1845, however, was a Board of Education formed, and several public-spirited men in the congregation, including Phineas B. Wilcox, James L. Bates, and Thomas Sparrow served on the board.

An organization with the grand name of the General Protestant Episcopal Sunday School Union put out a complete course of lessons and periodicals based on the Bible, the Book of Common Prayer, and the catechism. Students read small tracts containing moral dialogs and grim tales of children whose piety was rewarded by an early death. More exciting were the sensational stories such as "The Robber's Daughter, or the Sunday School Convert" and the story of a young man who rejected religion and found himself awaiting death in a jail cell.[19] The method of instruction, question-and-answer drills, required little skill or preparation from the teacher. Memorizing and reciting Scripture and the catechism must have been dull for students, but this was the usual method in day schools as well.

As congregations and Sunday schools grew, clergy allowed laymen to oversee the students. Bishop McIlvaine deplored this trend, maintaining that the pastor, like a shepherd, bore complete responsibility for the instruction of his lambs. The "Pastor is as much bound…personally to instruct the children of his charge, at regular times by *catechism*, as to appear before their elders in the pulpit and teach them every Sunday by sermons."[20] If William Preston was neglecting his duty by putting a layman in charge of Sunday school, the next rector, the Rev. Charles Fox, made it a point to correct that error. He reported to the convention of 1842 that during the year he was rector at Trinity, the "flourishing Sunday school has been superintended by the Rector in person" and that the children "have been catechised in Church each second Sunday." Fox's successor continued to teach the children in the church once a month, a practice that continued until the early 1860s.

Bishop McIlvaine also felt that parents were neglecting their duty to give religious instruction at home. In 1848 he published a collection of sermons for the use of families and congregations without a resident clergyman. Written by Anglican bishops and noted American clergy, the sermons treated such topics as "Christian Meekness and Forgiveness," "The Christian Character of Youth," "Readiness for Heaven," "The Corruption of Man," and "The Excellency of the Holy Scriptures." The two-volume work, published by Trinity's own Isaac N. Whiting, is evidence of Bishop McIlvaine's zeal in the matter of educating priests, parents, and the children in their charge.[21]

After the Civil War the practice of teaching the children once a month in the church was abandoned in larger urban congregations like Trinity's. The number of students made it impractical for the rector to call them together for a sermon or a recitation of the catechism. At Trinity in 1870, for example, there were 27 different classes, each with six to 12 students, not including the nursery division. So successful were church school programs, in fact, that children were seldom attending worship. This caused Bishop McIlvaine to warn that "Sunday school instruction must be subordinate to the duties of the sanctuary." In 1870 he approved a short liturgy to open and close the Sunday school, but he stressed that it was not intended to be a substitute for children worshipping with the congregation. Trinity's first mission, the Church of the Good Shepherd, was proud to claim in 1874 that 31 children worshipped with the small congregation on Sundays. The evangelical push for education had been so successful that a shift in emphasis was now necessary, so that children would develop the habit of liturgical worship.

Mission School for
Colored Students

From the earliest days of its Sunday school, Trinity was committed to educating the black children of the community. In 1831 the Sunday school was divided, or segregated, with 173 white pupils and 30 "colored" pupils. (It is unclear whether the Sunday school classes were originally mixed.) The following year the number of colored students more than doubled to 70. These children were not taught from the Episcopal Sunday school materials but from a basic reading and writing curriculum. In 1845 more than a third of the 348 Sunday school pupils were black. Despite an 1848 state law that mandated the establishment of schools for black children, few children attended these schools. From 1857 to 1869 Trinity maintained an afternoon Sunday school for about 120 black students. They joined the other parish children for Christmas and Easter celebrations.[22] Eventually black churches and schools took over the education of these children.

Forms of Worship at
Old Trinity Church

To a modern churchgoer, Sunday worship at Trinity in the years before the Civil War would seem simple and austere. While many prayers and collects would be familiar to users of a modern Prayer Book, other elements of the service have been changed by successive Prayer Book revisions. On Sunday mornings, morning prayer and the litany were followed by the ante-Communion. This was the portion of the service that followed the second reading, the recitation of the Creed, and prayers. It began with a collect, then the minister recited the Ten Commandments while the congregation responded by asking for mercy. Then followed the Gospel, notices of fast or holy days or marriage banns, and a sermon. Preaching was an important feature of all services. Robed in black, the evangelical minister favored long, extemporaneous sermons that were both instructive and emotionally arousing. Following the sermon came the offertory and collections. Before concluding, the minister announced the next occasion for Holy Communion. If Communion were to be celebrated that Sunday, he proceeded to a general confession, the prefaces and consecration, a hymn, the shared sacrament, and concluding prayers.

The entire congregation took part in the singing. They sang metrical versions of the Psalms that had been in use since the sixteenth century in England. Evangelicals

Symmes Evans Browne, who married his cousin Fannie Bassett, was the father of three sons, Louis, Morton, and Walter, and a daughter, Bertha. When Browne moved to Columbus in 1869, he joined Trinity and began to teach Sunday school. All the Brownes were communicants at Trinity, which means they were Sunday school graduates who had been confirmed. At the time boys and girls were taught in separate classes. Nineteen of the 25 teachers were women. There was no undercroft or parish house, so classes met in the chapel, which was then adjacent to the sanctuary. (Today the space holds parish offices.) The babel of voices and the summer heat must have been overwhelming. From Browne's 1869 class of eight boys, four were confirmed and four, he feared, were in danger of being lost. Five of the young men were fatherless and five were earning their own livelihood. Frequent absence and careless preparation were a problem for several of the boys. At times, Browne felt overwhelmed and inadequate to the task of educating the children.

Eventually Browne took over the Sunday school because there was no one else to do so. He lamented the lack of discipline and the faint loyalty of teachers, who in summertime "all deserted me save about half a dozen who did not find the weather too warm or exertion too great to devote an hour to the Sunday school."[23] The recommendations of the bishop, the Rt. Rev. Thomas A. Jaggar, regarding Sunday school were neglected. For example, the teachers agreed among themselves to discontinue the approved Sunday school liturgy and to follow instead the Book of Common Prayer and the hymnal. Bishop Jaggar was adamant that the morning hour of Sunday school should be devoted to teaching. For many it was becoming a substitute for worship. "I often meet with pain the children flocking home from the Sunday school…when they ought to be going with their parents and elders to Church," Jaggar lamented to the diocesan convention in 1884.

Symmes Browne operated a High Street business that sold hats, caps, and fur goods, umbrellas and gloves. He was chronically short of cash and often in arrears on his modest pledge to Trinity. But his level of involvement in Sunday school set a strong example in a congregation where men were usually less active than women in the education of Trinity's youth.

Sunday school teacher Symmes Evans Browne made certain that his family attended church regularly. From a 1904 photograph on the 40th anniversary of his wedding to Fannie Bassett.

brought in the use of hymns over the resistance of conservative bishops who argued that hymns (unlike Psalms) lacked scriptural foundation and might stir up improper emotions. But singing was popular with congregations, and in 1826 the General Convention approved a hymnal with 212 hymns.

Music was an important element of worship at Trinity. Charles Prczrminisky, the architect, also served as the first music director. He played the violoncello and bass viol in the gallery before there was an organ. Together with the Matthews children Dorrance and Adelaide, he also led the singing. An organ was installed at Trinity around 1840, about the same time as the Presbyterians obtained one. (There, over the doubts of the elders, the women of the parish simply raised the money to buy the organ.) By 1841 Trinity's organ and bell were cited in John Kilbourne's *Ohio Gazetteer* as city landmarks and harbingers of progress.[24] Soon a formal choir was organized, though they were expected to choose music that the entire congregation could sing. Choirs were out of sight in the rear galleries and did not wear robes or march in procession until after the Civil War.[25]

Holy Communion was celebrated on the first Sunday of the month in most churches. The priest wore no vestments, only a cassock. The elements were ordinary bread and unmixed wine. There would have been no flowers or candles, only a plain linen cloth covering the communion table. Bishop McIlvaine would not consecrate a church with an altar, seeing it as a sign of popery. Legend has it that he once used his walking stick to knock out the front and back panels of an altar, making it a proper table, before consecrating the church. After he left the rector simply replaced the panels.[26] Trinity Church, earning high praise from the Bishop as a "habitation of holiness," had a simple communion table with legs.

The number of occasions for worship, instruction, and conversion marked Trinity as an evangelical parish. Besides morning and afternoon Sunday worship, the congregation met on weekday evenings for prayer meetings and lectures on the Bible, the Book of Common Prayer, and other religious subjects. In 1835 attendance at a women's prayer meeting was growing, and Tuesday evening prayer meetings and Thursday evening lectures were well attended. These gatherings occurred in the church basement, which was also used for Sunday school and for a day school.

The move to the newly-built church in 1833 brought about some changes in worship practice. Kneeling had been the norm in Trinity's early days, as historian James Wilcox remembered:

> The injunction of the Prayer-book, "devoutly kneeling," was accepted literally, it being
> the practice of the congregation to turn around and kneel down while offering their
> devotions. And this custom was maintained at the lecture services on Wednesday and

Friday evenings, in the basement room, until the removal into the new church, when either the increased dressing, in both pulpit and pews, or some other cause, did away with it.[27]

The move to the new church coincided with or occasioned a growing formality in dress. Clerical vestments may have been introduced at the time. The congregation also ceased to kneel for prayers. Perhaps the habit of standing developed because the pews were not yet finished with kneelers. Possibly standing came to be favored over kneeling because women's fashionable big skirts made it difficult to maneuver with dignity in the pews.

While Trinity's leaders were evangelical in outlook and practice, the people in the pews were sometimes divided on issues like prayer. In high church parishes, all prayers were taken from the Prayer Book, while evangelicals included informal prayers. Many of Trinity's original parishioners, following their first bishop, stuck firmly to the rubrics. One of these was Matthew Matthews, who disagreed with a parishioner who favored informal prayers. Finally Matthews agreed that they should lead the next meeting with extemporaneous prayer:

At the appointed time, Mr. Matthews broke forth, in his earnest way, in a fervent, moving, extempore prayer; but his opponent, when called upon, could find no better words to express his devotion than the 'good old collects.' So the 'High Church' brother, who didn't like extempore prayer, vanquished the 'Low Church' brother, who thought he did, upon his own ground.[28]

Lucy Matthews, his wife, adhered even more rigorously to the rubrics. She disapproved when Preston occasionally omitted the ante-Communion service. When cholera struck, as it did repeatedly in the 1830s, she saw it as God's punishment for the errors and omissions in the service. Needless to say, many found Mrs. Matthews too rigid.

For the most part Trinity was able to accommodate the differences between its conservative members and those favoring evangelical practices. But as a stray ember can spark a wildfire, a seemingly trivial issue ignited passions at Trinity. The offending item was a piece of clergy clothing, the surplice, which waved like the flag of the advancing high church army to the settled evangelical congregation of Trinity.

Much Ado About a Surplice

As the evangelicals brought hymns to the Episcopal Church, the high churchmen brought the surplice, a loose white vestment worn over the black cassock. William Preston, a low churchman, wore a black gown for services, as did most Ohio clergymen. Only in two or three Ohio parishes was the surplice worn. Gradually, however, the surplice was introduced for the reading of the service. Afterwards the priest would retire to the vestry, remove the surplice, and emerge in his black gown to ascend the pulpit. After his sermon he would change back to the surplice, though some clergy omitted this second change.[29] To allow for the minister to change his garments, the sermon hymn was introduced. Thus innovations in one area led to other changes in the service, creating ripples like a stone dropped into a pool.

The surplice was unknown at Trinity when William Preston resigned as rector in 1841. He left partly out of frustration at being unable to improve the financial situation of the parish. Bishop McIlvaine, preaching a missionary sermon at Trinity in April, observed firsthand the congregation's grief at their separation from Preston. Several families left the parish to attend other churches.

Joel Buttles' diary entry of April 19, 1842, noting the congregation's decision to charge its current rector, Charles Fox, with slandering former rector William Preston.

Before Preston left, however, he helped select his successor, hoping to leave his flock in good hands. The vestry approved the invitation of the Rev. Charles Fox, an Englishman, as rector at an annual salary of $600. Fox accepted and took up his duties in May of 1841. He complicated the difficult task of following a much-loved minister by immediately introducing unfamiliar high church practices. His seemingly rigid rules and doctrines soon made him unpopular. Joel Buttles voiced the discontent of many in the congregation when he complained about Fox's "high and aristocratic notions of the Church of England" and deemed him "not a very agreeable preacher."[30] Buttles predicted a rupture that would formally divide the congregation, and he began to attend the Methodist church.

For whatever reasons the congregation disliked Fox, the one they seized on was his practice of wearing the surplice at the ante-Communion. Many perceived this to be a high church affectation. Word reached Preston that Fox had begun to wear a surplice. Preston felt betrayed, for he believed that Fox had promised him not to introduce such high church customs at Trinity. Unfortunately for Preston and his supporters as the drama unfolded, the letter containing Fox's alleged promise had been lost. Acrimonious correspondence passed between the two men, and the situation within the congregation also deteriorated.[31]

At the annual meeting on Easter Monday, March 28, 1842, the usual balloting occurred for the election of wardens and vestry. Then John A. Lazelle stood up and called for the return of Preston as rector. Isaac N. Whiting, who was high church in his sympathies and favored Fox, attempted to table Lazelle's resolution, but to no avail. It was discussed and supported by many before the meeting was adjourned. In the view of one correspondent, Lazelle's actions were highly improper. The polls were not the place to introduce other business and, furthermore, there was no vacancy in the rectorship to be filled. "Can it be wondered that a Rector should ...feel *goaded* under such an insult as that?" he wrote.

On April 2 Fox summoned the vestry and submitted his resignation. He felt that materially and spiritually, the congregation was in deep trouble and error, and he wrote:

> *I do not believe it to be possible to place it [the parish] upon a foundation either respectable or stable; even if, for a short while it could be maintained at all as at present. Error has been too far admitted in previous times.... Everything in my power has been done, and every talent has been exerted to improve the parish but in vain. Neither my health my duty my interest will allow me any longer to take a charge, so hopeless so burdensome, and unprofitable.*

He also predicted that unless the temporal affairs of the parish were overhauled, it would shortly die out altogether. With unanimity the vestry replied simply that they "deeply regret the circumstances which have induced the resignation of the Rector."

Fox did not leave without firing a final and explosive salvo. On his last Sunday, April 17, he preached morning and afternoon sermons that denounced Preston and the entire congregation. News of Fox's morning sermon, a "lecture of unparalleled abuse," reached Joel Buttles. He hurried to the afternoon service, where he heard "rather a malediction than a farewell." He took detailed notes and entered them in his diary. Fox declared, "I am certain that I preach the true doctrine and that all else is innovation and unsound." He accused the congregation of being established upon false principles, their error so deeply rooted as to be ineradicable. He blamed Preston for sowing this bad seed, but he held each member of the congregation accountable on the day of final retribution for their treatment of him, a messenger of God.

Many in the congregation found these sermons unbearably inflammatory. On April 18 an irate congregation gathered without wardens, vestry, or clergy author-ization. Cyrus Fay, Philander Chase's brother-in-law, chaired the meeting. As one of Trinity's founders and a leader for 23 years, Fay must have been deeply grieved at the direction Trinity had taken under Fox. Those gathered unanimously supported a resolution by Phineas B. Wilcox that condemned Fox as "a slanderer, a liar, guilty of forgery and fabrication" for his attack on Preston. They called for Fox to be brought before a church tribunal. The congregation instructed the vestry to supply copies of Fox's incendiary sermons and the correspondence between Fox and Preston, and to enter its proceedings in the church records.

The vestry obeyed the congregation's will. It forwarded the resolutions to the bishop and called for Preston to return. The minutes of the unorthodox meeting became part of the official vestry record. Only Isaac Whiting and Joel Buttles voted against the vestry's action. Whiting supported Fox, while Buttles abhorred anything that led to division and disorder. Bishop McIlvaine was incensed by the congrega-tion's move. He protested that they had no authority to give orders to the vestry. He exonerated Fox and deferred to his discretion, as rector, to conduct worship according to the laws of the church. He judged that "Mr. Preston is deeply in the wrong. Mr. F is greatly injured and most unjustly." Moreover, he forced the humiliated Preston to write an apology to Fox which he, McIlvaine, approved and forwarded.

After the decision in his favor, Fox wrote gratefully to his bishop but with a bitter and self-righteous tone. He castigated the members of Trinity's vestry who had opposed him. He wrote of his "contempt and pity" for their lamentable spiritual condition, and he recommended that for the sake of the church they dishonor they leave it "and seek in some sectarian congregation freedom for such loose opinions and conduct."

Effects of the
Preston-Fox Controversy

*N*o party in this dispute emerged unbloodied. The smug victor, Fox looked proud and vindictive. Preston behaved with paternalism towards his former congregation, and his attempts to control Fox undermined the new rector's authority. Bishop McIlvaine found himself in a difficult position. He did not share Fox's high church sympathies, but he realized that the conflict involved far more than the wearing of a surplice. He chose to uphold the authority of priests and bishops, while bowing to the realities of change. His response made him unpopular with the congregation. Joel Buttles criticized McIlvaine: "I think he was not just in his decisions…he treated the church and the principal part of its members with great indignity. And I do not feel disposed to swear allegiance to such despotism."[32]

The reputation of the congregation was also damaged. Its problems were now public. The conflict had made apparent its discomfort with church hierarchy. Fox had accused: "This congregation, with three or four worthy exceptions, are not professors of the true doctrines of the true Episcopal church….The church is more congregational than episcopal." This perception would make it difficult for Trinity to secure a new rector. The writer of a letter to Trinity's wardens, Arora Buttles (brother of Joel) and A. H. Pinney, summarized the business as "a charming example of what a minister may have to contend with who gives offense." He advised the wardens to raise the rector's salary and to levy a pew tax to ensure that pew holders would be invested in the welfare of the parish. This advice suggests that financial matters were a contributing factor to the conflict that focused on the ministers.

In July of 1842 the Rev. Alexander Dobb bravely took on the leadership of this capricious flock accused of being "more congregational than episcopal." He was encouraged by the attendance, finding "a good deal of zealous attachment to the order, orthodoxy, and sound spirituality of the Church." In the wake of Fox's departure, Bishop McIlvaine had written to Arora Buttles in a reproving tone, "I hope he [Dobb] will use both the surplice and ante communion service, and I hope some of these days to see a reading desk in the church." Dobb, however, discontinued use of the surplice and promised in his convention report of 1842 that "when the vestry furnish one to the Church and make arrangements for its use, 'decently and in order,' it will be cheerfully resumed." Wisely, Dobb drew back from the offending item, but while seeming to leave the matter in the hands of the vestry, he did not rule out future use of the surplice.

Formation of St. Paul's

During Preston's tenure there had been talk of organizing a mission in the southern party of the city, and Trinity began to raise funds for building a church. The rupture at Trinity hastened the process, and St. Paul's was formally organized in December of 1842. The Kilbourne imprint was on this new congregation, too. His nephew Dorrance Matthews, son of Trinity's Matthew Matthews, provided the property at Third and Mound where the first church was built. Dorrance's brother Fitch James Matthews was on the vestry. Arora Buttles and his wife Harriet Kilbourne joined, and Arora was elected senior warden. Isaac N. Whiting was elected junior warden, and he managed St. Paul's affairs for many years while remaining a communicant in good standing at Trinity as well. At its founding St. Paul' had 21 communicants but within a year had added 17 and organized a Sunday school with 50 pupils. It was founded on the ideal of being a free church, not relying on pew rentals. It took several years, however, to attain this goal.[33]

The surplice controversy at Trinity helped to define this new congregation. Many of Fox's supporters joined its small ranks, and St. Paul's became the high church alternative to the evangelical Trinity. St. Paul's often raised the ire of Bishop McIlvaine. McIlvaine refused to consecrate the new church until the altar installed by its rector, the Rev. Henry Richards, was converted to a proper communion table. Richard had read both Bishop McIlvaine's writings and those of the Tractarians, and he became convinced of the truth of the latter. Richards eventually converted to Roman Catholicism.[34]

Conclusion

The Oxford controversy was peripheral to the experience of most Episcopalians, but it reached the very chancel of Trinity church. The congregation was not torn asunder, as Buttles feared. Nor did the end that Fox predicted come about. But the troubled relationship with Fox forced the congregation to acknowledge and reaffirm its evangelical identity. It also made Trinity wary of clergy and episcopal leadership. For many years Trinity preferred to trust members of the congregation to direct its business and guide the struggle towards financial security. At the same time, seeds of change were sown, and forms of authority and ritual that the congregation found unthinkable in 1840 would in the future be accepted as natural.

Notes

[1] James A. Wilcox, *Historical Sketch of Trinity Church, Columbus, Ohio, from 1817 to 1876* (Columbus: Nevins and Myers, 1876), 14

[2] Holmes, *Brief History*, 101-103.

[3] Bill Arter, "The Kelley House," *Columbus Vignettes*, II (Columbus: Nida Eckstein Printing, 1967), 40. See also Abbott Lowell Cummings, *The Alfred Kelley House of Columbus, Ohio: The Home of a Pioneer Statesman* (Columbus: Franklin County Historical Society, 1953); James Bates, *Alfred Kelley: His Life and Work* (Cincinnati: Robert Clarke & Co., 1888); and city and county histories.

[4] *Ohio State Journal* April 28, 1840, 3; cited in Cummings, 8-9.

[5] His daughter Helen married Francis Collins in 1852. Alfred Kelley, Jr. and his wife, Matie Dunlevy were also on the communicant rolls.

[6] From a transcription of a diary entry of Maria Kelley Bates dated October 18, 1850 (Ohio Historical Society, Kelley Papers MSS 151, folder 5). The original journals are privately held.

[7] See *In Memoriam. James Lawrence Bates.* Columbus, n.d. Privately published memorial volume in Trinity Parish Archives.

[8] Ingraham, *History of Central Presbyterian*, 8.

[9] William Carus, ed., *Memorials of the Rt. Rev. Charles Pettit McIlvaine, D.D., D.C.L. Late Bishop of Ohio* (New York: Thomas Whittaker, 1882), 65.

[10] On the Oxford movement and high church vs. evangelical practices see William W. Manross, *A History of the American Episcopal Church* (New York: Morehouse Publishing Co., 1935), 213-219, 266-79; Holmes, *Brief History*, 103-112; Smythe, *History of the Diocese*, 238-40; Booty, *The Church in History*, 124-6. For a study of Bishop McIlvaine and the evangelical movement, see Diana Hochstedt Butler, *Standing Against the Whirlwind: Evangelical Episcopalians in Nineteenth-Century America.* (New York: Oxford University Press, 1995), 93-135.

[11] Cited by Butler, 101.

[12] Charles P. McIlvaine, *Justification by Faith: a charge delivered to the clergy,* (Columbus, Ohio: I. N. Whiting, 1840). In its published form, the sermon ran 127 pages.

[13] See Charles P. McIlvaine, "A Charge to the clergy of the Protestant Episcopal Church in the State of Ohio on the Preaching of Christ Crucified…Chillicothe, September 5, 1834" (Gambier, Ohio, 1834). For an account of his years as bishop, see B. Z. Stambaugh, "The McIlvaine Episcopate," *Historical Magazine of the Protestant Episcopal Church*, v. 6 (Sept. 1937).

[14] Lida Rose McCabe, *Don't You Remember* (Columbus: A. H. Smythe, 1884), 93-7, 103.

[15] Ruth Young White, *We Too Built Columbus* (1936), 107-8.

[16] Fanny A. H. Platt, *Letters of Fanny Arabella Hayes Platt.* Edited by Dorothy Hubbard Appleton, 1956. Copy in Ohio Historical Society.

[17] Wilcox, 11.

[18] Ahlstrom, *Religious History*, 640-41.

[19] James Thayer Addison, *The Episcopal Church in the United States 1789-1931* (New York: Charles Scribner's Sons, 1951), 115-6; Smythe, 234-5.

[20] Diocesan Journal, 1842.

[21] Charles P. McIlvaine, *A Series of Evangelical Discourses Selected for the Use of Families and Destitute Congregations* (Columbus: Isaac N. Whiting, 1848).

[22] Wilcox, 12.

[23] Symmes Evans Browne Papers 1803-1927, Ohio Historical Society MSS 133.

[24] John Kilbourne, *Ohio Gazetteer and Traveler's Guide* (1841). The first mention of an organist, Mr. Ward, occurs in the 1842 vestry minutes, and in 1843 a Mr. Gregory held the position. It is possible that Trinity had a small organ earlier, for a letter of Lucy Matthews to her son Fitch James, dated June 15, 1836, states that her other son "Dorrance is organist for the present" (Ohio Historical Society, James Kilbourne Papers, MSS 332).

[25] Smythe 221-24; see also Holmes 101-112.

[26] Stambaugh, 304.

[27] Wilcox, 16.

[28] Wilcox, 16-17.

[29] Smythe, 223.

[30] Diary of Joel Buttles, November 29, 1841.

[31] The correspondence regarding the Preston-Fox controversy and the congregation's role is preserved in the vestry minutes and in contemporary copies of correspondence in the church archives. One letter from an unknown correspondent is a fragment.

[32] Diary of Joel Buttles, January 19, 1843.

[33] Information on St. Paul's history comes from diocesan journals, Smythe's *History*, and documents in St. Paul's archives: vestry minutes; Record Book #2, and a pamphlet, "Centennial Celebration: St. Paul's Episcopal Church, Columbus, Ohio 1842-1942."

[34] On Henry Richards, see Butler, 113.

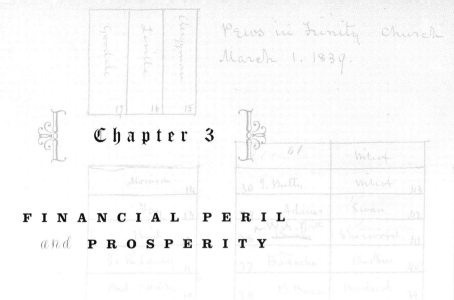

Chapter 3

FINANCIAL PERIL and PROSPERITY

Between 1840 and 1850, four rectors arrived at Trinity and soon departed. Ohio's clergymen, like the general population, were emigrating westward, causing the bishop much concern about the weakened state of the church. In addition, the boom in church-building in the 1830s left the diocese financially vulnerable. Then came the Panic of 1837 and the subsequent failure of banks and businesses throughout Ohio. In 1842 only about a quarter of Ohio's 60 Episcopal parishes had contributed anything to the General Missionary Society. The bishop took a voluntary pay cut. Trinity could not meet its mission share, nor could it afford the major repairs needed on its roof and tower. Bishop McIlvaine lamented to see "so much evil arise out of debts incurred in the building of churches, and which remain to injure the character of the congregations and prevent their growth."[1] Was this a reference to the recent controversy at Trinity? In truth, debt was a burden to the congregation, a severe test to its leadership, and an impediment to growth. None of the rectors was able to help Trinity climb out of debt or improve the system for raising funds. The persistent financial troubles of the congregation are hard to understand, however, for its members were among the most wealthy citizens of Columbus.

Pew Rental and Social Status

Episcopal congregations raised funds to cover operating expenses by gathering pledges, then known as subscriptions, from members. Once a congregation had its own church, its steadiest source of income was pew rental. In 1834 pews in the new Trinity church were offered for public auction after a minimum price was calculated. There were 60 pews: six in the chancel facing the altar, 26 side-by-side down the center, and two side rows of 14 pews each. Seats near the front of church offered a better view of the services, and their occupants were visible to the rest of the congregation. A front row pew sold for $210 in 1842, while a pew in the rear cost $90, or $10 in annual rent.

The location of family pews reflected social distinctions among the congregation. Of the six pews flanking the altar, one was reserved for the clergy and another was held by Lincoln Goodale, an important citizen and patron. Alfred Kelley owned one of these prominent pews, as did the Burr family, Worthington settlers with Connecticut roots. Both John and Charles Edward Burr were active at Trinity. John Lazelle, a publisher, judge, and foe of Charles Fox, held one of the pews. William Neil, the stagecoach magnate, held a front row pew in the nave. Founders Cyrus Fay and Demas Adams owned pews near the front, as did lawyer Joseph R. Swan, the jeweler William A. Platt, and John Bailhache, mayor of Columbus. Joel Buttles and Matthew Matthews initially purchased five pews, which may have been needed to

seat the extensive Buttles family. The church later transferred five additional pews to Joel Buttles to cancel its debt, for Buttles had financed much of the construction. By 1839 Buttles owned or had a share in ten of the 47 pews that had been purchased. Perhaps he in turn rented the pews or made them available to churchgoers who did not own pews.

Conflicts over pews were not unknown. Phineas B. Wilcox, who had also funded the new church, felt slighted when Joel Buttles was given the center front pew adjacent

---

Pews in Trinity Church March 1. 1839.

Nos. 18. 31. not completed.
Nos. 30. 23. 21. 48 & 6, transferred to J. Buttles May 15. 1839 in payment of his claim. See receipts —

Transferred to W. A. Platt March 12. 1839

1840 chart showing location of members' pews. The additional pews were added in the center front to resolve Phineas B. Wilcox's dispute with the vestry.

to his own. Wilcox struck an agreement with the vestry for an additional row of pews to be added in front of these, with the right one reserved for his sole use. As a result the center row of pews extended beyond the side rows. Wilcox must have felt that his stature in the congregation dictated this solution rather than a simpler one: purchase a second family pew from those available behind his current pew.

In 1843 an enlargement to the church was planned, for all the pews were sold or rented. Eighteen new pews were then to be added in the front. When the wardens and vestry called upon parishioners for pledges, Joel Buttles was dubious. He recalled how

> *Mr. Pinney called on me to subscribe to support of Mr. Dobb in the Episcopal Church but I suspect, with some doubts in his mind whether he should get anything. I subscribed $25 for the year. He also had a proposition for enlarging the church, that is for making it 30 feet longer. I could not consent to that but told him that I would not oppose it if others were desirous to be done.*[2]

Buttles predicted trouble among the pew holders who would find themselves farther from the pulpit. Indeed several petitioned to change their pews. They wished to occupy the same position relative to the pulpit as before. The vestry, however, felt that those who had paid for the additions to the church by purchasing the new pews were entitled to occupy them. Finally a compromise was reached; for a surcharge, old pew owners could switch to "better" pews, as long as the rights of new pew owners were not infringed. Joel Buttles was one who found that his pews were suddenly diminished in value. He insisted on an adjustment, venting in his diary outrage at this "robbery" and "injustice" that almost made him sever his ties to Trinity altogether. The vestry settled his claim separately and presumably to his satisfaction. In 1846 Buttles made a donation of four of his pews back to the church.

A pew was more than a smooth place to sit during services. Ownership of a pew was, of course, a qualification for being a voter or vestryman. Pews were property, the rights to which could be bought and sold. They became vital markers of social status. One's place in church reflected one's prominence in the city, and in a time of rapid social mobility and change, neither position was secure or uncontested.

Financial Difficulties
Close Trinity

The improvements to the church exceeded the initial estimates and totaled about $3,500. They included not only new pews, but a reading desk in the chancel and a vestry room convenient to the pulpit. Due to the generosity of one of the ladies, carpeting was also installed. The result, announced rector Alexander Dobb proudly to the convention of 1844, was a church "thoroughly renewed…one of the neatest and most commodious in the Diocese." Membership had rebounded from a low of less than 100 communicants around the time of Fox's departure to a total of about 125 in 1844, and it reached a high of 160 in 1846.

Despite this modest growth, financial problems continued to mount. In January of 1845 the parish had accumulated a debt of about $300, which was equivalent to a year's operating expenses, including lighting, firewood, an organist, and a sexton. Frequently vestrymen found themselves calling on members of the congregation to collect pledges and overdue pew rents. They considered passing a pew tax, a step favored by clergy as a reliable form of income. Pew-owners, however, strongly opposed taxation.

With no other alternative to raise money for the chronic shortfall, the vestry instituted a collection at Sunday services. (Communion days were excepted.) One-third of the collection would go to retire the old debt, and the vestry would aim to raise Dobb's salary from $700 to $800 annually. Any excess would fund domestic missions. Some members of the congregation, however, blamed the rector for the church's financial problems. In 1846 the vestry stated their confidence in Dobb's ministry and maintained that the same financial troubles, arising from "a defective mode of raising money," had persisted for years. Having lost both Preston and Fox in part because of these financial problems, the vestry was eager to retain the current rector.

The Sunday collection did not solve the church's financial problems. The vestry then took the extraordinary step of closing the church until pew owners agreed to a tax or some other fair and effective means of meeting expenses. At this Dobb resigned in July of 1846, citing the financial system that had been a source of "painful anxiety to its ministers, and of embarrassment to the congregation."[3] Abandoning parish work for the scholarly life, he eventually took a position as professor of Latin and Greek at Kenyon College.

Immediately, the vestry appealed to its former rector, William Preston, promising to cover expenses by any means, including the hated pew tax, if he would return as their rector. Preston declined as did another candidate. Finally in February

The Rev. Dudley A. Tyng,
rector from 1847–1850.
Tyng later became a vocal
opponent of slavery.

of 1847 the Rev. Dudley Tyng accepted at a salary of $1,000 for one year. He was 24 years old with a wife and an infant child on the way. The son of Episcopal clergyman Stephen Tyng, a longtime associate of Bishop McIlvaine, his evangelical credentials were excellent. This was his first ministerial assignment, and he was probably unaware of the extent of the difficulties he was taking on. Joel Buttles invited Tyng to stay at his house and advised the youthful cleric that he should "take a firm dignified stand, which should control the waywardness of the various tendencies" in the congregation.[4] Tyng immediately suggested several improvements to the management of the church's affairs, and the vestry resolved to borrow money to pay its past debts.

Tyng remained about two years and went on to serve as rector of Christ Church in Cincinnati. After his departure Trinity closed again, and the congregation was without a rector for a year.[5] This time William Preston was moved by the pleas of his former congregation. In July of 1850 his return was eagerly awaited by Maria Kelley Bates: "We have no minister now and our church is shut up; we hope Mr. Preston will be here soon." In the meantime she attended the Presbyterian church with her husband, Judge James Bates, and her mother. The second coming of William Preston occurred that October; Maria Bates exulted that "the same beloved clergyman…now preaches once more for us after nine years' absence."[6]

On his return Preston reported to his bishop that the congregation was "feebler, both in strength and numbers, than when I left ten years ago."[7] Lack of clergy leadership and the closure of the church had resulted in a one-third drop in membership. Several members had also died in the recent cholera epidemic. Trinity was a full year behind on its diocesan assessment of $100. Preston remained at Trinity for four years, managing only modest growth to 125 communicants. He settled the parish's debt to the diocese.

The City and the Congregation in 1850

One night in 1852 the old Statehouse burned spectacularly to the ground as Trinity and other buildings on Capitol Square reflected the fiery glow. Fortunately a new Statehouse was already under construction. Trinity also faced the end of an era. In 1853 the congregation received word of the death of Philander Chase, Trinity's first rector and bishop. Then in 1854 William Preston left the congregation a second time, bound for Connecticut. The congregation embarked upon another difficult transition. The city, too, was in the midst of rapid change. One had only to step outside Trinity's front door to see the traffic crossing

the land on the National Road and pausing for business in the bustling city. Dust billowed and wheels churned the mud as families in covered wagons rode westward. Lumbering Conestoga wagons filled with raw materials and newly manufactured goods crossed paths with stagecoaches carrying passengers, mail, and newspapers. In 1850 the first railroad cars rolled into Columbus.

Several Trinity men made their wealth in the new industrial economy that was transforming Columbus. Alfred Kelley, the canal builder, and William Neil, the stagecoach magnate, saw the new future of transportation and switched their investments into railroads. Kelley was president of the Columbus and Xenia Railroad Company, and several Trinity men were on its board of directors. The Ridgways, foundry owners, began to manufacture railroad cars. Railroads enabled Peter Hayden, banker, iron merchant, and mine owner, to extract and transport a million tons of coal by 1872.

In 1850 some of the wealthiest citizens of Columbus attended Trinity. Out of 33 parish members located in the 1850 census, there were eight lawyers, six merchants, three bankers, two editors, a foundry owner, and a railroad president. Lincoln Goodale, whose real estate was valued at $160,000, was the wealthiest man in Columbus after the Neil brothers, William and Robert, whose property was worth $600,000 combined.[8] The average value of real estate owned by Trinity members (excluding Goodale) was $22,000. This includes Joel Buttles, who valued his real estate at $110,000, the Ridgway family, whose property was worth $91,000, and the publisher Samuel

1846 view of South High Street drawn by Henry Howe. The steepled building is the original Statehouse, adjacent to the state offices and the court house. Across the roadway are the Neil House and American Hotels and, nestled between them, the Eagle Coffee House where Whig politicians conducted their business.

Medary, who claimed $75,000 in real estate. Trinity's two clergymen held considerably less real estate than the average member of the congregation, William Preston owning $3,000 in real estate and Dudley Tyng $4,000.

At a time of increased immigration, Trinity's congregation was overwhelmingly American-born. The only immigrant among the 33 heads of households was Richard Page. He, his wife, and four of their eight children were born in England. Some German, Irish, and Welsh immigrants found homes with Trinity families as servants. All but six of the 33 families had servants, and these 27 households averaged two servants each. The average number of family members (excluding servants) in all households was 5.4.

Free blacks worked in a third of the households with servants. Philo Olmstead, a hotel keeper, employed Mary Jackson. Thirty-year-old Hannah Butcher lived with Joel Buttles's family, along with servants from Wales and Germany. The clergyman Dudley Tyng housed Robert Montfort, age 14. Joseph Ridgway, John W. Andrews, Phineas Wilcox, and Demas Adams also listed household members who were black.[9] There is no evidence that these servants accompanied their employers to services at Trinity. Most likely they attended either St. Paul's African Methodist Episcopal Church or Second Baptist Church, black congregations founded in 1823 and 1836 respectively. They were located within a stone's throw of each other on East Long St.[10]

Among the most prosperous families at Trinity was that of William A. Platt, who reported $55,000 worth of real estate in the 1850 census. Trained as a watchmaker and jeweler, Platt had become a successful capitalist and was president of the city's first gas company. His wife complained in 1848 of their crowded house, with so many children and servants constantly running over each other. In 1855 the Platts moved to a splendid new house at 8th Avenue (now Cleveland Avenue) and Broad Street, an area that was practically rural. Their three-acre estate was given over to gardening, a passion of Platt's. In 1860 they had a servant and a cook, and Platt's daughters helped with the gardening and preserving.[11]

By the mid 1860s the congregation was slightly more diverse. From a large and approximate list of

William A. Platt (1809–1882). His first wife, Frances A. Hayes, was the sister of President Rutherford B. Hayes. She died in 1856 just a few days after bearing infant twin daughters, who also died. Four of their other six children survived to adulthood. Platt also had three daughters by his second wife. The Platt family is deeply entwined with Trinity's history.

Trinity member George F. Wheeler exemplified the enterprising spirit of the times. Wheeler came to Columbus from Germany as a boy. He went to work in a grocery store, where he fell in love with Emma Waterman, daughter of a customer. As she was well above him in social status, he lacked the means to court her seriously. In 1849, hoping to strike it rich, Wheeler joined the ranks of Forty-niners heading for California. Luckily he returned with some gold and was able to purchase a half interest in the grocery business at 15 North High Street. Still feeling unworthy of Miss Waterman, however, he made a second trip in 1856. On his return he was shipwrecked off of South America but survived and even saved the gold he had mined. He married Emma, who was a staunch Episcopalian. Their first son died in infancy, but they named their second son Charles Reynolds Wheeler after T r i n i t y ' s rector. They also had a daughter Fanny and a son Edwin.

Wheeler's fortune was eventually made not by prospecting gold, but in local real estate. After the Civil War he bought a lot at 5 West Broad Street, where he built the tallest building in Columbus. Skeptics called it "Wheeler's Folly," for assuredly no building nine stories high could possibly stand. It stood until it was torn down in 1975.[12] Five generations of this family have been married at Trinity, including Wheeler's great-granddaughter, Molly Morris, and her

communicants compiled during the Civil War, 49 members were found in the 1860 census. Over half comprised the usual troika of lawyers, bankers, or merchants. On the other hand, more immigrant families had joined Trinity. Samuel McClelland, a land agent, was born in Nova Scotia, and William Bracken, a laborer, and his wife were Irish and the parents of five American-born children. Four families hailed from England, including the brewer William Say and the painter William Herd. With the exception of the Herds, who reported property worth $10,500, the other English emigrants were members of the working class. Several single women were communicants, including Mary Wing and Maria Wells, who lived at the Ohio Institute for the Blind, and a few German and Irish women who were servants. George Wheeler was the only German-born head of household, prospering modestly in his grocery business with $7,000 in assets.

Between 1850 and 1860 more families of modest means were attending Trinity. The proportion of households with servants declined from four out of five in 1850 to two out of three in 1860. Of the seventeen households without servants, six owned no property. Still, wealthy households (those with servants) accounted for 93 percent of the real estate wealth of the parish, an average of $24,400 per household. The average value of property among modest households (those without servants) was $6,300. At a time when the average wealth of a Franklin County family of 5.4 members was $3,818,[13] even modest Trinity families were far above average socio-economically. Many newcomers and immigrants may have been attracted to Trinity out of social ambition as much as piety, for the Episcopal Church represented the height of respectability. At Trinity one could rub shoulders with some of the wealthiest and most influential citizens of Columbus.

Standing at the corner of Third and Broad Streets before the Civil War, you were in the most desirable residential neighborhood in Columbus. Looking south on Third Street, you would see the home that Joel Buttles's widow shared with the family of her son-in-law, Charles Hardy. Next door was the home of John W. Andrews, and a few doors away lived Phineas B. Wilcox and his son James. All were lawyers. At 64 South Third Street lived Isaac Whiting, the retired book publisher who had founded Trinity's Sunday school. Facing the Statehouse at 106 East State Street was the home of Dr. Ichabod Jones's widow, Cynthia, and her family. On East Town Street lived the families of founders John Broderick and Cyrus Fay.

Looking west from the same corner you would see the Ridgway and Swan homes on Broad Street, facing Capitol Square. At the northwest corner of Third and Broad lived the banker William G. Deshler, next to First Congregational Church. Looking east you could pick out among the stately residences the homes of the banker John W. Andrews and Albert Buttles, Joel's son. Three homes stood on the distant Kelley estate, housing his widow and the families of his daughters Helen (Collins) and Maria (Bates). The homes of Charles Wetmore, W. S. Prentice, and William Platt, whose daughters were close friends and active at Trinity, completed the vista as far as Cleveland Avenue.

Trinity's congregation was proof that Episcopalians were generally wealthy. Material wealth, however, was not always an index of the congregation's spiritual or financial health. At Trinity much wealth was hoarded. In some years mission contributions lagged relative to those of comparable parishes in the diocese.[14] Lacking consistent clergy leadership, a clear sense of mission, and consensus on the matter of building a church, members of the congregation could not commit their substantial financial resources to solve the church's many problems.

"We Have Been So Long Destitute of a Pastor"

After Preston's second departure, Trinity had difficulty attracting a new rector. In the interim the congregation attempted to guide the vestry, and lay leaders alternately cooperated and clashed as the parish struggled to make important decisions. Chief among these was what to do with the aging church building. In 1854 the timbers of the cupola were rotted, so it was dismantled and the bell sold to the public schools for $200. The money was used to meet church expenses. Those who were saddened by the loss were promised that the money would be reallocated for the purchase of another bell. It never was.

Some members of the congregation were eager to abandon the old building, while others preferred to repair and maintain it. At a meeting of the congregation in 1854 Dr. Ichabod G. Jones, a son-in-law of James Kilbourne, advocated selling the church and finding a new building site. This proposal caused a stir, but any decision was postponed until key members of the congregation returned from out of town. Others felt that finding a rector and paying his salary was a higher priority than a new building.

To deal with this crisis, a committee of four respected members of the congregation was appointed to work with the vestry. The committee consisted of Phineas B. Wilcox and James Bates (son-in-law of the financier Alfred Kelley), and Judge Joseph R. Swan and his son-in-law, John W. Andrews (who had recently resigned from the vestry). The formation of this committee suggested a lack of confidence in the vestry and a need to mediate between the opposing groups within the congregation.

Together the committee and vestry decided to defer the sale of the current church and lot while raising funds to purchase a new lot. They also agreed to call a clergyman as soon as possible, but on a temporary basis. They were cautious about the commitment involved in making a permanent call. In light of the plans for expansion, they wanted a rector who would help them realize their goals, not question their means to achieve them.

The vestry began to woo a number of candidates, first extending an invitation to the Rev. Charles Reynolds at a salary of $1,300 plus moving expenses. Perhaps anticipating Reynolds' rejection (which came in November), vestryman John A. Lazelle also wrote to another candidate with the disingenuous assurance that Trinity was financially stable and that this call was the "unanimous voice of the wardens and vestry…backed up by the equally harmonious voice of the parish." He promised a salary increase if the candidate accepted at once, and the tone of desperation comes across: "We have been so long destitute of a pastor."

The Rev. Charles Reynolds,
rector from 1855–1858.

Trinity was not alone in its struggles to find a rector. St. Paul's had also been without a rector, forcing it to close its doors for eight months. Trinity investigated or called at least four other candidates without result. Finally in February of 1855 the vestry dispatched John W. Andrews eastward with instructions to make any arrangements for a suitable pastor. He returned in March to report the hiring of none other than the first candidate, Charles Reynolds, who had earlier declined. Reynolds came at a high price: a salary of $1,500 plus $100 in moving expenses and six weeks' vacation in summer and autumn.

With a rector on board, plans for building a new church progressed. In June negotiations were underway to purchase a lot owned by John G. Work on Broad Street at Sixth Avenue. Several thousand dollars in subscriptions had been raised, and the vestry approved plans drawn up by Cincinnati architects Hamilton and Rankin. In 1858, however, Reynolds joined the westward migration, resigning to take a post at a mission in Kansas.

One reason Trinity had trouble retaining rectors was that they were so poorly paid. The contrast between the rector of humble means and his wealthy vestrymen was stark. Speaking to lay delegates at the 1857 convention, Bishop McIlvaine urged parishes to provide their pastors with a parsonage and

John A. Lazelle (1789–1870) and his wife, Bathsheba Patch, were French pioneers who came to Columbus around 1829.

some land for a garden in order to extend their meager salaries and induce them to stay more permanently. Accordingly Trinity offered its next rector, the Rev. G. H. Norton, a package worth $1,900 including a rectory, which Trinity rented from William A. Platt.

Even this concession, however, was not enough to ensure a permanent tie. Norton arrived in 1858 and resigned in May of 1859 not, he said, because he doubted Trinity's prosperity, but for "reasons powerful and immovable, which need not be enumerated." He admitted that physical weakness was a factor. Though the vestry offered him a leave of absence and an assistant, Norton could not be swayed. Poor health, so often cited in the rectors' resignations, was either a polite excuse for other dissatisfactions, or pastoral work truly drove many clergymen to exhaustion and illness.

Trinity's next rector, the Rev. William D. Hanson of Princeton, New Jersey, also had a short tenure. Barely a year after his arrival in 1859, pledges for his salary fell short by $500, despite increasing membership. The vestry decided that the drop in contributions was due to a "want of interest on the part of the congregation in the prosperity of the parish." They commended Hanson's "pure and earnest Christian character," but they could not encourage him to remain permanently. Perceiving a lack of confidence in his ministry, Hanson immediately resigned. The vestry protested that they never meant to bring about his departure, but they accepted his resignation. Later they asked him to withdraw it, but Hanson would only consider resuming his position if Trinity issued him another call. The vestry would not oblige. This exchange, occurring over two weeks, involved mutual misunderstandings and bad feelings as both sides sought to preserve their pride and a measure of authority.

That November the Rev. Julius Grammar was offered the rectorship, though he declined. The vestry prevailed upon him to visit, and after seeing "what a wide field of usefulness it presents," Grammer agreed to become rector. He took up his post in February of 1861, just before the start of the Civil War. While at Trinity he became close friends with Lincoln Goodale. Grammer resigned a few years later, just as the foundation of the present church was being dug. Citing poor health, he took up a post in Baltimore. From September of 1864 until July of 1865 Trinity was without a rector, until the Rev. Charles A. L. Richards of Philadelphia arrived.

Building Plans
Abandoned and Resumed

The lack of strong and consistent clergy leadership, together with divisions within the congregation, contributed to the church's failure to complete the planned church at Sixth and Broad Streets. Once the foundation was laid, the work stalled. The vestry was unable even to assemble a committee to raise the money needed to protect the exposed stone foundations. Then, in 1858 John Work sued for the balance due him on the property; the $3,000 debt had swelled to $3,800. Noah H. Swayne, William Dennison, Joseph Swan, John W. Andrews, William A. Platt, and William G. Deshler dug into their pockets to make up the last $1000 of the debt. That December the vestry and principal investors in the new church unanimously decided to sell part of the lot, including the foundation, to the Board of Education for $8,800.

The congregation still needed a new church building. In 1861 the church was full at most services. All the pews were rented, so new revenue was limited and newcomers could not be accommodated. The sale of the Work lot, however, had put the congregation on firmer financial ground. In 1861 the vestry was able to balance current operating expenses and income. The major expenses were the rector's salary of $1,600; rental of the parsonage for $300; stipends for the organist ($156) and sextons ($100); and the cost of gas, wood, and coal ($150). Income from subscriptions was $1,218 and from pew rents $1,170.

While the annual budget of $2,300 was now manageable, the church was carrying an old debt of approximately $3,000. No one knew the exact amount. It would be prudent, all agreed, to determine and pay that debt before beginning another building effort. At the same time, the old church had to be minimally maintained. Six hundred dollars was needed for a thorough cleaning and repair of the church interior. The vestry decided to sell the rest of the Work lot and to crack down on pew renters who were behind in their payments.

By 1862 the financial picture continued to improve. With the final payment from the Board of Education for the Work lot, Trinity was able to pay off its debts and rebuild the trust fund for the purchase of a new church lot. William G. Deshler and James A. Wilcox were negotiating the purchase of a piece of land owned by Governor William Dennison. Dennison's terms were generous, including a conditional subscription of $1,000 should the building be commenced within ten years. On November 24, 1862, the sale was completed and Trinity owned a lot at the corner of Third and Broad Streets.

Conclusion

F rom the 1840s to the onset of the Civil War, Trinity saw seven rectors arrive in hope and leave for greener or calmer pastures. The unpopular Charles Fox may have hit upon a truth when he charged in 1841 that Trinity was "more congregational than Episcopal." The congregation sought spiritual leadership in a rector, and they needed a force to inspire them to greater generosity and unity. But they clearly expected to run the church's business themselves. After all, they were capitalists, lawyers, merchants, men of wealth and influence in the thriving capital city.

Notes

[1] Diocesan Journal, 1842.

[2] Diary of Joel Buttles, February 7, 1843.

[3] From the parish report in the Diocesan Journal of 1846.

[4] Diary of Joel Buttles, February 19, 1847.

[5] The details of Tyng's departure and Preston's second tenure will never be known, for there are no vestry records for the years 1848-1854.

[6] Maria Kelley Bates, Family Journal, Ohio Historical Society, MSS 151.

[7] From the parish report in the Diocesan Journal, 1851.

[8] Charles C. Cole, Jr., *A Fragile Capital: Identity and the Early Years of Columbus, Ohio* (Columbus: Ohio State University Press, 2001), 215.

[9] In 1860 blacks represented only 6% of the servants employed by Trinity members (six out of 64), as compared to 16% in 1850.

[10] Richard Clyde Minor, *The Negro in Columbus, Ohio* (Ph.D. Diss. Ohio State University, 1936), 81-85.

[11] I am grateful to David E. Platt for a copy of his book, *"Spacious, Sightly and Comfortable": The William A. Platt house,*
1853-1929.

[12] Family reminiscences provided by Molly Morris and her brother, Arleigh D. Richardson.

[13] *Statistics of the United States in 1860* (Washington, D.C.: Government Printing Office, 1866), v. 4, 310.

[14] According to reports in the diocesan journals, in 1854, $150, or 22% of its total collections of $670, went to missions. Trinity Church in Cleveland, having just completed a new church, earmarked over 50% ($340 of $636) of its collections for the missions. Similarly, over half of St. Paul's, Cleveland, total of $700 was earmarked for missionary purposes.

Chapter 4

PRESERVING THE UNION: FIGHTING THE CIVIL WAR *and* BUILDING A CHURCH

The Civil War was the crucible in which the American nation, not yet a century old, was refined by fire. The moral and spiritual values of all its people of faith were tested. Though the Episcopal Church tried to stay aloof from politics, peoples' experiences of war and the sudden assassination of Lincoln inspired a spiritual narrative of sin, suffering, and redemption, revealing the vexed but vital relatedness of the church and civic matters. Trinity's clergy and lay leaders individually wrestled with the issue of slavery while they sought to unify the congregation and the citizenry. Men from Trinity battled their southern brothers while women and children threw themselves into relief work. Drawn together by the task of winning the war, the congregation was also able to plan, fund, and build a magnificent new church.

Politics and Anti-slavery Views

Trinity's founders were mostly Whigs, men of means with New England roots, or landowners from the South. Their political opponents were the Democrats, the party of common men, workers, and immigrants. Joel Buttles expressed the views of his fellow Whigs, an elite minority, when he wrote of his fears that the Democratic party would ruin the nation. The two parties disagreed on economic issues, Democrats pressing for banking reform and regulation and Whigs trying to preserve the system that favored businessmen and bankers.

In the mid-nineteenth century, opposition to slavery was growing, especially in Ohio's capital city. Five percent of the city's population was colored, compared to two percent in Cincinnati.[1] Blacks were a familiar sight, and evidence of suffering and oppression was just beneath the surface of daily life. Next door to Trinity

Church, separated from it by the narrow Pearl Alley, was the Buckeye House, a tavern that was known to be a station on the Underground Railroad. From time to time new faces would appear on the kitchen staff and disappear again.

The issue of slavery forced a major realignment of political parties. Membership in the Whig party declined and the Republican party took shape in the mid-1850s, drawing members from various factions who opposed the extension of slavery into new territories. Bishop McIlvaine joined the Republican party and supported Lincoln for president. Trinity's wealthy bankers and businessmen found themselves drawn to the Republican party for its economic policies.

The views of congregation members regarding slavery were no doubt complex and changing. The lawyer Noah H. Swayne was born in Virginia of Quaker parents. His wife Sarah Ann Wager, also of Virginia, celebrated their marriage by freeing all of her slaves. Swayne was a vocal opponent of the extension of slavery to new states. Of the Trinity families who had black servants in 1850, all were from Connecticut, New York, or Pennsylvania. Those with origins in slave-holding states had only American or European-born servants. Whatever their views regarding blacks, it is clear that the number of Trinity households with free black servants declined in the decade before the Civil War.

Generally evangelical Protestant churches gave less attention to slavery than they did to moral reforms such as temperance. Quakers and Congregationalists were more likely than other Protestants to be involved in the abolition movement. At Columbus's First Congregational Church the Rev. E. P. Goodwin actively preached the abolition of slavery, and when the war started he stated that he was willing to take up arms.[2] Episcopalians, by contrast, were generally conservative politically and favored the status quo. One notable exception was dry goods merchant Fernando Kelton and his wife Sophia, Episcopalians who gave refuge to runaway slaves at their home at 586 East Town Street.

Noah H. Swayne. Swayne and his wife lived at the end of State Street, where the Columbus Metropolitan Library now stands. One Sunday morning they came out of the house expecting to find their horse and carriage waiting for them, but it was nowhere to be seen. They walked to church, the tall man and his short, heavy wife, and arrived to see their horse standing in front of the church. Their groom had brought the carriage to the front of the house as usual, but when the church bell rang, the horse trotted off to church by itself. When Swayne became a Supreme Court justice and moved to Washington, D. C., his home became the residence of a number of Ohio governors, including Rutherford B. Hayes.

John Whiting Andrews, an attorney and longtime vestryman, exemplified the attitude of many Trinity men regarding the issue of slavery. Speaking in 1858 of the growing tensions between North and South, Andrews remarked: "We, at the North, do not like the institution of slavery; we would not tolerate it among ourselves. But we have no idea of making war upon those among whom it exists." He favored a live-and-let-live approach, harkening back to the inviolable constitutional compromise that permitted slavery in order to maintain the Union. On those constitutional grounds he also supported enforcement of Ohio's fugitive slave law in an 1839 speech.[3] The moral basis for his views was that an infinitely wise and powerful God "tolerates, in his plans of reform, the existence of evils for ages," and that man's job is to be a patient co-worker with God.[4]

Andrews and others who condemned slavery were not necessarily abolitionists. They wanted slavery isolated to the South, not allowed to spread to new territories.

On another occasion, in 1854 Andrews spoke against the Nebraska Bill to an audience assembled at First Presbyterian Church. He called for the new territories to be kept as the "home of free labor," fearing that slave labor in the territories would diminish opportunities for Ohioans who wished to emigrate there. The group's resolutions on that occasion were crafted by a committee

Monument to John W. Andrews (1811–1893) in Trinity. Andrews married Lavinia Gwynne, whose parents were early settlers of Franklinton. A lawyer, Andrews resided on South Third Street, a neighbor of Joel Buttles.

that included Fernando Kelton, Peter Hayden, Joseph Ridgway, Lincoln Goodale, and Joseph Swan, all Episcopalians who evidently agreed with Andrews.

Andrews's view that slavery should be contained and patiently opposed represented a radical position for Episcopalians. Trinity's former rector Dudley Tyng preached a sermon expounding this view and was forced to resign from his Philadelphia congregation in 1856. He then founded a new congregation where he openly preached against slavery.[5] Few people at the time favored racial equality. Their attitude towards blacks was one of charitable paternalism. The Rev. Julius

The Rev. Julius Grammer, rector of Trinity from 1861–1864. Most of Trinity's leaders opposed slavery but were not as extreme as the abolitionists. Grammer believed the Civil War was just and preached the duty of supporting the Union.

Grammer, Trinity's rector during the Civil War, called for teachers for the mission school for colored children, stating, "The African should be regarded as a trust from God to America."[6] Joel Buttles, for all the goodness shown to his young black servant Mary Shepherd, saw her as a morally inferior child in need of his protection.

Many well-meaning opponents of slavery were involved in the colonization movement to return freed blacks to Africa, rather than helping them to settle in northern cities. In 1854 Lincoln Goodale responded to an appeal to purchase the freedom of a family of 71 slaves and pay their passage to Liberia.[7] He employed a colored man, Joseph Harris, for more than twenty years and considered him a member of the family. Harris was widely respected by his white neighbors. When Harris died in 1845 Joel Buttles noted in his diary the passing of this "worthy man."[8] Many who supported colonization eventually embraced more radical solutions to the suffering of blacks.

An event that galvanized anti-slavery sentiment in Columbus was the kidnapping of Jerry Finney, a black man who lived with his wife and children in Columbus. Finney was a waiter at the Eagle Coffee House and known to the members of Trinity who were its patrons. One night in March of 1846 he was lured to Franklinton, kidnapped by four men, and returned to Kentucky as a fugitive slave. Citizens were outraged and demanded justice. Trinity's William Dennison was a prosecuting attorney in the subsequent trial. Noah Swayne represented the kidnappers, who were in the end acquitted. Finney was returned to his family in Columbus after his supporters raised $500 to pay for his release.

Bishop McIlvaine set a powerful example for the equal treatment of blacks. In

1859 he discovered that a Kenyon student, Mr. Alston, who was black, was not allowed to receive Holy Communion until the clergy and the other students had partaken. The next day, the bishop entered the chapel and joined the man, who sat apart from the other students. When the time for Communion approached McIlvaine "waited until the clergy of the place had communicated, and then stepping forward, and bidding Alston follow him, advanced and knelt at the chancel, placing the coloured man by his side."[9] Thereafter Alston communed with his fellow seminarians.

It is unlikely that this uplifting scenario played itself out in Episcopal churches in McIlvaine's diocese. Even if members of Trinity agreed that their black servants were their equals in God's eyes, and even as they taught the city's black children in Sunday school, they continued to worship separately.

Several members of Trinity with public roles and political ambitions found themselves caught up in the turmoil of the pre-war period. One was Joseph R. Swan, who began as a law student of his uncle, Gustavus Swan of Franklinton, and eventually became chief justice of the Ohio Supreme Court. Swan was at first a Democrat, but because he opposed the extension of slavery he joined the Republican party. While a justice, however, he upheld the fugitive slave law in a case against Oberlin abolitionists who sought to protect a runaway slave. This decision lost him the favor of the Republican party, which in the next election nominated William Dennison for governor.

Swan served on Trinity's vestry almost continuously between 1841 and 1858, but he stepped down the year after his political rival, William Dennison, was elected to the vestry. Dennison, a banker and railroad executive, served as Ohio's governor from 1860–1862 while remaining a vestryman at Trinity. He did not sign Trinity's articles

Joseph R. Swan (1802–1884). The drawing room of Judge Swan's home at the corner of East Broad and Fourth Streets was deemed "the pinnacle of social recognition" by journalist William Dean Howells.

William G. Dennison (1815–1882), a long-time member of Trinity, served as Ohio's governor from 1860–62. Dennison's wife, Ann Eliza Neil, was the daughter of William and Hannah Neil. The Dennisons were parents of 11 children.

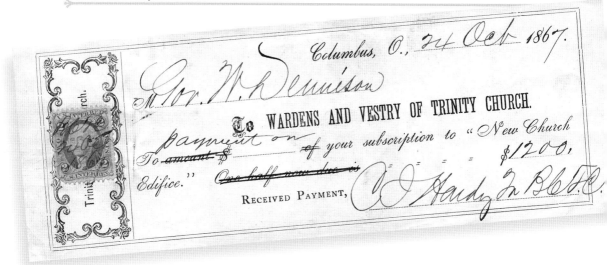

Receipt showing Dennison's payment of $1,200 toward his subscription to the new church, signed by Charles J. Hardy, son-in-law of Joel Buttles.

until 1869. Thus he had not been a qualified voter or a legitimate vestryman. He did, however, contribute more than $10,000 to the construction of the new church, so the small matter of a signature could be overlooked.

During the 1859 campaign, Abraham Lincoln campaigned in Columbus on behalf of Dennison while Stephen Douglas spoke in support of the Democratic candidate. A Trinity member with the imposing name of Richard Plantagenet Llewellyn Baber was instrumental in bringing Lincoln to the city. No doubt Baber and other members of the congregation turned out to support Dennison, swelling the crowd that heard Lincoln speak from the east terrace of the Statehouse. It was Baber who persuaded Lincoln to publish his debates with Douglas, and he arranged for William Dean Howells, then a newspaperman with the *Ohio State Journal*, to edit the volume.

Partisan politics occasionally produced tensions within the congregation. The Democrat Samuel Medary, editor of the *Ohio Statesman*, was an anomaly in a congregation of Republican lawyers and Whig businessmen. Medary was a member around 1850, and two of his daughters were baptized there as adults. His rival editors at the *Ohio State Journal*, the Whig newspaper, were members of Trinity. When Medary attempted to put up a Democratic judicial candidate to run against James Bates, Alfred Kelley's son-in-law, Republican colleagues blocked Medary's move so that Bates ran unopposed.[10] Just prior to the Civil War, Medary began editing the anti-war *Crisis*, a newspaper that condemned Lincoln. Medary's extreme political views made him a strange and possibly unwelcome pew-fellow in a congregation dominated by Republicans who supported the Union and their president. Medary died in 1864 but his widow was still a pew holder in 1868.

Trinity and the War Effort

When war was declared in April of 1862, thousands of volunteers poured into Columbus anticipating a hasty war and an easy victory.

James Kilbourne Jones, son of Dr. Ichabod Jones and grandson of James Kilbourne, was reputed to be the first Ohioan to enlist. He served with the 2nd Ohio Volunteer Infantry, fought in the first Battle of Bull Run, and was promoted to first lieutenant. But he was discharged in 1862 suffering from sunstroke. His health never recovered and, unable to resume his legal studies, he went into the hardware business with his uncle, Lincoln Kilbourne.[11] John B. Neil, nephew of William Neil, enlisted at age 19 and was wounded at the Battle of Shiloh. After the war Neil became a member of Trinity. In 1864 Fernando Kelton's eldest son was killed in action at the Battle of Brice's Crossing in Mississippi. It was a loss felt by the entire city.

Several Trinity men were assigned to commanding roles. James A. Wilcox resigned from the vestry to enlist in September of 1862. He was soon appointed colonel of the 113th Ohio Volunteer Infantry, a position that brought him more grief than glory. His efforts to prepare his regiment for duty met with their ill will and insubordination.[12] Before the regiment saw combat, Wilcox resigned his post and returned to Columbus. When the draft was instituted in 1864, he had the unpleasant task of drawing names of Columbus men.[13] The burden of the draft fell on the poorest wards of the city, where the citizens were unable to meet their quota or to raise enough bounty money to pay soldiers. No one from Trinity was drafted.

After Wilcox's resignation his position in the regiment was taken by another Trinity member, John G. Mitchell, a son-in-law of William Platt. Mitchell spent several months on leave recovering from a smallpox-like disease, but he was back in command at the Battle of Chickamauga. It was a terrible loss for the Union; Mitchell's regiment alone numbered 27 killed, 98 wounded, and 66 missing, and one company left the field with only eight men standing. Mitchell was promoted to brigadier general just a few months before the war's end.

J. Wager Swayne, a lawyer like his father Noah, was another of Trinity's war heroes. He volunteered in July of 1861 and was appointed major of the 43rd Ohio Volunteer Infantry. He accompanied General William T. Sherman on his infamous march to the sea, a campaign in which an exploding shell claimed Swayne's right leg. He was later promoted to brigadier general. After the war he was commissioner of the Freedman's Bureau in Alabama.[14] The Bureau worked closely with Episcopal mission organizations to provide education and jobs to former slaves. In 1867 Trinity contributed $158.95 towards the work of the Freedman's Commission.

Lincoln supporter Richard P. L. Baber also played a small role in the war effort. He practiced law with his uncle, Noah H. Swayne, and lived with his father, a Methodist Episcopal minister, in a boarding house. He was considered "impossible in polite society," for he was disorganized, neglectful of his dress, and lacked a sense of decorum. This honest but eccentric man was rewarded with the minor post of paymaster in the army. While stationed in Illinois, he left for several weeks to visit a friend, one of the Sullivants who had settled there. He returned to find himself dismissed for absence without leave but was soon reinstated.[15]

Civilian men also practiced military readiness. William A. Platt, William G. Deshler, and Albert Buttles (Joel's son) were among the citizens who met for evening military drill on the east terrace of the Capitol.[16] Their citizen militia prepared for the possibility of a rebel attack on Ohio's capital city. Fears were heightened in 1863 when Confederate General John Hunt Morgan led his troops on a raid throughout the southern and eastern counties of Ohio, coming within 60 miles of Columbus. Morgan was captured and brought to the Ohio Penitentiary in Columbus, but he and six of his men escaped from this bastion, to the dismay and embarrassment of the city, and made their way to Tennessee.[17]

Women and the War Effort

*W*ithin a week of the start of the war, Columbus women met in the basement of First Presbyterian Church to form a Soldier's Aid Society. The meeting began at 9 a.m on April 23, and by noon a workshop was operating at a hall donated by Peter Ambos, the city's premier caterer. Sewing machines were set up, bolts of cloth were spread over tables, and women clipped, basted, and sewed uniforms for the soldiers. One woman took home supplies to make a hundred shirts.[18] Every day the women sewed and collected donations door to door. As a grassroots organization, the Soldier's Aid Society was a model of efficiency and effectiveness.

At least a dozen Trinity women were among the organizers and officers of the society. They were the wives and daughters of civic leaders and had deep roots in the community. Among the women were the governor's wife, Ann Eliza Dennison, daughter of William and Hannah Neil; Mary Elizabeth Deshler, wife of the banker William G. Deshler and daughter of James Kilbourne and Cynthia Goodale; and Mary Llewellyn Swayne, sister of J. Wager Swayne. Alfred Kelley's daughter, 19-year-old Kate, was elected an officer. Lauretta Buttles, Joel's widow, was on the garment-cutting committee, and her daughter-in-law, Mary Buttles, solicited funds and donations.

John W. Andrews, who had opposed fighting a war over slavery, was a tireless relief worker together with his wife, the former Lavinia Gwynne, and their daughter Jennie, 19. This was their family's contribution to the Union cause, for Andrews at 50 was too old to enlist and their 12-year-old son was too young.

Besides working from their homes and churches to provide clothing and supplies for soldiers, women also served as nurses at local military hospitals. The Esther Institute, a girl's school at the northeast corner of Third and Broad Streets, was converted into a hospital in 1862. The governor's daughter Eliza and Dr. Jones' daughter Emma, whose brother had enlisted at the start of the war, probably nursed wounded veterans at their former school. Years later, the building was purchased by Trinity and used as a parish house.[19] Today it is the site of the Athletic Club.

Not all women stayed close to home, however. Laura Platt Mitchell, wife of John G. Mitchell, accompanied her husband's regiment as it mustered first at Camp Chase, then at Zanesville and Louisville, which the soldiers called "Camp Laura" in her honor. Barely nineteen and newly married, she was something of a free spirit remembered for climbing around Mammoth Cave on a family vacation wearing red flannel bloomers.[20] When Mitchell's finger was injured in a drill exercise, his wife attended to him, prompting one of his men to observe that "A woman is a handy piece of furniture, even in camp."[21] When her husband was hospitalized in Tennessee for a smallpox-like illness, she packed her trunk and went to join him, accompanied by her father-in-law. On her return to Columbus she was delayed near Nashville as rebel troops blocked the tracks.

Laura Platt Mitchell, daughter of William A. Platt, with her daughter Jean around 1872. Jean Mitchell married Nicholas D. Monsarrat, who served on the vestry from 1908 until his death in 1928. Five generations of this family have been active members of Trinity.

Laura Mitchell's younger sister, Fanny Platt, was active in Trinity's fund-raising efforts during the war. In June of 1863 Fanny and her friends staffed the candy table at a Trinity church festival. They raised $8.75 by selling all their candy plus bouquets hastily made of flowers from the centerpiece. Money collected in Sunday school was used to purchase supplies and treats for soldiers. Fanny herself made "four pairs of shoulder-straps and three needle-books" embroidered with flags and patriotic mottoes. Together the students assembled more than 150 bundles.[22]

In 1864 the men in Mitchell's regiment, camped in snowy Georgia, received a shipment of bags made by a Sunday school class, possibly Fanny's. Francis McAdams's parcel contained paper, pencil, and an envelope, tea, pepper, and cloves, a bit of soap, sugar, yarn, a comb, pins, needles, and thread. A Bible was enclosed with a letter from "Anna," who wrote, "I hope God will spare your life and bring you to your home again; but if he sees best to have you die, far away from home and friends, I hope Jesus will be with you then, and hope we may meet in heaven."[23] Such pious sentiments helped children to understand and accept the harsh realities of war.

The ministry of Trinity's women and children probably did not extend to those Confederate prisoners housed at Camp Chase, located four miles west of Columbus. While 500 Franklin county men died in the Civil War, thousands of Confederate soldiers died in appalling misery at Camp Chase.[24] For Fanny Platt, Laura Mitchell's younger sister, that reality was remote. At a party in February of 1865 she met an officer stationed at Camp Chase and wrote in her journal: "he says they have a splendid band there, and that he will send it out to serenade me before long."

The Church Responds
to the War

*P*rizing unity over moral purity, the Episcopal Church avoided taking a position regarding slavery. Historically tolerant and wary of any involvement in politics, the church tried to remain focused on spiritual matters during the war. Despite the church's official neutrality, many in the ranks of laity and clergy found it difficult to stay out of the political fray. Bishop McIlvaine was one. Addressing the diocesan convention in June of 1861, he condemned the rebellion as "the most unjustifiable outbreak of sinful prejudice and passion." He stated in no uncertain terms the duty of Christians to support the government and use all lawful means to preserve the Union. Fearing schism, McIlvaine called for mercy and the persistence of brotherly love between enemies. McIlvaine urged Lincoln to emancipate the slaves on religious and moral grounds.[25] He even found himself in the role of a diplomat. At the request of Secretary of State William Seward, he traveled to England after Union troops had fired upon and boarded an English vessel, the *Trent*, in order to capture a Confederate privateer. Insisting his trip was a "mission of peace," he felt he had some success in soothing British feelings.[26]

It was left to the assistant bishop, the Rt. Rev. Gregory Bedell, to keep the Ohio church focused on spiritual concerns. Citing the separation of church and state, he urged the clergy of the diocese to "withstand the temptations to enter the political arena from the pulpit. Let the Sabbath be…devoted entirely to spiritual interests."[27] That he felt compelled to emphasize this point suggests that clergymen were indeed preaching politics on Sundays. To maintain the church's spiritual focus, he assigned special collects for thanksgiving after victory and prayers for wounded, sick, and dying soldiers to be recited in parishes.

Many clergy were troubled about how to separate the political and spiritual dimensions of the war between the states, which was an archetypal Cain and Abel conflict. At the outbreak of the war Trinity's rector, Julius Grammer, preached to thousands of men and women gathered at Camp Jackson. Grammer assured the soldiers that although a war for fame or plunder was wrong, a war for the defense of one's country was right. He exhorted them to "endure hardships as faithful soldiers, and sooner than yield or dishonor the flag of their country, to lay down their lives upon the field of battle." In the event of their death, "their names would be enrolled in the dome of the Capitol and their memories embalmed in the hearts of the people."[28] Grammer did not claim that their names would be enrolled on the dome of *heaven*; he avoided sanctioning war and promising a martyr's crown to the fallen soldier.

Spiritual metaphors, however, were readily available for the country's travail. In response to the Emancipation Proclamation, Bishop Bedell praised God's providence "in turning the rebellion of slave-holding States into a great instrument for the destruction of slavery. God has made a way in the sea, and a path in the mighty waters of this awful war."[29] Lincoln freeing the slaves was likened to Moses leading the Israelites from captivity. Evangelicals exulted but their joy was soon turned to despair. After Lincoln's assassination Bedell consoled the grieving Ohio delegation: "These waves of troublous times change no purpose of God towards the church; they but roll the ark on towards its haven; heavily rolling, in these latter days, and tossing their huge caps madly in the light."[30]

Celebration Turns to Mourning

Columbus began celebrating the end of the war as soon as news of the fall of Richmond and Petersburg reached the city. "The rebellion is crushed and our country is saved," exulted Fanny Platt in her diary entry of April 3, 1865. After Lee's surrender to Grant on April 9, people poured into the streets and rushed to the *Ohio State Journal* office though it was the middle of the night. "Then the bells commenced ringing, the cannon belched forth its thunder tones, huge bonfires were kindled, and, for the remainder of the night, joy and rejoicing reigned supreme. But none of our family knew anything of all this until morning. We slept through it all," Fanny wrote ruefully. She did not miss church services on the morning of April 14, when the cacophony of cannons firing from the Statehouse and the church bells ringing forced the preacher to bring his sermon to an early end.

News of Lincoln's assassination reached Columbus the next day. Stunned by grief and unable to write, Fanny later recalled, "The rejoicing of the whole city was suddenly changed into mourning. It seemed as though there had been a death in each family. Nearly every house in the city was draped in mourning which the day before was bright with flags."[31] Sunday evening thousands gathered on Capitol Square for community worship. One preacher spoke from the west terrace of the Capitol, while the Reverend Granville Moody preached from the east terrace on this text: "And the victory of that day was turned into mourning unto all the people" (2 Samuel 19,2).[32]

On April 29, 1865, Lincoln's funeral cortege passed through Columbus enroute to the cemetery in Springfield, Illinois. Several of the honorary pallbearers were from Trinity: Lincoln Goodale, banker William B. Hubbard, publisher William B. Thrall, and Joseph R. Swan, whom Lincoln had appointed to the United States Supreme Court. A black-canopied hearse drawn by six white horses bore the body from Union Depot to the Statehouse, where the tall columns were draped in spirals of black crepe. Every window, housetop, and balcony along High Street was crowded with silent observers. The president's body lay on a catafalque in the Statehouse rotunda where those passing by could see his face and upper body. By the time the procession returned to the station late in the afternoon, more than 50,000 people had paid their respects. The line of mourners, four abreast, stretched north to Long Street and south to Rich Street. Charles Reynolds Wheeler, son of George Wheeler, was one of this vast crowd. He remembered seeing the president's body, packed in ice and turning black.[33] Though he was only five years old at the time, the event left an indelible mark on him.

The separation of church and state that helped carry the Episcopal Church through the Civil War without breaking apart was blurred as the nation mourned its

murdered president. Ohio Governor John Brough joined in declaring Thursday June 1, 1865, a "Sabbath of the nation," calling citizens to close their businesses and to unite in prayer at their churches. Bishop McIlvaine appointed a special prayer in which the faithful confessed, "in this time of sore national bereavement and affliction, how deeply, as a nation, we have deserved Thy wrath…and bow to Thy holy will in submission and humiliation."[34] Congregations throughout Ohio were led to see the loss of their great leader as an angry God's punishment of his proud and wayward people. No doubt this penitential prayer left a deep impression on Trinity's congregation, especially those who had so recently seen the coffin of the slain president.

Abraham Lincoln's funeral cortege heads east on Broad Street on April 29, 1865. This scene occurs from the vantage point of Trinity Church.

Financial Plan for Building the New Church

*I*n times of national trial, spiritual needs often receive renewed priority. During the Civil War members of Trinity gave what they could to sustain their country at war, and their patriotic generosity spilled over into support for the church. Even in the midst of war, the congregation was able to find the resources to undertake a new church building. In 1863 the pewholders adopted a financial blueprint that guided them throughout the entire building process. It included among other measures a provision for the vestry to levy the much-debated and long-needed pew taxes.

A key element of financing the new church was the sale of the existing building. Dr. John Andrews, a member of the congregation not to be confused with attorney John W. Andrews, purchased the old Trinity church in 1863 for $10,000. He allowed the congregation to continue using it for worship. Shortly thereafter, Andrews died and his heirs tried to cancel the contract, asking that the $5,000 already paid be refunded with interest. The vestry refused but apparently without alienating Andrews's widow, who remained a member of Trinity. When Andrews's estate was finally settled, his heirs sold the land to Peter Hayden, the banking, mining, and railroad mogul. Hayden tore down the church and erected a modern office building, a four-story brownstone crowned by a massive cornice, with tall French glass windows at ground level. The only remnant of the old church is a single block of stone; it was installed in the key-stone of the arch of the great window over the main entrance of the new church.[35]

The lion's share of funding for the new church came from 16 subscribers in the congregation, each of whom pledged around $2,000. They included John W. Andrews, William Dennison, William G. Deshler, Joseph R. Swan, Peter Hayden, William A. Platt, Noah H. Swayne, Mrs. Alfred Kelley, Mrs. William B. Hubbard, and Baldwin Gwynne. For every $100 subscribed and paid, a subscriber had one vote, and decisions were made by majority vote. Thus these parishioners had a correspondingly loud voice in matters related to the new church.

It now remained to select an architect and a plan. In July of 1863 the building committee, consisting of William A. Platt, William Deshler, and Francis Collins (son-in-law of Alfred Kelley), travelled to Detroit to look at churches there. The group included several women, among them Lucy (Mrs. James) Wilcox, Miss Grammer, the rector's sister, and Fanny Platt, a teenager more interested in the secular sights than in church architecture.

Christ Church in Detroit impressed the Columbus visitors so much that upon returning, they hired its architect, Gordon W. Lloyd. Lloyd was a young Englishman who had recently arrived in Detroit to establish a practice. Trinity paid him an advance of $350 to design a virtual copy of Christ Church. The chancel would be deeper and the south transept narrower than the north one in order to fit Trinity's lot. Even before construction began, cost estimates exceeded the budget and Lloyd was summoned to Columbus to modify his plans. A less expensive stone was selected, a sandstone quarried in Newark. The spire and ornaments were abandoned. Plans for the chapel were scrapped but subsequently restored. The vestry negotiated a temporary loan, and income from the Andrews purchase enabled the church to undertake construction.

The master builder of Trinity was William Fish, founder of the Fish Stone

Gordon W. Lloyd of
Detroit, Michigan,
architect of Trinity
Episcopal Church.

company. He was trained as a mason and stone cutter in England and came to
Columbus with the hope of working on the new Statehouse, but he was not hired.[36]
To lay the foundation of Trinity, Fish's company was paid $5.00 per day. Work began
in 1866. Bishop McIlvaine refused to lay the cornerstone, on the grounds that he
had done so in the past and nothing had come of it.

By 1867 the foundation had reached the surface of the ground, where the first
project had stalled. This time the work continued. A new building committee
relieved the original one and oversaw the completion of the project. By the middle
of 1868 costs for the church and lot had mounted to $47,000, the amount pledged
by the congregation. The building, however, was far from complete. Alfred Kelley,
the financial wizard, helped the committee negotiate a loan for $15,000 to be paid
out of future pew sales. A year later the finishing details were being worked out. A
committee of ladies, including Mary (Mrs. Albert) Buttles, Laura (Mrs. John G.)
Mitchell, and Ann Eliza (Mrs. William) Dennison, representing also their natal
Trinity families the Ridgways, Platts and Neils, gave advice on upholstery and carpeting. Historian Jacob Studer described the interior, finished in white walnut and
ash "in a chaste and beautiful manner," and he approved the "modern style" of its furnishings.[37] The total cost of the church was now pegged at $70,000.

Trinity's rector, the Rev. Charles A. L. Richards, a Yale graduate and former
medical doctor, recalled a terrible moment in the church's construction. When the

THE FISH STONE CO.
Contractors and Builders

FISH'S STEAM STONE WOI

William Fish (b. ca. 1823) and the Fish Stone Company. Building Trinity gave the Fish family a unique tie to the church, and they became members and communicants. Fish's only son, William Fish Jr., followed his father's calling as a stonemason. In 1874 a double wedding at Trinity united him and his sister Jane to their respective spouses.

roof timbers were put in place, it was evident that the peak of the roof was not directly over the church's center aisle. "The rector and the building committee and contractor wrung their hands and tried to disbelieve their eyes…it seemed as if the Gospel itself could hardly go straight to its mark under such adverse conditions."[38] Nothing could be done, and the defect remained, though it is not apparent today.

In the midst of this work, another clergy crisis loomed. In January of 1868 Richards complained to the vestry of his serious financial straits. His salary no longer covered even his daily living expenses and he had been unable to save even a dollar for his family in case of death or disability. Only two rooms of his house were furnished. When he came to Trinity from Philadelphia in 1865, he was promised a

The Rev. C. A. L. Richards, rector from 1865–1869,
oversaw the building of the present church.

salary increase when the church was finished. Two and
a half years later the church was still a work in
progress. Apparently the vestry was able to placate
Richards for a time. But at a vestry meeting the following year, he pointed out that $425 of his salary was
still unpaid, then he withdrew. After deliberation the
vestry decided to take out a loan—which was used to
pay construction debts and to cushion the pews.
Richards resigned, surely dismayed that his livelihood was so little valued. The salary
due him was soon paid. He became rector of a parish in Providence, Rhode Island,
where he served for the next 33 years.

Pews in the New Church

The sale of pews was an integral piece of the plan to finance the new church.
Sufficient revenue was needed to cover the cost overruns and operating
expenses for the new building, but the price of pews had to remain within reach of
all who wanted to buy or rent them. A wide sliding scale was put into effect. The
16 principal subscribers to the new church each purchased a pew for $800, leaving
100 pews for general sale. One-tenth of the pews were set aside for the poor, for
strangers, and for longtime members who could not afford to pay for them.

The actual sale of pews, scheduled for Easter Monday in 1869, proceeded by
strict rules. Free market forces were given full play as pews were sold to the highest
bidder at or above their assessed value. If two or more bids came in for the same
pew, it went to the one whose original subscription to the building was higher and
had been paid. Following the sale, remaining pews were offered for rent at two-
thirds of their appraised value. Renting a pew was thus the more economical
option. Pew taxes could be levied at the discretion of the vestry; for 1869 the
assessment was 15 percent for purchasers, 23 percent for renters. If one fell six
months behind in pew rent or accumulated two years' worth of unpaid taxes, the
pew was repossessed. This happened very shortly to Richard Page, who owed $150
when the vestry reclaimed his pew in April of 1870.

The vestry was stern about finances, keeping close tabs on every dollar in over-
due pew rents. In 1870 the church's annual budget was around $5,800 and it owed

TRINITY CHURCH.

Lithograph of Trinity Episcopal Church. The congregation could not afford to build the proposed steeple, estimated to cost between $10,000 and $12,000 in 1872.

a $15,000 mortgage. Three years later that mortgage fell due. Under the threat of an auction of the church and its property, the pew owners ponied up the assessed amounts to pay off the debt. In June of 1871 work on the tower was begun, and when the funds ran out, the work stopped at the belfry window. The tower was not completed until 1910, when the church was finally dedicated.

Conclusion

Trinity's Gothic Revival style, with its implied reverence for medieval times, was an unusual choice for a congregation with a strong evangelical background and little sympathy for high church practices. Perhaps following the upheaval of the Civil War, leaders wanted their church building to reflect a time in history when Christianity was a stronghold. The magnificent new church expressed the social and religious aspirations of its members. It also strengthened morale in the congregation, which pulled in unison to complete the project. A more business-like attitude prevailed, and improved bookkeeping practices and standing committees were instituted to oversee finances, care of the church, and music. The spokesman for the building committee envisioned the vestry and congregation united by the mutual performance of their fiscal duties. When all in the congregation understood that "a promise to pay money to a church is as binding and important as a like promise to a Bank," he predicted with confidence that Trinity would experience no more financial difficulty. Unfortunately this golden age would never materialize.

Notes

[1] *Fourth Annual Report of the Commissioner of Statistics to the Governor of the State of Ohio. 1860* (Columbus: Richard Nevins, 1961), 130, 132.

[2] *The Golden Jubilee of the First Congregational Church, Columbus, Ohio 1852-1902*, 91.

[3] John W. Andrews, "The Nebraska Bill Speech. . . at a Meeting of the Citizens of Columbus, Ohio, February 14, 1854; "Address Delivered Before the New England Society of Columbus, December 22, 1858," (Columbus: Follet, Foster, and Co., 1859), 16-17; "Speech of J. W. Andrews on the Engrossment of the Bill Relating to Fugitives from Labor or Service from Other States," Delivered in the Ohio House of Representatives, February 9, 1839. Copies available at Ohio Historical Society.

[4] Andrews, "Address" (1858), 18, 22.

[5] Butler, 156, 173 n. 101.

[6] Julius Grammer, *Parish Statistics of Trinity Church, Columbus from June 1863 to June 1864* (Columbus, 1864), 8.

[7] Jones, *State*, 98-99.

[8] Diary of Joel Buttles, January 18, 1845.

[9] Carus, ed., *Memorials*, 258.

[10] *In Memoriam: James Lawrence Bates* (Columbus, n.d.), 49. Copy in Trinity parish archives.

[11] Lee, 2, 807.

[12] F. M. McAdams, *Every-Day Soldier Life or a History of the One Hundred and Thirteenth Ohio Volunteer Infantry* (Columbus, 1884), 10.

[13] *Ohio State Journal*, May 4, 1864.

[14] Lee, II, 837-8, 808-9.

[15] Duane Mowry, "Richard Plantagenet Llewellyn Baber: A Sketch and Some of his Letters," *Ohio Archaeological and Historical Quarterly* 19 (1910), 370-81.

[16] Lee, II, 122.

[17] Sources for information on Columbus during the Civil War are Francis P. Weisenburger, "Columbus During the Civil War," *Publications of the Ohio Civil War Centennial Commission* 12 (Columbus: Ohio State University Press, 1963); Lee's history (including biographical sketches); George W. Knepper, *Ohio and its People* (Kent, Ohio: Kent State University Press, 1997); Eugene Roseboom and Francis P. Weisenburger, *A History of Ohio* (Columbus: Ohio Historical Society, 1996); Whitelaw Reid, *Ohio in the War: Her Statesmen, Generals and Soldiers*, 2 vols. (Cincinnati: Robert Clarke Co., 1895; rpt. 1995). On the political landscape of Columbus in the pre-war years, see Cole, *A Fragile Capital*.

[18] *Ohio State Journal*, April 23, 1861.

[19] Bill Arter, "Esther Institute," *Columbus Vignettes IV* (Columbus: Nida-Eckstein Printing, 1971), 30.

[20] *We Too Built Columbus*, 120.

[21] McAdams, 14.

[22] Diary of Fanny Platt, June 6, 1863.

[23] McAdams, 70.

[24] Estimates range as high as 5000, though 2260 are buried at the cemetery there. See Garrett, 75; Mike Harden, *Columbus Celebrates the Millennium* (Montgomery, AL: Community Communications, Inc., 2000), 70.

[25] Butler, 152.

[26] Carus, ed., 217-18, 222.

[27] Diocesan Journal, 1862, 20-21; 1863, 25.

[28] *Ohio State Journal*, April 22, 1861.

[29] Diocesan Journal, 1864, 28.

[30] Diocesan Journal, 1865, 59.

[31] Diary of Fanny Platt, April 12, 1865; May 18, 1865.

[32] Lee, II, 150.

[33] Manuscript reminiscences of Arleigh D. Richardson, courtesy of Molly Morris (both grand-children of Charles R. Wheeler).

[34] Diocesan Journal, 1865, 140-41.

[35] Wilcox, 25.

[36] See "Trinity Episcopal Church," *Keystone: The Newsletter of the Columbus Historic Preservation Office* (Winter 2001), 1-2.

[37] Jacob H. Studer, *Columbus, Ohio: Its History, Resources, and Progress* (1873), 178.

[38] "Trinity Observes its Nonagenary," *The Ohio State Journal*, May 13, 1907.

Chapter 5

RITUALISM *and* REFORM
AFTER THE WAR

o sooner was the divided country reunited than conflict broke out in the Episcopal Church over matters of churchmanship. Ritualism brought innovations in worship associated with Anglo-Catholicism, while science and historical criticism threatened to undermine the authority of the Bible. While evangelicals strongly resisted these trends, Trinity's congregation took a middle course, the broad church way. While remaining true to its evangelical heritage, Trinity slowly accepted innovations in worship. Its leaders embraced a more liberal theology and active social ministry, working to alleviate poverty and social problems in the city.[1] While men supported missions with their dollars, the charity work was done primarily by women. Indeed, in the nineteenth century most of the worshippers in the pews were women. Their influence on the church was profound, extending from the décor within its walls to the work in the world outside its doors.

Controversy Over Ritualism

larmed and depressed by the errors gaining ground in the church, Bishop McIlvaine continued to fight against ritualism. "I have contended all my life against it, and expect to do so, in the name of the Lord, till I die," he wrote in 1867.[2] McIlvaine joined with 28 bishops who condemned innovations in church worship, such as the use of incense and candles during Holy Communion, reverences to the elements, and changes in clerical dress.

Once again, ritual practices at St. Paul's provoked McIlvaine's wrath. Their rector, the Rev. Colin C. Tate, introduced a vested choir that began morning and evening service with a hymn sung in processional. In 1869 this was wholly unknown in Ohio and contrary to the rubric stating that morning and evening prayer be opened by reading sentences of scripture. For the choir to wear surplices was also not allowed. Soon, McIlvaine feared, the organist and church wardens would wear surplices, and the clergy would hanker after popish priestly robes. He ordered Tate to cease the practice, but his admonitions had no effect. Nor did the threat of a trial. Twice an ecclesiastical court was convened and then dissolved when it could not reach a resolution. (Trinity members Judge Joseph Swan and General John G. Mitchell served on the prosecution.) Tate finally deferred to his bishop after defying him for a full year.

Trinity's rector took a less controversial approach to music. In 1864 Julius Grammer insisted on the subordinate role of music in worship, declaring, "The choir is to be an auxiliary to the desk and the pulpit."[3] Still, the congregation was proud of its choir. In 1876 its dozen members included young women. The purchase of a $2,600 organ in 1878 and the subsequent expansion of the music program, however, triggered a budget crisis.[4] In 1883 a committee consisting of both men and women, pew-owners and pew-renters, was appointed to determine what kind of choir the congregation desired and how to pay for it. On a parish-wide survey, many called for simple music the congregation could sing. "We should have worship, not musical performances," wrote one critic. The committee recommended the money-saving measure of employing a choir of five men and training Sunday school boys as choristers. The choir would never be put into surplices, they promised. This compromise, which sought to avoid the appearance of Anglo-Catholicism, was short-lived. Within ten years, Trinity had a professional-quality choir of 40 men and boys who wore surplices and sang in processional.

Not all Episcopalians accepted the gradual increase of ceremony. Some evangelicals, disappointed that the church's pronouncements against ritualism were not stronger, withdrew and established the Reformed Episcopal Church in 1874. James Bates, who married Alfred Kelley's daughter in 1837 and later became a respected judge, affiliated himself with the Reformed Episcopal Church of Philadelphia, as there was no organized congregation in Columbus.[5] His wife Maria remained a member of Trinity, where she and her children Fanny, Mary, and Alfred were communicants. Throughout her life

James Bates (1815–1890), who became dissatisfied with the increase of ritual at Trinity and joined the Reformed Episcopal Church.

she exercised the independent spirit she exhibited at her wedding, when she persuaded the minister to omit "obey" from her vows. Her husband may have been dissatisfied with Trinity, but she maintained her ties with the church of her childhood.

Embellishing the Church

Trinity's splendid Gothic Revival building swept its congregation into the tide of ritualism, for its very design encouraged profound changes in worship practice.[6] Classical-styled churches and simple meeting houses that featured a central pulpit focused attention on the reading of scripture and preaching. Trinity's new Gothic church, by contrast, had a deep chancel that provided a distinct place for sacramental worship. A plan to modify the church in 1876 called for cutting down the pulpit and moving it to the north wall. One reason for removing the pulpit was that it was awkward for a robed preacher to ascend and descend the pulpit steps. Occupants of nearby pews also had to crane their necks to see the preacher, which made these pews less valuable. No doubt there were objections to the changes, and the pulpit was merely lowered. The plan also called for adding ornamental seating in the chancel and a railing. Now the communion table became the focal point, instead of the pulpit, suggesting a shift of emphasis from preaching the word to celebrating the sacrament.[7]

Another fashion was polychrome painting, which replaced simple

The earliest-known photograph of Trinity's interior, decorated for Easter around 1908, just after the installation of electric lights. The elaborate decorations of the chancel were matched by greater ritual expression in the liturgy.

whitewashed interiors. According to the 1876 plan, the reredos was decorated with the symbol of the Trinity and a cross and crown in the center panel, with the scripture "God so loved the world," and "The Spirit and the Bride say come." Panels on either side would contain scripture such as "Do this in remembrance of me" and "Go unto all the world and preach the Gospel." In terms of the controversy over ritualism, the plan sent a mixed message. Moving the pulpit suggested that emphasis on the Word was being sidelined and a space cleared for presentation of the sacrament. At the same time, the scriptural verses printed on the reredos reaffirmed the congregation's evangelical heritage.

A series of misunderstanding plagued the painting project and led to the departure of the rector, the Rev. Rufus W. Clark. Junior warden Robert S. Smith had engaged the painter Charles Jansen to do the frescoing. After Jansen visited the Church of the Holy Spirit in Gambier for inspiration, he presented a design which the rector and vestry approved. The work began shortly and was completed by November. In the meantime, the rector moved to Gambier and was seldom around. When he saw the finished work, he was dissatisfied with the design and implied that

The Rev. Rufus W. Clark, rector from 1871–1877. In 1874, Clark married Lucy G. Dennison, daughter of parishioner and former governor William G. Dennison. When Clark died in Columbus in 1909, his funeral was held at Trinity.

Smith had acted without authority. Some members of the congregation who disapproved of the work also blamed Smith. One issue was the cheap cost. Jansen's fee was only $200, while Clark had envisioned a style of work that would have cost about $1,000.

Smith felt unfairly maligned, and the vestry agreed that the rector was at fault for not conveying his wishes more clearly. Then they discussed with Clark the condition of the parish, a conference that resulted in the rector offering his resignation. The vestry, however, declined to accept it, hoping to save face and avoid the appearance of a rector leaving over a decorating dispute. It is not clear why Clark moved to Gambier, but an absentee rector was hardly good for the church. Several months later Clark was allowed to leave for a parish in Detroit.

Two years later the entire church interior was cleaned, painted, and frescoed. At first only the side walls were to be cleaned, since they were blackened by soot from the furnace registers. But once they were restored, it was decided to complete the entire interior, including the ceiling. Over the central arch separating the nave from the chancel was inscribed "The Temple of God is Holy, Which Temple Ye Are." Henry Butenshoen completed the work at a cost of $1,150. A recent inspection by the Ohio Historical Society's building conservators revealed an area behind the paneling in the south gallery that bears traces of paint from this period. The church was then brilliant with color, its arches and ceilings painted with intricate designs of acanthus leaves in silver, blue, and red.

Many of the improvements and decorations in the church were underwritten by women in the congregation. The Ladies' Society contributed most of Jansen's fee for painting the chancel. Women paid for the new carpeting and contributed to the purchase of the organ. A few years later Mrs. Dennison paid for the installation of woodwork in the chancel. Women gave gifts that enhanced worship, including ornamental hangings for the chancel and embroideries and furnishings for the communion table.

Ultimately, fashion as much as theology determined the decoration of the church. The women of the parish rose eagerly to the task of embellishing the Lord's house as richly as they did their own Victorian homes. Much deliberation went into small details, such as fabric for chancel chairs and the choice of foam rubber over horsehair for new pew cushions. Those who wanted to use their cushions from the old church had to refurbish them to exacting standards. It was important that the new church reflect the prosperity and high status of its members, especially those who had contributed substantially to its erection.

Trinity's grand new church was a desirable site for weddings. The only royal wedding Columbus has ever seen was celebrated at Trinity on May 16, 1871. The bride was Amelia "May" Parsons and the groom was Prince Alexander Ernst de Lynar of Bavaria. The couple had met while May was studying in Europe and the Prince was an aide to Emperor William I at the German embassy in Paris. The bride's father, George Parsons, was one of the city's wealthiest men, living in a Greek Revival mansion at the corner of Parsons Avenue and Bryden Road. St. Paul's rector Colin Tate and Bishop McIlvaine conducted the service.

Hours before the wedding, crowds gathered, enough ladies, the *Ohio State Journal* reported, "to make a good sized sewing society." Police were stationed near the entrance, but the crowd was peaceful. No one was excluded from the church, not even the chattering girls on their way home from school. Seats in the north gallery offered the best view of the bride, who wore a dress of heavy white corded silk with a moderate train, a long overskirt looped with orange blossoms, a long tulle veil, and a necklace of diamonds and pearls. The Prince was in full ceremonial dress, with decorations about his neck and "a profusion of rings" on his fingers.[8]

A less dignified occasion was the wedding of Sallie Maybell Monypeny, a member of Trinity, and Logan Conway Newson, in December of 1885. Fanny Fullerton, who was married at Trinity just five months after May Parsons's royal wedding, wrote an account of the Monypeny wedding to her sister, Minnie:

The crowd at the church was the greatest jam I think I ever was in, and seemed to be quite beyond the control of the ushers, for although there were cards of admittance securing, as they supposed,

Amelia (May) Parsons, daughter of George Parsons, married Prince Alexander Lynar at Trinity on May 16, 1871 and left Columbus to live in his castle in Lindenau, Germany. After May's death in 1920, her children sued to recover her Columbus property that had been seized by the United States during WWI.

Rutherford H. Platt (1853–1928) and
Maryette Smith Platt (1863–1929).

good seats for those invited to the recep-
tion, the crowd pushed forward so that
when those dressed in full evening costume
arrived there were no seats for them, and
most of them had to…stand in the side
aisles under the gallery, and some stood
up on the seats in order to see."

From her pew near the back, Fanny
enjoyed the confusion of the ushers and
the indignation of invited guests who
arrived to find there were no seats.[9]

Many brides still opted to be married
at home. The new custom of a church
wedding was slow to displace the tradition of home weddings. The size of the
wedding and the suitability of the bride's
home were two factors to consider.
Fanny's younger brother, Rutherford H.
Platt, married Maryette Smith at her home
on a January evening in 1887. Her father,
Robert S. Smith, was a long-time warden
and vestryman at Trinity and her mother,
Anna Swan, the daughter of Judge Swan,
was active in Trinity's Bee Hive Society.

The Smiths lived just steps from Trinity
Church. Guests entered the library, which
was decorated with palms and roses, lilies
and hyacinths. In an adjacent room, the
bride and groom knelt at a prie-dieu
before a bay window draped in lace. The
reception occurred in the dining room.

One of the guests was former
President Rutherford B. Hayes, the
groom's uncle. Another was Fanny and
Rutherford's half-sister Susan, who wore
the dress from her own recent wedding to
Herman Hubbard. Herman was the grandson of Joel Buttles' nemesis in the world of
banking, William Hubbard. Susan wore a
relatively plain dress of white silk mull
with short train, high neck, long sleeves
and carried no flowers.[10] She had insisted
on a simple wedding to be held at Trinity
Church with only about 40 relatives
attending. No doubt the event was a
marked contrast to the mayhem of the
Monypeny wedding.

Postwar Changes in
Episcopal Leadership

After the Civil War, there was a shortage of clergy to serve the growing Episcopal Church. Ohio's evangelical clergymen were moving to parishes in the west, leaving their congregations bereft. In 1866, 20 of the 97 Episcopal parishes in Ohio lacked a resident minister.[11]

After Charles A. L. Richards left in 1869, Trinity had difficulty replacing him. Three candidates had turned down the position when Bishop Bedell intervened. Though the vestry preferred to make its own decisions, they reluctantly agreed to call the candidate favored by the bishop. They made it clear that this course of action, which violated their procedure for calling a rector, would not become a precedent. As it turns out, the candidate's request for a two-month annual vacation was unacceptable. No doubt relieved to have a good excuse, they did not hire him. A number of other candidates were invited or considered before Rufus Clark of New Hampshire accepted the position in 1871. He departed six years later following the misunderstanding over decorating the chancel.

Trinity was experiencing a new, more direct relationship with the bishops, particularly in the matter of calling a new rector. When the Diocese of Southern Ohio was formed in 1874, an advantage was that the bishop would have a smaller territory to oversee and hence be more available to parishes. While Bishop Bedell's involvement had been resented, Trinity welcomed the assistance of southern Ohio's new bishop, the Rt. Rev. Thomas A. Jaggar, in their search for a rector after Rufus Clark's departure. After five candidates had turned them down, Jaggar sat down with the vestry. Several vestrymen made pledges in order to raise the salary offer to $3,500. With Jaggar's help, Trinity finally hired the Rev. Charles H. Babcock, who had been trained at Kenyon College.

In the 1870s Trinity was thriving, with two services on Sunday and a lecture in the chapel on Wednesday evening. The 200-member congregation grew to 350 members

The Rev. Charles H. Babcock, rector from 1879–1888.

in 1874. In 1872 the Sunday evening service was made a "free" service with pews open to anyone. This was a way to expand the congregation beyond current pewholders. Under rectors Rufus Clark and Charles Babcock, Trinity was a healthy congregation with a growing commitment to the city beyond its doors.

Mission Churches Established

As industry expanded and the population of Columbus grew in the years after the Civil War, the need for mission outreach to the poor and unchurched became acute. Speaking to the 1867 convention, Bishop Bedell had urged the church to plant itself where people were settling. In Ohio people were moving from rural areas to new towns and to cites like Columbus. The growing network of railroads was responsible for this migration. In fact, the railroads were among the largest employers in the city of Columbus.

Trinity's first mission was a school for the children of railway workers. It was held in the waiting room of the Union Depot, just east of the present-day Columbus Convention Center. In 1871 Trinity's congregation raised money to erect a chapel near the depot. This mission outpost became the thriving Church of the Good Shepherd. Though 34 communicants of Trinity transferred their membership to Good Shepherd, this did not hurt Trinity's congregation. Within a few years the mission church's Sunday school enrolled 181 pupils. It was supervised by General John G. Mitchell, Trinity's Civil War hero, and Augustus N. Whiting, son of the founder of Trinity's Sunday school. Pews at the mission were free, for the church served a poorer neighborhood. All expenses, including the minister's salary, were raised by subscription. By 1875 Trinity was recommending parish status for its offspring, which meant that it would be governed by its own vestry. In 1885 the congregation built a new church at the southeast corner of Park Street and Buttles Avenue.

Trinity also established the St. Andrew's Mission east of what is today known as German Village. St. John's Mission, west of the Scioto in the area then known as Middletown, began with a Sunday school in 1873. The relationship between Trinity and St. John's remained close, with the vestry overseeing its finances and the congregation contributing toward its expenses. Youth from Trinity lent their labor to build a new church in 1900. Income from endowments and various legacies also favored the mission. There was a good deal of hand-holding while St. John's took steps to become an independent parish in 1914.

St. Philip's Mission, founded in 1891 to serve the African-American neighborhood, was not so well nurtured by its parent church. From its origins in a former saloon at Cleveland Avenue and Naghten Street, the mission survived due to the work of Augustus N. Whiting and his wife, Ellen. Whiting suspended his term as junior warden of Trinity to organize St. Philip's. The Rev. Julius Atwood, then rector of Trinity, was a strong supporter of the new congregation, and he engaged Robert Brown, a minister "of their own race," as vicar. In 1907, after Atwood's resignation, the congregation of St. Philip's felt bereft, as no further support seemed forthcoming from Trinity. They asked and were allowed to separate from Trinity in order to become a diocesan mission that could seek support from other parishes.

Before the establishment of St. Philip's, a handful of families identified as "colored" were on Trinity's parish roll. This is the first evidence of any racial diversity in the congregation. The spirit of the times, however, favored segregation, and no doubt those of both races preferred the establishment of a separate congregation.

A unique outreach was All Saint's Mission for the Deaf, founded at Trinity in 1876 by the Rev. Austin Ward Mann. Mann was only the second person who was both deaf and mute to be ordained in the Episcopal Church. For many years he worked alone in a vast field stretching from Pennsylvania to Nebraska and from Michigan to Kentucky, traveling tens of thousands of miles every year. Three to six times a year he visited Columbus, conducting services for pupils and teachers at the deaf asylum and preaching to a congregation at Trinity that numbered from 100–150 persons.[12] They came from throughout the city, and only about a quarter of them were Episcopalians. When Mann was not present, the service was interpreted in sign language in one of the church's galleries.[13] In 1911 Mann died after suffering a stroke as he emerged from a train at Columbus.

One of the first baptisms in 1884 was 37-year-old George Fancher, who was the deaf son of hearing parents, William and Eveline Brown Fancher. His descendant, David Fancher, has worshipped regularly at Trinity for many years, the sole remaining member of the All Saint's Mission congregation.

Women and the Spirit of Reform

Establishing local mission congregations was an important form of outreach for members of Trinity. It laid the foundation for the movement that became known as the Social Gospel, the commitment to relieve suffering and bring justice to all citizens. By and large, missionary work depended on the efforts of women, the silent majority of American Protestants. In the nineteenth century, religion provided women the motivation and means to engage in reform activities. While men wrote and preached the gospel of service, it was primarily women who actively ministered to the poor, the suffering, and the unchurched. One church historian argues that "from 1850 through 1920 women transformed the Episcopal Church by providing the labor force and the moral initiative" behind social service ministries.[14]

Nineteenth-century women had long been taught that their sphere of influence was the home, their responsibility the care and education of children. The role of mother was ennobled with a political purpose, for she was the builder of nations. Mrs. Sigourney, whose popular column was frequently carried in the diocesan newspaper, the *Western Episcopalian Observer*, wrote that a mother is part of the "mighty experiment, whether a republic can ever be permanent.... Kneeling by the cradle-bed, [she] hath her hand upon the ark of a nation."[15] The same newspaper quoted a clergyman who said, "I have often thought that women's unlimited influence in private, would preponderate over that of man in his most public character."[16] These attitudes encouraged women to believe that their domestic roles were far-reaching in influence.

The church was the other acceptable arena for women, for it occupied a middle ground between their domestic world and the male world of business and politics. Though barred from preaching and leadership in the Episcopal Church, women taught Sunday school, organized parish fairs, raised money, and fed and clothed the poor. These works were an extension of their obligations to educate godly children and to serve others.

Though church records do not focus on women's activities, it is clear that from the earliest days, women at Trinity gathered for the purpose of helping others. In 1829 a Female Missionary Society was begun and a charitable association was active. In the mid-1830s female prayer meetings were growing. Beginning in 1841 women met to sew clothes for the missions and for needy church school children. The sewing society continued during the Civil War as the Mrs. Bedell Society, named for the bishop's wife. The rector praised their efforts in 1864: "In the noble and expansive benevolence of the church, woman is privileged to sustain an important part."[17]

Well before the Episcopal Church established the Women's Auxiliary to the Board of Missions in 1876, parishes such as Trinity had women's missionary societies. In 1870 the Trinity Church Society had 106 women members who met regularly for social purposes and for mission work in the city. Another group was the Women's Five-Cent Missionary Society. Girls and women pledged five cents weekly, bi-weekly, or monthly. Men could be contributing members, but women officiated and managed the group's funds. When they turned money over to the vestry, they specified how it was to be spent.

Women's groups were skilled at raising money for various causes, in effect increasing their husbands' contributions to the church. As Joel Buttles grumbled, the raising of money by ladies at parish fairs "does not differ much from a donation from their husbands made through them."[18] To his credit, Buttles also realized that church work provided women an outlet for their zeal.

Trinity's mission congregations were sustained by the voluntary work of women and girls. When a new chapel was built for St. John's on McDowell Street in 1876, the Ladies' Society contributed nearly a third of the cost. Mary (Mrs. Ezra) Bliss paid for a bell and a new organ, and she left the chapel $3,000 in her will. Laura Platt Mitchell and her daughter, together with Mary (Mrs. George) Hardy and others, held mother's meetings and sewing circles. When the church needed a new organ in 1891, 25 girls made and sold aprons to raise the money. Women made clothing for the poor and a gown and surplice for the minister. In 1893 a ladies' society formed, pledging their help to the rector in any church work on the west side. The women were even trying to organize the men into a chapter of the Brotherhood of St. Andrew and a boy's club.[19]

Columbus Female Benevolent Society

As Columbus grew, more charitable work occurred beyond the boundaries of congregations. Trinity women were often leaders in the city's charitable organizations.[20] This was due to several factors. Barred by convention from taking paid employment, women were encouraged to undertake charitable work. Because they were economically privileged, they could afford domestic help that freed them for volunteer work. They were well educated and able to organize effective programs. Many of them had been empowered by their participation in relief work during the Civil War.[21]

One of the earliest outreach efforts by women was the Columbus Female Benevolent Society, organized in 1835 in response to the cholera epidemic that left thousands of widows and orphans. The society was ecumenical. Its first president was Mary Hoge, wife of the Presbyterian minister. The group met in the Town Street Methodist Episcopal Church and started their meetings with scripture and prayer. Several Trinity women were leaders, including Sarah Wager (Mrs. Noah H.) Swayne, Lucy Sullivant (Mrs. James) Wilcox, and the wife of mayor John Bailhache.

Girls practice their needlework skills at the
Industrial School, an early welfare organization
supported by churches such as Trinity.

Ann Eliza (Mrs. William) Dennison, the daughter of William and Hannah Neil, was president in 1872. The society built the first free school for city children in 1838 on a lot donated by Alfred Kelley and his wife (now the site of the YWCA). The society was supported by donations from the city's major Episcopal, Congregational, and Presbyterian congregations.

Some Trinity women went into the homes of the poor, bringing clothes, food, money, and sometimes a doctor. Among the caseworkers were Emma Waterman (Mrs. George F.) Wheeler, Anna Swan (Mrs. Robert S.) Smith, and Laura Platt (Mrs. John G.) Mitchell. The reality they encountered was a stark contrast to their comfortable lives. They visited families with fifteen children living in a dirty hut. They helped a new mother whose crippled husband earned 75 cents a day ripping rags. They taught a teenaged mother and father how to feed a baby. They helped gladly the "deserving poor," those who were humble, thankful, and willing but unable to work. The undeserving poor were judged harshly: "We would hardly help again as they display little gratitude and are so unworthy"; "The woman is dirty and shiftless, and withall very lofty in her notions."[22] Despite their condescending attitude, women found personal and spiritual satisfaction in relieving the suffering of the city's poor.

Another city-wide charitable organization was the Industrial School, organized in 1855 as a day school for orphaned and abandoned children. William Hubbard's wife was its first president. The young Fanny Platt and her friend Clara Wetmore taught classes there on Saturday afternoon. In her journal Fanny described one icy January day in 1864 when, despite being tired from a late-night party, she fulfilled her duty to the five little girls in her class, who had to walk so far in the snow. Another founder of the Industrial School was Hannah Neil, who had been confirmed by Bishop McIlvaine at Trinity. Maria (Mrs. William) Monypeny persuaded local churches, including Trinity, to contribute to this mission. Maria (Mrs. James) Bates was the first president of the Woman's Home, organized in 1869 by ladies from several Protestant churches. Its mission was to reform "fallen" girls and help the destitute to find employment.

Without William G. Deshler, Trinity's women could not have done their benevolent work. A banker, Deshler was the son of David Deshler and Betsy Green Deshler, who were among the earliest settlers in Columbus. His was the grand home on the northwest corner of Third and Broad Streets. His son, John G. Deshler, built the hotel that was a landmark at Broad and High until it was torn down in 1968. It was the elder Deshler's idea to line Broad Street with elm trees, creating a grand avenue worthy of a fine city. Deshler also pledged nearly $3,000 to help build the new Trinity Church, which was visible from his parlor window.

The church, however, was not always the primary recipient of a man's wealth. Deshler's donations to Trinity were mere pocket change compared to his patronage of the Columbus Female Benevolent Society. Deshler's mother died when he was an infant, the first of his many losses. In her honor he established a $100,000 trust for the society, a gift that prompted the incredulous women to sing "Praise God from whom all blessings flow." Deshler's first wife died at age 19, and his second wife, Mary Elizabeth Jones (a granddaughter of James Kilbourne), died after bearing him three children. In 1887 his daughter, Kate Deshler Hunter, died in childbirth at the age of 33. In her honor he gave the society a gift of $33,000 for the relief of worthy poor or widowed mothers. When his daughter's only child died in 1889, Deshler gave the Society $17,000 to aid crippled children. Though his wealth could not shelter him from tragedy, it could help relieve the sufferings of others.

Many Trinity women did charity work for the Deshler Hunter Fund. They knew Kate Hunter and her family. They knew that suffering and loss did not respect boundaries of class. Between 1879 and 1889, four out the seven deaths of Trinity women aged 21–40 were related to childbirth complications. One of these was the rector's wife, Emily Babcock, who died giving birth at the age of 36.

William G. Deshler (1827–1916), banker and philanthropist.

William Blackstone Hubbard (1795–1866), patriarch of a family with a long history at Trinity.

W. B. Hubbard

William Blackstone Hubbard and Joel Buttles were presidents of rival banks, and Buttles wrote in his diary that Hubbard was hard to do business with, greedy, and rigid.[23] At one point he sued Hubbard, alleging a fraudulent transaction.

Hubbard was an educated and witty man who could quote Shakespeare and converse in Latin. Following his years in the state legislature, he settled in Columbus and purchased a 40–50 acre lot on North High Street. There he built a vast home known as Park Place. He had five children who survived him.

One of his daughters, Mary (1819–1889), married Dr. Ezra Bliss and bore two sons who died as infants. Sadly released from maternal duties, she traveled widely, visiting Europe, Africa,

Russia, and the Holy Land. In 1874, at the age of 55, she was presented to Queen Victoria, her exact contemporary. The art treasures she collected during her travels adorned her father's house where she lived. Her means were ample and her benevolence was great. In 1878 her gift of $15,000 to the Columbus Gallery of Fine Arts made her its largest single donor.

Mary Bliss's numerous small charities reveal her character and the extent of her largesse. She was a member of Trinity with a particular interest in the St. John's mission. Between 1874 and 1876 she gave well over $500 to Trinity and its missions and organizations, including support for the Trinity fair, decorating the reredos, the music program, and the church schools. She also paid her pew assess-

Mary Hubbard Bliss (1819–1889), whose charity extended beyond the support of Trinity and the St. John's mission.

ment, pledged for the clergymen's salaries, and purchased a new suit and coat for the assistant, Mr. Kendrick. She helped to retire Trinity's debt on the new church. She was also among the first at Trinity to relinquish her pew in favor of free pews, a move that belied any sense of elitism. When she died in 1889, she left $3,000 in her will to sustain the St. John's Mission.

Under the notebook heading "Heavenly Accounts," Bliss kept track of her charitable giving, which ranged from a few hundred dollars to nearly a thousand dollars annually. Her contributions were not limited to Trinity. She donated a bell for the Methodist church, gave $1,000 to the Home of the Friendless and various sums to the Women's Home, the Hannah Neil Mission, St. Paul's Episcopal Church, the "colored church," the Industrial school, and the Female Benevolent Society. Yet this was a woman who on her European travels could coolly drop $3,400 for a pair of diamond solitaire earrings, nine carats total weight.[24]

Another of William Hubbard's sons, Herman, married Mary Jane Whiton, who was for 36 years president of the Female Benevolent Society yet who apparently thought so little of her sex that she opposed women's suffrage. Their eldest son, Herman, married Susan Platt in 1886, and in 1900 their second son, Fred, married Dorothy Fullerton. These weddings united two of Trinity's (and Columbus's) eldest families. Tragedy struck when Fred Hubbard died in March of 1913, leaving a wife and four children. A few weeks later his 83-year old mother died. Fred Hubbard had served on the vestry from 1894 until his death and had been the treasurer of Kilbourne-Jacobs Company. A memorial window in the south transept of Trinity is dedicated to Hubbard and his mother.

William Hubbard's great-grandson, John Xerxes Farrar was active at Trinity and served on the vestry. His daughter Jane Seymour represents the fifth generation of the Hubbard family to be a member of Trinity.

Mary Jane Whiton, born in 1831, married Herman Hubbard (son of William) at Trinity. A leader in benevolent organizations at Trinity and in the city, she died on March 28, 1913, a few days after the devastating flood that struck Columbus. Here she is shown with her grandson, Winslow Hubbard.

Women's Participation
in Church Life

Throughout the 19th century, religion and church work were the province of women. Women participated in church life more fully and in greater numbers than men. Between 1847 and 1867, three times as many women as men were confirmed at Trinity. Because one had to be confirmed before becoming a communicant, the imbalance extended to the communicant lists, the official measure of church membership. In 1864 only 37 of 211 communicants (17 percent) were male. In 1875 the number had increased slightly to 21 percent. Though they probably attended services with their families and supported the church financially, most men were not active communicants. Even two or three vestrymen in 1864 and 1875 were not on the communicant rolls.

The problem of men's low participation was serious enough that the bishop addressed it at the 1880 diocesan convention. The number of confirmations in the diocese was well below expectations. Moreover, fully nine-tenths were women. The bishop blamed the family, particularly the poor example set by fathers:

> *There is a weakening of parental authority…a neglect of family worship…an irreligious, worldly atmosphere. Parents, and especially fathers of families, seem not to realize their great responsibility to God and to society. The force of a father's example too often tells against church-going…"*

Habits did change, though slowly. Parish records in 1895 show that 51 out of 121 adult men (42 percent) were communicants, a ratio that had doubled in 20 years. But 34 were not even baptized. Of the 197 adult women, 77 percent were communicants and fewer than ten were not baptized.

Not only were women more active in church life than their husbands, but they also bore primary responsibility for ensuring that their children attended services and Sunday school. They had some success, for Sunday school enrollment was almost equal for boys and girls. But mothers could not compel their children—especially their sons—to be confirmed or to receive communion. Where both parents were communicants, it was more likely that all the children were baptized, confirmed, and active communicants. Symmes Browne, his wife Frances, and their three sons were an exemplary family, as was Charles E. Burr, his wife, and their four children. Burr was the scion of a strong Episcopalian family that came to Ohio with James Kilbourne; his son, Karl, would serve on the vestry for many years.

Conclusion

Throughout the nineteenth century, but particularly in the post-Civil War years of ritualism and reform, women played a significant role in Trinity's life. But the ideology of separate spheres for men and women resulted in a similarly separated church. Excluded from the public governance of the church, women developed their own social and mission groups and raised money for favorite projects. This gave them a measure of independence within the hierarchical structure of the Episcopal Church.[25] At Trinity, women influenced the very fabric of the church, for their tastes and the fruits of their work shaped the interior worship space. In response to the feminization of church life would come a concerted effort to bring men back to the church. Meanwhile, through their church-related work, women had broken through some domestic boundaries and found themselves in contact with the world beyond—a world of poverty and need that surely changed them even as they worked to change it.

Notes

[1] On the evangelical movement after the Civil War, its battles against sacramentalism, and accommodation to broad church ideology, see Butler 178-225.

[2] Carus, ed., *Memorials*, 265.

[3] Grammer, *Parish Statistics*.

[4] Installed by Derrick and Felgemaker Pipe Organ Company of Erie, Pennsylvania, it had 28 stops and 1415 pipes, according to the *Trinity Parish Record*, January, 1879.

[5] *In Memorian: James Lawrence Bates*, 14.

[6] Schultz makes the point that Gothic style invited ritual experimentation (*The Church and the City*, 84.)

[7] On architectural change and theology, see Williams, *Houses of God*, esp. chapter 1.

[8] See *The Ohio State Journal*, May 17, 1871; John Switzer, "For Columbus, a wedding of the century," *Columbus Dispatch*, Aug. 22, 1999; "Columbus's Royal Wedding," *Columbus Metropolitan Library Metroscene* (Winter, 2000), p. 8.

[9] *Letters of Fanny Arabella Hayes Platt*, letter dated December 6, 1885.

[10] Ibid., letters dated January 11, 1887 and October 19, 1886.

[11] Diocesan Journal, 1866.

[12] Austin Ward Mann, *Record of Church Work Among Deaf-Mutes in the Diocese of Southern Ohio*, manuscript in Trinity Church archives.

[13] *Historical Outline of Trinity Parish*, Columbus, Ohio, 1817-1910. (Columbus: Franklin Press, 1910).

[14] Mary Sudman Donovan, *A Different Call: Women's Ministries in the Episcopal Church 1850-1919* (Wilton, CT: Morehouse-Barlow, 1986), 6.

[15] "Mrs. Signourney's Letters to Mothers," *Western Episcopalian Observer*, Gambier, Ohio, May 1, 1841.

[16] *Western Episcopalian Observer*, April 2, 1842.

[17] Grammer, *Parish Statistics*.

[18] Diary of Joel Buttles, January 11, 1846.

[19] Clara C. Wetmore, from a manuscript history of St. John's Chapel, ca. 1894, Trinity Parish archives.

[20] This corresponds to the findings of Elizabeth Hayes Turner for a later period, "Episcopal Women as Community Leaders: Galveston, 1900-1989, in Catherine M. Prelinger, ed. *Episcopal Women: Gender, Spirituality and Commitment in an American Mainline Denomination* (New York: Oxford University Press, 1992), 72-110.

[21] Donovan, 11-16. See also Susan Hill Lindley, *"You Have Stept out of Your Place": A History of Women and Religion in America* (Louisville, KY: Westminster John Knox Press, 1996), chapter 10. On the ideal of womanhood, see chapter 6, and on women's church work during the early nineteenth century, see chapter 7.

[22] Notes from Kate Deshler Hunter Fund Cases, 1890-1898. Ohio Historical Society MSS 837/5/6. Confidentiality agreement prohibits identification of individuals associated with particular cases.

[23] Diary of Joel Buttles, April 22, 1842; February 15, 1845.

[24] I am grateful to Sally Larrimer of Columbus, Ohio, great-great granddaughter of William B. Hubbard, for sharing with me a photostat of Mary Bliss's expense book from 1868-76.

[25] For the idea of a "parallel church," see Joan Gunderson, "Women and the Parallel Church: A View from Congregations," in Prelinger, ed., *Episcopal Women*, 111-132.

A mother and child listen to Christ's word. Detail from the south transept window in memory of Mary Jane Hubbard and her son, Fred W. Hubbard.

Chapter 6

"BREAKING *from* OLD MOORINGS": TRINITY AT THE TURN OF THE CENTURY

*B*etween 1860 and 1900 the population of Columbus grew from 18,000 to 125,000 inhabitants. The city expanded to the north and east where the neighborhoods now known as Victorian Village and Old Towne East developed. With the advent of streetcars and automobiles, people built homes farther from the noise and bustle of downtown. Churches followed the people. St. Paul's moved from Third and Mound Streets to East Broad and Monroe Streets, building a frame church in 1882 and a Gothic stone church in 1903. Trinity, however, remained in the heart of the city. Its membership base expanded and became more middle class. By 1900 Trinity had become a metropolitan congregation with a strong urban mission, an identity it would carry throughout the next century.

In 1889 Trinity Church was located in Columbus's prime residential neighborhood. Note the incomplete tower; construction was halted when funds were depleted.

Trinity Becomes a Free Church

The year 1889 marked a turning point for Trinity. The vestry acknowledged it had done nothing to attract new members from the thousands who were coming to Columbus each year. They realized the need for Trinity to change in order to survive.

One obstacle to growth was the system of pew ownership, which created a closed, elite congregation that did not encourage newcomers. Supporters of the system argued that members would maintain ties to the congregation only if they had an investment in the church, like a stockholder has in a company. To make all pews free had profound implications some were reluctant to embrace: it would open the door to everyone and affirm the social as well as spiritual equality of all worshippers in the congregation.

The catalyst for change was the Rev. Robert Ellis Jones, who was called to become Trinity's rector in 1889. Jones made it clear that he would not accept the call until Trinity became a free church. The vestry immediately adopted a resolution in support of free pews, and within a month had secured 20 of the 30 pews that were owned. Among those who were first to relinquish their pews were senior warden Henry P. Smythe and his son, Arthur; James A. Wilcox; Eliza Dennison, the governor's widow; and Mary (Mrs. Ezra) Bliss. Edward L. Hinman, a vestryman since 1870, was opposed to the change but consented to it. Several pews were tied up through inheritance, and four owners simply refused to give up their pews. The vestry also stirred the congregation and raised the salary offer from a pitiful $2,500 to a respectable $3,500. Sensing their over-eagerness, Jones cautioned them not to expect a rector to solve the congregation's problems. He called on the church's lay leaders to inspire the congregation from within to accept change.[1]

The Rev. Robert Ellis Jones, rector from 1889–1893. "The spectacle of a parish equipping to stay in the lower part of the city and work among the masses when others are following the pocket-books up town, is one that tells of the power of a Christly faith," Jones wrote to fellow clergyman William Bodine on June 12, 1889.

Jones visited Trinity in July and afterwards conferred with the Rt. Rev. Boyd Vincent, assistant to Bishop Jaggar in Cincinnati. Reluctant to leave his Kalamazoo congregation, Jones had hit upon another plan for Trinity—establishing it as a cathedral church. Securing Bishop Vincent at Trinity would be the key. Junior warden

Charles Burr admitted that Jones's proposal "came near to taking our breath away."[2] They invited the bishop, who visited but declined to settle at Trinity, for he needed time to survey the diocese before attaching himself to a parish.

Instead Bishop Vincent assisted the negotiations between Jones and the vestry. He wrote to Jones with advice about taking charge at Trinity. Vincent had noted a "dislike of your reading in monotone and still more the prospect of intoning the service," and he advised Jones to move slowly regarding changes. "They are not ready for work yet. They want feeding first. They are literally starving for the Gospel."[3] Vincent also reported complaints about Jones's morning sermon, though the congregation liked the evening sermon. Jones dismissed the congregation's criticisms. His evening sermon was, he said, a low-class sermon with "very little spirituality, or Gospel, in it," preached "for a test to discover the existence of the Gospel thirst."[4] The congregation's favorable view of this sermon reflected poorly on their spiritual state.

After receiving the bishop's advisory letter, Jones wrote to Burr that he was reconsidering his acceptance, for it seemed that the parish was not united in support of a new rector and the new order he would impose. Jones also wrote to the Rev. William Bodine, president of Kenyon College and a critic of old-style evangelical religion,[5] "I should judge that all the people whose heads are set backward upon their shoulders made their moan to the Bishop, expressed their fears of impending rationalism and ritualism and impressed him that my usefulness in Columbus is very uncertain." He saw the congregation as a sick patient and himself as the doctor, unwilling to force the medicine down their throats but unable to change the cure to their liking.[6]

When Jones was assured that his hands were not to be tied in any way by the congregation or by the bishop, he accepted the position. He admitted a feeling of dread at "assuming the burden" of Trinity.[7] The wardens and vestry were aware that they were engaging an authoritarian rector who disdained them. Yet both parties proceeded, for the congregation had already made sweeping changes in anticipation of Jones's coming. Burr was afraid that to lose Jones would discourage and divide the congregation, "render[ing] the future of our slowly dying church very dark."[8] The vestry also dreaded the "long harassing business" of a new search process. Trinity had fixed its sights upon one man and, despite being warned, they hoped for him to perform a miracle on the moribund congregation.

Jones had definite ideas for changes he would introduce at Trinity. He favored an expanded role for the choir, believing its purpose was "to lead in worship." He wanted to introduce music to revive poor attendance at the evening service. His choir would be vested, and he was in favor of processional and recessional hymns as a "dignified and attractive way of getting a choir in and out of the chancel."[9] Bishop Vincent disagreed regarding the choral evening service and processionals, but he recognized Jones's right, as rector, to determine these matters. Finally, Jones maintained, if Trinity were serious about expanding its congregational base, it had to consider adopting a liturgy that would appeal to a wider class of people. Tastes were changing, and ritual and ceremony seemed the key to attracting new members.

In 1889, members of the boys' choir pose on the church steps with choirmaster Julius G. Bierck and the rector.

The New Order at Trinity

Despite the prickly personality that came across in Jones's letters, the changes he brought made him popular with the congregation. Among those who welcomed the new order was 42-year-old Fanny Platt Fullerton, daughter of William Platt and younger sister of Laura Platt Mitchell. Fanny wrote to her sister of Jones's success at Trinity, observing that her niece "will not know Trinity when she comes back. We all like Mr. Jones so much, and he is putting new life into old Trinity. He seems to take an *individual* interest in each member of his congregation, and is such a good earnest man that even Erskine already thinks a great deal of him." Dr. Erskine Fullerton, whom Fanny married in 1871, was not an Episcopalian. He was not even baptized. He once feared that his young son, who enjoyed reading Bible stories, would become a minister. (His father and two brothers were Presbyterian preachers.) Yet he began attending evening service with his children when Jones was rector.

Fanny's family also liked the changes in the service. On another occasion she wrote to her sister, "We have never had as beautiful a service in the church as we had Christmas day. The choir of men and boys sang downstairs for the first time, and with their white vestments and the boys' sweet earnest faces it seemed like an angelic host indeed.... The church is crowded at every service, even in the evening."[10] Jones had succeeded in resurrecting the moribund evening service with music. And in a move unthinkable a generation earlier, his choir was outfitted with surplices.

The Fullertons were a typical family in their pattern of church involvement. Fanny's activities drew in her children and even her husband. Fanny began a Saturday sewing society in her home with 20 Sunday school girls. Her nine-year-old son Rutherford then begged that the five boys of his Sunday school class be allowed to meet as well. Fanny put them to work making lamp-lighters and shaving cases for an upcoming church fair. Within a few months her "Circle of King's Daughters and King's Sons" numbered 43 children who filled the house on Saturday mornings. The rector came to the sewing circle one Saturday morning and took the time to become acquainted with every girl, which endeared him further to Mrs. Fullerton.

While Jones was instituting a new order, James A. Wilcox, a man who exemplified the old order at

James A. Wilcox, longtime secretary of the vestry and author of the 1876 "Historical Sketch of Trinity Church." Wilcox's wife Lucy, granddaughter of Franklinton founder Lucas Sullivant, was also a mainstay of Trinity.

Trinity, died. Born in 1828, his family ties to Trinity were deep, for his father was one of Trinity's founders. His wife Lucy, the granddaughter of Franklinton founder Lucas Sullivant, was an active churchwoman. Wilcox was a staunch evangelical churchman of the Bishop McIlvaine school. He remained loyal to Trinity, however, and "when in recent years he consented to changes in the service, which seemed to him like breaking from old moorings and which cost him more personal grief than many know, he stipulated only *that the Gospel should still be preached.*"[11] Wilcox first joined the vestry in 1857. When he attempted to resign in 1883 on account of his hearing loss, his colleagues refused and made accommodations to enable him to continue. For more then 30 years he wrote the vestry minutes in an even, rounded hand with a backward slant. A new hand took over the minutes in 1890, foreshadowing an era of change.

A 1902 view of East Broad Street, showing First Congregational Church on the left, the William G. Deshler home, Trinity's parish house, and the tower of Trinity Episcopal Church at right.

Trinity Purchases a Parish House

*J*ones was dedicated to preaching the gospel, even beyond Trinity's doors. When he was hired he stipulated that Trinity should obtain a parish house to serve as a "workshop" in the city. The chapel was no longer adequate for the business of a large city parish. In 1891 Trinity initiated the purchase of the Irving House, a hotel owned by George M. Parsons, whose daughter had married the Prussian prince at Trinity in 1871. Five parishioners each subscribed $5,000 towards its purchase, and shortly more than $45,000 had been pledged, so the sale was completed.

The gala fundraiser for the parish house was a typical church social function of the so-called Gilded Age. Julius Bierck, the choirmaster, was allowed to operate a music school from the parish house. In exchange he offered to give a benefit concert. Maria (Mrs. William) Monypeny, president of the ladies' society, organized the event, which featured Bierck's students and Gertrude Parsons as soloist. The location was Columbus's Grand Opera House, where the stage was set as a parlor

for the musical entertainment. Three hundred tickets were sent to the M. E. Lilley Regalia Factory to enable the young working women to enjoy an evening of high-class music. The event netted $750 for remodeling and furnishing the new parish house.[12]

Trinity House was soon in constant use by a dozen parish organizations, including a ladies' aid society and the Woman's Auxiliary, the Trinity Cadets, the Boys' Brigade, and the Brotherhood of St. Andrew. It was also used by the choir, the Sunday school, the vestry, and the altar guild. Despite the enthusiasm that drove the purchase of the parish house, the mortgage burdened the congregation for many years. In the 1890s when a national financial depression affected Columbus, parishioners of ample means, such as Mrs. Monypeny, and those of modest means, like Symmes Browne, could not make their pledges to the parish house fund. In 1898 the vestry decided to sell Trinity House, admitting that it had been only a temporary solution to the need for a "workshop" in the city. In 1904 the vestry sold the property for $50,000, though Trinity continued to occupy the building until the new parish house was completed in 1910.

Supporting a Free Church

As a free church Trinity was modestly successful at raising revenue and membership. Before Jones arrived in 1889, income from the 72 pews was $3,860. Three years later there were 189 pledges for a total of $4,880.[13] Though the average pledge amount ($26) was half that of the former average pew rental, overall revenues increased somewhat. During the financial depression of the next several years, the number of pledges rose slowly, while the average pledge amount declined slightly. Some doubted whether the new system would succeed.

When the Rev. Julius Atwood succeeded Jones as rector in 1894, he urged the congregation to put aside their past differences and make the system work. Trinity, he said, was no longer a church of rich laymen. All who attended, even children,

The Rev. Julius W. Atwood, rector from 1894–1906.

had to assume the responsibility of giving. In 1895 collection boxes at the door were abandoned in favor of the more direct method of passing the offertory plate. Pledge cards explaining the system of church support were placed in the pews. Vestry members called on those who had not pledged. In many families, husbands and wives and children pledged individually.

At the turn of the twentieth century, old and new habits of giving were both evident. Twelve members, including the widows of William Dennison and William G. Deshler, former vestryman Robert S. Smith, and Henry M. Neil, accounted for a third of the total pledge income. The pledges of the ten vestrymen, averaging $83.38, were almost 20 percent of the total.[14] The average household pledge was $25.50, a figure that represents between 2.5 percent and 5 percent of the average worker's income in 1900.[15] Comparatively poor members probably gave a more generous proportion of their income than did the wealthy.[16] For instance, Lucretia Phelps, a teacher, pledged $50 and Edward K. Hayes, the owner of a buggy manufacturing company, pledged only $26. Of the 400 families in the parish, more than half did not pledge.

Annual pledging was only one form of giving to Trinity. Mission congregations also received support from Trinity parishioners. Joseph Outhwaite and his wife, Ellen Peabody Outhwaite, not only pledged $234 in 1900, but they also gave $1,000 to build the new St. John's chapel on Avondale and Town Streets. All the societies of the church raised money for their needs separately. Subscriptions were solicited when an assistant minister was needed. A major source of revenue was the Easter collection, which was designated for the operating expenses of the church. In 1901 the $1,500 Easter collection was a major portion of the $9,000 annual budget. Many parishioners gave far more than they pledged, while others fell short.

Though the congregation ended the nineteenth century carrying a deficit, a small endowment of $4,000 was being nurtured for the future. Atwood repeatedly called for memorial gifts and legacies to beautify the church, deepen its historical significance, and ensure its future.

Trinity's Congregation in 1895

*I*n an 1892 sermon Jones reflected on the future of Trinity and the prospects for growth:

Just think of the grade and character of our new population, the very best; fully nine-ty percent are native born Americans! . . . . They are prosperous and earnest and strong people, the very class from which the leaders and makes of progress chiefly come. . . . How encouraging it is to work among such people! In the great cities of the East the Churches are fighting abject poverty, trying to sweep back the rising tide of pauperism that surges from the European shores.[17]

As Jones recognized, immigration was changing the face of America, especially its eastern cities. The new surge of immigrants between 1870 and 1900 came primarily from southern and eastern Europe. Their clothing and customs were strange, and they were often stigmatized for being different. They flocked to the cities, where they swelled the ranks of the working poor and unemployed. The attitude of proud nativism in Jones's sermon reflected an unfortunate but common prejudice against these immigrants.[18]

The seismic shifts in population barely registered in the pews of Trinity. Columbus was the least ethnic of Ohio's three major cities. Only four percent of Columbus residents, for example, were non-English speaking.[19] Most newcomers to Columbus who found themselves at Trinity were at least a generation removed from their European roots. Despite their European surnames, the Aughenbaugh family hailed from Pennsylvania and the Pompellys were all born in Ohio. Some new members came from small towns and farm settlements around Ohio. By and large, American-born members of the middle class expanded Trinity's membership, while the mission congregations were planted where the city's poor and immigrant populations lived.

In 1895 Trinity's congregation included members of the growing middle class, but it was still an economically privileged group. Nineteen percent of male heads of household were doctors, lawyers, or professors, and an equal number were business owners. Managers made up an additional 15 percent. The largest group (22 percent) was made up of clerical workers: bookkeepers, accountants, sales clerks or representatives. Civil servants and government employees made up seven percent, while tradesmen and artisans constituted six percent. A mere handful worked as laborers.[20]

Working Women and Society Women

A sign of the changing times was the more than 30 working women who were members of Trinity. The three Pompelly sisters and Fanny and Clara Dale worked to support their aging parents. Jemima Broadfoot, who boarded on West Rich Street in the Scioto peninsula, was a forewoman. Other women worked as clerks, secretaries, and dressmakers. Several teachers attended Trinity, among them Lucretia M. Phelps, principal of the Phelps English and Classical School, and her associate principal, Bertha Hall. Harriet Townshend was a university librarian, and Miss Van Horn worked at the pension office. Emma T. Windle co-owned a decorating company. Nine women employees of the State Asylum for the Insane came regularly to Trinity.

The Girls' Friendly Society at Trinity, around 1910. This Episcopal social organization aided single and working women of any denomination.

Many working women were drawn to Trinity by the Girls' Friendly Society. Like the YMCA and the YWCA, the society was founded to assist those who came to the city to work in the factories and offices. Trinity women offered moral and spiritual guidance to the young workers, who did not have to be church members.[21] The branch at Trinity was active by 1892, meeting Monday evenings at the parish house. One meeting featured a calisthenics class, and another time the women were entertained by a violin and piano duo. Instruction in current events, American literature, music, and the history of the Prayer Book was also offered.

Another form of urban ministry were the mothers' meetings held at the parish house on Thursdays. About 30 working class mothers regularly brought their young children for an afternoon of tea, prayer, and fellowship. Women of Trinity gave advice on caring for a household and children. The mothers could purchase clothing for a few pennies. Often they were put in touch with Trinity women who could employ them to do laundry or sewing.

The growing reality of women's employment helped to change attitudes about working women. Mary Hardy, whose husband George was a banker, believed that a woman should be equipped to earn her livelihood, even if she never had the opportunity to do so. Matie (Mrs. Alfred) Kelley, who lived in the family's Greek-inspired home, felt that interior decorating was appropriate work for young women. Penelope Smythe was a staff writer at the *Dispatch*, though her family faced no financial need.[22] (They even had a telephone, a rare novelty in those days.) Her husband owned an artist's supply company, and her father-in-law, Henry P. Smythe, was a warden of Trinity for over 40 years.

On the other end of the social scale from the working-class women were those who belonged to the city's elite social clubs. Mrs. Kelley, who favored a violet-scented, purple silk gown with amethysts gleaming among its folds, exemplified the society matron of the Gilded Age. She was the president of the Columbus Art Association. She was also a charter member of the Saturday Club, which met from 1885–1915 at the home of Sarah Wilcox Henderson, daughter of James Wilcox. The women took turns presenting topics of intellectual or general interest. A group organized on a similar model was the Eclectic Club, to which a number of Trinity ladies belonged. Though the stereotype persists of stiff society women playing whist all day, these clubs also raised money for charities and worked to improve the quality of life in Columbus. The first circulating library in Columbus was organized by such women after the Civil War. Lucy Wilcox, Mrs. A. N. Whiting, and Mrs. Benjamin Huntington were among the women who consolidated their books and opened a lending library in a music store on East State Street.[23]

Muscular Christianity

*I*n the decades after the Civil War, organizations for men became a part of parish life. A men's group, the Trinity Guild, was organized in 1873 but was apparently short-lived. The Brotherhood of St. Andrew, founded in Chicago in 1883, later became established at Trinity. In 1892 its 65 members organized concerts, social events, and solicited advertising for the parish newsletter, the *Trinity*

Hundreds of these tickets were distributed by members of the Brotherhood of St. Andrew. By advertising its free pews and good preaching, Trinity hoped to attract new members to the congregation.

Trinity Church,
THIRD AND BROAD STREETS, COLUMBUS.
Services for Sunday, February 14.
MORNING SERVICE AT 11.
Sermon: "TRINITY'S FUTURE WORK,"
BY REV. ROBERT ELLIS JONES.
SPECIAL CHORAL SERVICE AT 7:30. (CITY TIME)
Sermon: "Some Elements of Church Life."
BY REV. FREDERICK W. CLAMPETT.
YOU ARE CORDIALLY INVITED TO JOIN HEARTILY IN THE SERVICES.

ALL SEATS ARE FREE.

Record. Their motto was "Work and Prayer." As a missionary organization they were charged with bringing new members to Trinity from the ranks of their everyday associates. Jones exhorted the men, "The great cry of many modern preachers is 'How to reach the masses?' The way to reach the masses is to reach the man next to you."[24] Jones was part of the movement known as "muscular Christianity," a concerted effort to counteract the feminization of church life by drawing men back into the ranks of active churchgoers.

Jones resigned in 1893, his health weakened by recurrent malarial fever. (He then served at Grace Church in New York City before becoming President of Hobart College in Geneva, New York, in 1897.) Under his successor, Julius Atwood, the work of the brotherhood increased. On Saturday nights the men distributed more than 200 invitations to Sunday services at hotels and restaurants frequented by men. They visited between five and 20 newcomers each week.[25] In 1896 the Trinity Club was formed for those who were more interested in socializing. Its talks and events were so popular that the club drew members away from the brotherhood, leaving only a core of 15 men to do religious work.

In the effort to revive the participation of men, the church realized it had to enlist them as boys and young men. Paying the choir boys was one way to ensure a level of commitment and loyalty. Another means of recruiting members was the Boy's Brigade, a paramilitary organization with chapters in several Columbus churches. Its goal was the promotion of "reverence, discipline, self-respect. . . [and] Christian manliness."[26] The Trinity Guards, boys between the ages of 13 and 21, were required to refrain from tobacco, alcoholic beverages, and foul language and to attend Sunday school. Those younger than 13 joined as cadets. In 1896, 40 Trinity Cadets were commended for attending both drill and Sunday school.

Boys being boys, however, they clamored for guns so they could perform authentic drills, and they raised the money to equip themselves with Springfield rifles, leather belts, and bayonet scabbards to go with their uniforms. About a quarter of the boys, however, were dismissed as "unstable material."[27] Perhaps the skirmishes held at Minerva Park were becoming too realistic. The younger cadets, more easily satisfied, had play guns. Eventually two rooms in the basement of Trinity

House were cleared for the boys to reduce the wear and tear on other parts of the building.

The outbreak of the Spanish-American War in 1898 only increased the zeal of the boys. Several young men enlisted though apparently none were killed in this brief, distant conflict. Those remaining took up basketball. The group evolved into a regular boy's club that focused its activities on sports and games.

The movement to revive Christian manhood through activity and service was slowly beefing up the ranks of male Episcopalians. In 1895 men made up one-third of the communicants at Trinity, a figure that had doubled since 1863.

A view of South Third Street around 1900, showing Trinity at lower left. A nineteenth-century parishioner who took his country relatives to the Statehouse dome to view the city related an encounter there with two visiting gentlemen. He pointed out Trinity Church, and in response to their inquiries replied that yes, it had a large congregation and a fine minister whom everyone liked. "The next Sunday those two men were in Church and then the next thing I found out was that they had given our minister a call to go some place else and I thought it would be a good thing to advise people not to speak too highly of their ministers" to strangers.

Trinity as a Metropolitan Church

*J*n 1895 Trinity's members no longer lived only in the immediate environs of Capitol Square and East Broad Street. New modes of transportation enabled Trinity to become a metropolitan church, drawing members from the farthest reaches of the city. About four in ten parishioners lived in the swath of land that extended east from Capitol Square all the way to Franklin Park, bounded on the north by railroad tracks and by Oak Street (in today's Old Towne East) on the south. About half of these clustered in the fashionable East Park Place neighborhood that included Jefferson Avenue where the Thurber House still stands. Three in ten families lived south and east of Capitol Square. Just over one in ten inhabited the outlying areas known today as German Village, Victorian Village, and the University District. A similar number lived west of the Scioto in flood-prone Franklinton. Even the farthest verges of the city were represented at Trinity. Peter Hayden lived on East Broad Street near Alum Creek, the very eastern edge of the city. Dr. R. Gilbert Warner, a dentist, resided on West Broad Street beyond the western limit of the city.[28]

Only about one-quarter of Trinity's members lived within easy walking distance of the church. The rest traveled in horse-drawn carriages or by streetcars.

Henry M. Neil, youngest son of William and Hannah Neil and brother of Governor Dennison's widow, was a member of Trinity in 1895. He and his wife and six children lived on Indianola Place near the Ohio State University campus. Like his father the stagecoach magnate, Neil was a transportation pioneer. One of the first owners of a motorcar in Columbus, he traveled an amazing 5,000 miles by car one summer near the turn of the century. Said Neil, "I am so much attached to my motor that I go out to the barn, stand around and look at it and examine the different parts with as much interest as I once bestowed upon horses."[29] No doubt he caused a sensation when he arrived at Trinity by motorcar.

Charles Reynolds Wheeler, George Wheeler's son, was one of the first owners of a Packard in Columbus. In preparation for the ritual Sunday afternoon drive, he spent Sunday mornings washing and polishing his car. When traffic lights were first installed in Columbus, he refused to take notice, as he didn't believe in them. Wheeler's sister Fanny drove an electric car controlled by a kind of joystick. She did attend to the traffic lights, and once when she was stopped at a light on Broad Street, another car struck her from behind. The impact knocked the wheels off Fanny's car, and she was left sitting regally in the wheel-less cab in the middle of Broad Street.[30]

People little guessed how the automobile would change American social life and with it, patterns of church attendance. The Sunday drive and new opportunities for leisure beckoned the churchgoer away from traditional observance of the Sabbath.

Dressed for Sunday school, Elizabeth Wheeler, granddaughter of George Wheeler, stands next to the family car, the first Packard in Columbus.

Virtually everyone lived within a block or two of a streetcar line. In the 1890s lines ran from north to south along High Street from the university to Schiller Park (then City Park). East-west lines traversed Mt. Vernon Avenue and Long, Oak, and East Main Streets from High Street to the streetcar stables near Franklin Park. A line ran from downtown west to the asylum on the hill overlooking the city, enabling its resident workers to reach Trinity. Streetcars, though convenient, were very slow.

In the days before private cars were common, attending a church up to two miles from one's home was a choice that involved some inconvenience. Four out of ten Trinity members bypassed another Episcopal church, either St. Paul's, Church of the Good Shepherd, or St. John's, on their way to Third and Broad Streets. Their reasons for attending Trinity were varied: family tradition, the style of worship, the music, the rector. For the socially ambitious, Trinity was still considered the most elite Episcopal congregation in the city. And though people spread along its branching arteries, downtown was still the city's heart.

Conclusion: Trinity in the Modern City

Although we imagine that life 100 years ago was simple and slow to change, people at the time felt the rapidity of change and worried that materialism was a dangerous trend. An essay in the *Trinity Record* of April, 1903, offered this advice: "Make your life more simple, even if you have to make it less fashionable.... The world wants to see a real difference between Christians and other people in their attitude toward money."

Prosperity was welcome, but it was often blamed for the decline in religious observance. Forty years earlier, observant Episcopalians regularly attended both Sunday services at Trinity. Now the rector pleaded for those who missed the morning service to do their duty by worshipping at the evening service. Attendance also declined during the summer, prompting clergy to remark with a droll irony, "There is no rubric in the Prayer Book which says: 'In July and August these services may be omitted.'"[31]

Already the problems of being a downtown church were apparent. It was difficult, the rector realized, to engage a scattered congregation in the work of the church. In a sermon preached in 1904, the tenth year of Atwood's rectorship, he described Trinity:

It is more than a neighborhood church, more than a parish church. Its constituents come from every part of the city. It embraces all classes and conditions of men.... [We] minister to a large body of strangers who come here for a season and then pass on. In fact, it sometimes seems as if I were a minister of an endless procession, constantly coming and going into this church, and then passing away from my knowledge and influence.[32]

A hundred years later these words still characterize Trinity's vital role in the city and its diverse and ever-shifting congregation.

N o t e s

1. R. E. Jones to C. E. Burr, January 10, 1889. Copies of the correspondence surrounding Jones's call are bound in a volume in the church archives.
2. C. E. Burr to R. E. Jones, June 18, 1889.
3. Bishop Vincent to R. E. Jones, July 5, 1889.
4. R. E. Jones to Bishop Vincent, July 17, 1889.
5. Butler, *Standing Against the Whirlwind*, 225.
6. R. E. Jones to William Bodine, July 11, 1889.
7. R. E. Jones to Bishop Vincent, July 23, 1889.
8. C. E. Burr to William Bodine, July 15, 1889.
9. R. E. Jones to Bishop Vincent, July 17, 1889.
10. Fanny Fullerton to Emily Hastings, December 31, 1889, in *Letters of Fanny Arabella Hayes Platt*. Other letters consulted are dated March 3, 1890 and December 1, 1889.
11. From the tribute included in the vestry minutes after Wilcox's death in September, 1891.
12. *Trinity Record*, November, 1892. Copies in parish archives.
13. Ibid.
14. One vestryman's pledge was out of line with the rest. Henry Warren, the secretary, who owned an insurance agency, pledged only $7.80. The average of the other nine vestrymen was $92 per year.
15. In 1900, the average annual income of Americans in all jobs was $490. The income of clerical workers and those in finance, insurance and real estate was about $1040. Scott Derks, ed., *The Value of a Dollar: Prices and Income in the United States 1860-1999* (Lakeville, CT), 52-3.
16. *Trinity Record*, December, 1896.
17. Robert Ellis Jones, "The Opportunity and Responsibility of Trinity Church," Sermon preached Nov. 6, 1892, in *Three Years' Work 1889-1892* (Columbus: Trinity Church, 1892), 25-6.
18. Ahlstrom, *Religious History*, 849-52.
19. 1900 Census Reports, vol II, p. clxxii (Washington, D.C.: U. S. Census Office, 1901).
20. The 1895 parish roll, which includes names of all family members, place of residence, and indicates who was baptized, confirmed, and communicants, was cross-referenced with city directories for occupational status and with a contemporary map for geographical distributions of members. See Josiah Kinnear, *Commercial Map of Columbus, Ohio* (New York: American Publishing Co., 1890.) Selected families were looked up in 1900 census records as well.
21. Donovan, *A Different Call*, 84-86.
22. Mary Robson McGill, *You and Your Friends* (Columbus: F. J. Heer, 1906), 243, 242, 156-7.
23. White, *We Too Built Columbus*, 342-51;. Studer, *Columbus, Ohio*, 295-6.
24. *Trinity Parish Record*, November, 1892.
25. *Trinity Record*, February, 1895.
26. *Trinity Record*, November, 1895.
27. *Trinity Record*, May, 1897.
28. First Congregational Church had a similar pattern, with nearly all the families living from one to five miles distant, according to *The Golden Jubilee of the First Congregational Church, Columbus, Ohio 1852-1902* (n.d.), p. 52.
29. McGill, 214.
30. Reminiscence of Arleigh D. Richardson, courtesy of Molly Morris.
31. *St. John's Record*, cited in *Trinity Record*, June, 1895.
32. Julius W. Atwood, "Ten Years in Trinity Church," a sermon preached in Trinity Church, Nov. 13, 1904, 7-8. Printed for the congregation.

Chapter 7

STEWARDSHIP *of* THE CHURCH AND SOCIETY TO WWI

*I*n the years leading up to World War I, economic prosperity benefitted Trinity. Wealthy members helped secure the endowment, beautify the church interior, and build a parish house. As a downtown church with strong clergy leadership, Trinity also became closely identified with social reform. Building Trinity's wealth while combating poverty and other forms of social injustice, however, required a delicate balance.

In the early decades of the twentieth century, Trinity became a place where civic values were celebrated and public morality was shaped. Trinity maintained close ties to government and civic leaders. During the "splendid little war" with Spain in 1898 and the First World War, religious faith and national patriotism mutually reinforced one another. These wars brought forth a militarism echoed by the churches, but they also inspired people to great personal sacrifice. Fighting social injustice at home and tyranny oversees, Trinity Church and the secular state worked side by side, sometimes closely hand in hand.

In 1914, a visitor to Trinity sent this postcard, praising its well-known boy choir.

Gifts and Memorials
Transform Trinity

Rector Julius Atwood repeatedly urged members to invest in Trinity's future. Giving a stained glass window, a baptismal font, or a candlestick in memory of a loved one became a sanctioned way to own a piece of the church now that pew ownership was abolished. Such gifts also ensured families a permanent and historic association with the church. Every issue of the parish bulletin included a form for making a bequest to Trinity. Atwood's persuasions together with those of his successor, the Rev. Theodore Irving Reese, began to have an effect. With the return of prosperity in the new century, money from Trinity's prominent nineteenth-century families flowed into the treasury and transformed the church interior dramatically.

Endowing a fund was a less visible but no less effective way of purchasing a stake in Trinity's future. By 1913 the endowment stood at $40,000, an amount four times the annual parish budget of $10,000. (By comparison, in 2001 the endowment was only three times as great as the annual budget.) To celebrate the 1917 centennial the vestry launched a drive to raise $60,000 for the endowment, though they managed to raise only a third of that amount. No doubt anxieties about the country's recent entry into World War I affected people's giving. Nonetheless by 1920 the endowment had increased to almost $100,000, thanks to a few large donations and many modest bequests.

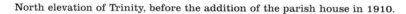

North elevation of Trinity, before the addition of the parish house in 1910.

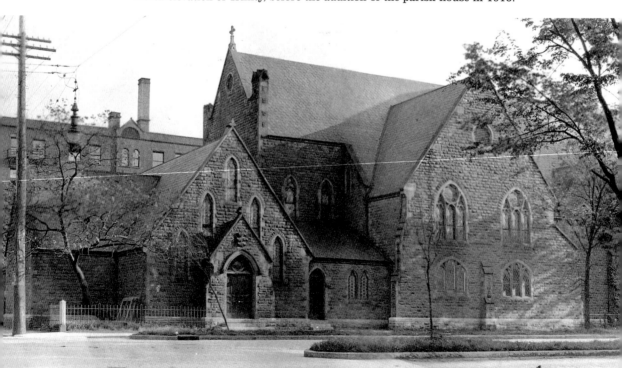

Atwood nurtured a vision of Trinity Church as a building of historical significance with monuments to the great leaders of the church and the nation. He called
for memorials to the "men of national reputation" connected with Trinity—Chief
Justice Swayne, Governor Dennison, and John W. Andrews. An Andrews memorial
was duly funded. But 12 of the 14 memorial funds existing in 1913 were begun by
or in memory of women of the congregation, not its famous men. It was not Swayne
but his wife who was honored with a fund established by her daughter, Mrs. Edwin
Parsons of New York. Mrs. John G. Battelle, who gave $2 million to endow the
Battelle Memorial Institute, contributed $10,000 to the endowment. Mrs. Benjamin
N. Hungtington gave $25,000 worth of securities in her husband's name, stipulat-
ing only that a tablet be erected. Robert S. Smith began a fund in memory of his
wife Annie Swan, daughter of Judge Swan. This fund was enriched by contributions
from her daughter Maryette A. Platt, wife of vestryman Rutherford H. Platt.[1]

Generous parishioners also enabled Trinity to purchase a rectory. In 1907 Helen
Collins, Alfred Kelley's daughter, gave $10,000 for this purpose. Flora Deshler
Brent then offered to sell Trinity her property at 85 Jefferson Avenue at a cost of
$8,750. It was a fine house, with a parlor,
dining room, and study on the first floor and
four bedrooms and two baths on the second
floor. A proud addition to Trinity's property
was the new parish house, designed by
Columbus architects Howell and Thomas.
Begun in 1909, it was completed in 1910. The
new parish house encompassed the existing
chapel, which remained on the first floor. The
building boasted all-electric fixtures and a
gymnasium on the third floor. The process of
wiring the church and replacing gas with electric lights began in 1906 and took several years.

Residence of Charles H. Hayden at
East State and Sixth Streets. The
Haydens, who gave Trinity its
altar, reredos, and chimes, lived in
a home with arched lancet windows
and other architectural features
reminiscent of their Gothic Revival
church.

While bequests swelled Trinity's bank
accounts, memorial gifts transformed the
church interior. In 1906 William Neil King offered to install the memorial window
in the chancel in memory of his mother, Elizabeth J. McMillen, and his brother,
Thomas Worthington King. McMillen, a longtime member, died in 1897 and King
and his family were lost at sea the following year. The window, designed by stained
glass artist David Maitland Armstrong, was completed in 1910. The estate of Jane
Case offered $6,000 for the remodeling of the organ, which was renamed in honor
of her husband, Dr. Douglas Case, a grandson of James Kilbourne. One after another,

memorial windows were spoken for, and plain glass was replaced with brilliant stained glass. A chancel screen was installed with 26 panels bearing individual plates commemorating the donors. The marble sanctuary flooring, altar steps, and communion railing were also memorial gifts.

Gifts of liturgical items including chalices, altar vases, alms basins, and a processional cross encouraged greater ritual expression. Evangelical clergy resisted at first. Atwood made it clear that accepting a gift of candlesticks did not imply his consent to the use of lighted candles in the service. However, the once-forbidden processionals and vested choirs had become accepted practice, and the taboo against lighted candles would also expire.

Trinity Episcopal Church after 1910, with the newly completed parish house and the tower housing the chimes.

Gifts in memory of dozens of forerunners enabled the completion of All Saints Tower, though not the steeple that had been originally planned. Charles H. Hayden and his wife, Louise Irving Hayden, donated the chimes in memory of five of their children who died young. Hayden, the son of millionaire mine owner and manufacturer Peter Hayden, instructed Trinity to procure the best chimes available. Cast by the Meneely Bell Co. of Troy, New York, they were dedicated on All Saints Day of 1910 in a memorable service. Maryette Smith Platt wrote to her son Robert, "They rang out first the Doxology—I as usual wept but didn't wipe my tears so no one knew." Then followed the hymn "All the Saints who Rest from their Labors," as people gathered on the corner and wagons, carriages, and autos crowded the intersection. Even after arriving home at 414 East Broad Street, the Platts sat in their car listening to the strains of the chimes.[2] The church was finally consecrated on this day, with due ceremony, two bishops, and ten clergymen. Many in the congregation probably felt that the work-in-progress had been completed.

More changes were soon accomplished. The white marble altar, designed by Howell and Thomas after one in Ravenna, Italy, was installed in 1912 at a cost of $1,000. The reredos was also completed, the work of woodcarver Johannes Kirchmayer, a native of Oberammergau who worked in Cambridge, Massachusetts. Both gifts commemorated Louise Hayden and were given by her husband and children. It was the Hayden family and other wealthy donors who defined the worship space and the character of Trinity's building for several generations to come.

The elaborate interior of Trinity Church gave witness that the ritual movement in the Episcopal Church, long resisted by many, was now a fact of church life. Only a decade earlier in 1901, the rector and vestry had rejected a plan to redecorate the reredos with wood panels, not wanting to change the sections which bore the Lord's prayer and the Creed. Now they were covered by the new reredos and the eye was drawn to the massive altar set off by the dark wood, above which glowed the Maitland Armstrong window depicting Christ and the archangels. The Gothic potential of Trinity's chancel was fully realized.

The Social Gospel

Trinity and its members welcomed the prosperity that came with the growth of cities and industry. But the unchecked power of business barons and political bosses threatened the promises of democracy and left many people mired in poverty and hopelessness. The Progressive movement that rose in the early years of the twentieth century attempted to reform the abuses of government and big business, especially in the cities. The social gospel, a religious movement sometimes called "the praying wing of Progressivism," shared with this political movement the goals of civil service reform, government regulation of business, and higher moral and ethical standards for government leaders.[3]

The social gospel was shaped by several forces. Historical criticism of the Bible, new fossil discoveries, and Darwinian theory led to doubts about the literal accuracy of the Bible. While fundamentalists rejected anything that challenged orthodox beliefs, other theologians sought to reconcile the new science with traditional Christianity. They emphasized man's freedom and capacity for moral action. This "liberal" theology led many Protestants to react against political corruption, laissez-faire economic policies, and the growing gap between rich and poor that characterized the so-called Gilded Age.

A leader of national prominence in the social gospel movement made his church home on Capitol Square, just a stone's throw from Trinity. The Rev. Washington Gladden was pastor of First Congregational Church from 1882–1914. During his tenure the congregation grew from fewer than 500 members to more than 1,200.[4] Week after week, many of Columbus's most successful businessmen heard Gladden preach the social gospel with its critique of capitalism. His evening sermons drew a wide audience beyond his congregation and the *Ohio State Journal* reprinted his sermons on Monday.[5] Gladden even served a term on the city council, where he successfully labored to secure municipal ownership of the electric power plant.[6] But the immorality of the political world discouraged him from that course of action.[7]

Washington Gladden (1836–1918), pastor of Trinity's neighbor, the First Congregational Church, and leader of the social gospel movement.

Trinity and Gladden's congregation had a neighborly relationship and a common mission. Both ministered to the needy downtown while attracting economically privileged members throughout the city. When his church was undergoing repairs in the summer of 1902, Gladden's congregation met in Trinity's parish house. Atwood spoke on the occasion of First Congregational's golden jubilee, and in turn Gladden preached at the celebration of Trinity's centennial in 1917. Gladden was always a popular speaker at parish meetings.

Gladden inspired Trinity and other churches to do the work of the social gospel. Among the first settlement houses was Gladden Community House, founded in 1905 and still in existence nearly one hundred years later. Following suit in 1909, St. Paul's Episcopal Church organized the Neighborhood House on Curtis Avenue to minister to the families of railroad workers who lived nearby. English classes were offered, as well as the city's first free dental clinic.[8] Soon all the Columbus

Episcopal churches, including Trinity, supported this ministry. Trinity's parish house was another urban refuge offering assistance to working mothers, a society for working single women, and cooking and sewing classes for girls. For a short time the parish also supported a deaconess, Mrs. McDowell, who was paid $15 per month and lodged at the parish house. Her job was to work among women and children of the city and to organize the women of the parish for missionary work. Though Atwood wished to support a full-time deaconess, no one in the parish or vestry made this a priority.

Episcopalians would not seem to be natural leaders in the social gospel movement, for they had long stressed the separation of church and state. A contemporary joke had it that a man moved to a new town, where he looked for a church home. He tried the Presbyterians but found too much religion there. He visited the Methodist church but found them too addicted to politics. Finally he found the most restful home to be among the Episcopalian, for they were overburdened with neither religion nor politics.[9]

Bishop Vincent believed that the church was not to be used for political purposes, and he avoided all mention of social problems in his convention addresses.[10] Preaching at Trinity on March 25, 1900, Vincent acknowledged social changes but declared that the church could not change, that it remained today the same "divine Institution" as it was 2,000 years ago. Reluctant to endorse social action, the bishop stressed, in true evangelical fashion, that it had to emanate from righteous and godly individuals. Change in the human condition comes "not by the direct effort of the Church as a body…but by his Spirit working silently and steadily upon the moral consciousness of the world."[11]

Many at Trinity did not follow the bishop's lead on this issue. One lay leader at Trinity who preached the social gospel was Dr. James H. Canfield, president of Ohio State University from 1895–1899. Addressing the congregation at the Thanksgiving service in 1896, he called for the church to change social conditions so that each man received his honest share. His critique of capitalism challenged listeners "not always to follow the iron law of wages…to insist upon the results of competition" or to worship the law of supply and demand. Set aside the desire for wealth and the tendency to measure value by material standards, he urged; go back to the Master and walk humbly with Him in service to one's fellow men.[12]

Julius Atwood, Trinity's rector from 1894–1906, believed that the sacred mission of the church could not be divorced from secular concerns. In his ten-year anniversary sermon to the congregation, he stated his allegiance to the social gospel movement:

I have believed that the pulpit of this Church, while proclaiming the Gospel of Jesus Christ in its simplicity and in its unity, should not lose sight of the truth that that same Gospel touches upon human life at every point and that here should be proclaimed not only a personal but a civic and national righteousness.[13]

Atwood wanted to place Trinity at the center of civic life. Unlike other churches in the city, Trinity, he said, "owes a duty to the city and to the State." He often held services to commemorate public events. In 1898 he officiated at a memorial service for the officers and men of the 17th Regiment who died in Cuba. Governor Asa Bushnell, at the close of his term of office in January, 1900, attended Trinity with his military staff to hear Atwood preach on "Sons of God: What Constitutes a Righteous Nation." After the death of Queen Victoria, Atwood held a memorial service at Trinity. Later that month a special service was offered for the Sons and Daughters of the American Revolution, featuring a sermon about George Washington.

Tribute to William McKinley

The William McKinley Memorial is a reminder of the days when Trinity had a close relationship to secular powers. McKinley, Ohio's Republican governor from 1892–96, defeated William Jennings Bryan in the presidential race of 1896. Although McKinley has become an icon of big business and American imperialism, in his time he was a popular president who had won a war and brought about an economic recovery. He had been handily re-elected when he was suddenly assassinated by an anarchist. At a memorial service held at Trinity in 1901, the governor and an Ohio Supreme Court justice addressed the congregation. Atwood later urged the parish to erect a memorial to McKinley and the major event of his administration, the Spanish-American War, sometimes referred to as the war for Cuban freedom. Because the Seventeenth Regiment was stationed at Columbus and the officers who died were all connected with the Episcopal Church, the memorial would celebrate a historic link between the city, the church, and the country. McKinley had been a charter member of the Sons and Daughters of the American Revolution, backers of the memorial, and Atwood was the group's chaplain. The plaque designed by the Tiffany Glass Company of New York can be seen on the south wall of Trinity's nave.

Theodore Irving Reese, rector of Trinity from 1907-1913 and subsequently bishop of Southern Ohio, was known for his classes in personal religion. When Reese died in 1931, six bishops and 50 clergymen presided at his funeral at Trinity, which hundreds attended. This painting by Mary Coleman Allen was given to Trinity by Bishop Boyd Vincent.

Atwood, who had served Trinity longer than any other rector in its history, resigned in 1906 to accept a post in Phoenix. His wife's ill health made a move to a warm, dry climate imperative. (Eventually he was elected bishop of Arizona.) His successor, the Rev. Theodore Irving Reese, rector from 1907 to 1913, was a graduate of the Episcopal Theological School of Cambridge. His father and grandfather were Episcopal clergymen. Reese's sermons were "like himself; straightforward, natural, intelligent, and spiritual." He was a "steadfast foe of ignorance, of injustice, of inhumanity" who preached the social gospel and lived it. Reese was appointed by Governor Harmon to chair the State Board of Arbitration while Columbus was in the midst of a bloody streetcar strike and months of civil unrest. In this role, said Cox, Reese "lifted this arm of the commonwealth so far above the practices and standards which had previously prevailed that the government was appraised in new terms." Reese was skilled at finding fair solutions to labor disputes, and he always carried his card declaring him a master machinist of the American Federation of Labor.[14]

In 1913 Trinity's rector, Theodore Irving Reese, was selected to become bishop coadjutor, the successor to Bishop Vincent. On Easter Sunday, March 23, the ladies of Trinity presented to their departing rector the robes they had made for him to wear at his consecration. The theme of Reese's sermon that day was the assurance of personal immortality. On that resurrection day, however, people across the Midwest were anxious as storms and tornados swept 20 states, killing hundreds.

Two days later as bishops and clergy gathered for Reese's consecration at Trinity, the worst flood in history devastated the west side of Columbus. Thousands of homes were swept away and bridges collapsed, cutting Franklinton off from the rest of the city. Water service and electricity were knocked out. There were stories of dramatic rescues and reunions but also of heartbreaking losses. One boy, crazed with grief, was rescued after being trapped in the branches of a tree for two days with the body of his sister.

The entire city rallied to aid the stricken west side. Bishop Reese, newly-consecrated and "quietly confident in the new authority and grace given him," plunged at once into relief work.[15] He set out by any means possible to find and aid his people. Members of Trinity, thankful for their own deliverance, gave assistance to St. John's mission, which was in the midst of the flooded area. The women's guild met for several days to sew clothing for flood victims. One woman took a basket of toys to the children of St. John's. In the three months following the disaster, the congregation contributed over $800 to help St. John's flood victims.

By the following year, St. John's had recovered from the flood and was seeking

St. John's chapel in 1910, before the mission became an independent parish.

to become an independent congregation. In 1915 the chapel at Town and Avondale Streets was extended into a full-sized church. In the long-term, however, the area never fully recovered from the catastrophic flood. Many residents relocated to the Hilltop, and property values in Franklinton dropped by as much as half. The neighborhood, continually vulnerable to flooding and economic instability, has never been prosperous. These facts have defined the mission and ministry of St. John's to this day.[16]

Patrols stationed near Trinity control access to East Broad Street during the 1910 streetcar strike.

Trinity's Centennial

Events of national and international significance threatened to eclipse Trinity's centennial in mid-May of 1817. America had just entered World War I. Patriotic fervor was high as thousands of college students, dismissed from Ohio's public universities, rushed to enlist. The Civil War epic, *Birth of a Nation*, was in its fifth big week at the Hartman Theatre. Suffragists from 21 states rallied in Columbus, and many were hosted by Trinity women. A crowd of 3,500 cheered the speeches of national suffrage leader Carrie Chapman Catt and Governor Cox.

In the year of its centennial Trinity was the second-largest Episcopal congregation in southern Ohio, with 1,246 baptized members, 965 of whom were communicants. Christ Church in Cincinnati was the largest with 1,200 communicants, and Christ Church in Dayton was a close third. While Cincinnati had several successful Episcopal congregations, activity in Columbus was centered at Trinity. St. Paul's on the east side was struggling with a debt of $15,000, and St. John's in Franklinton was still in its infancy as a parish. Trinity boasted the greatest number of organizations of any parish in the diocese. The parish house vibrated with constant noise and activity, from women's guild meetings and choir rehearsals to boy scout meetings and basketball practice.

At its one hundredth anniversary service on May 11, 1917, Trinity could justly celebrate its vital parish life, its financial health, its magnificent buildings, and its positive relationship with the city. Washington Gladden and Governor Cox addressed the congregation. Cox was a Democrat who had supported many progressive reforms. (In 1920, with Franklin Delano Roosevelt as his running mate, he would campaign against Warren G. Harding for president.) His speech at Trinity testified to the church's moral authority in the secular world. For 100 years, he said,

> *Trinity Church has cast a watchful, inspiring and sometimes probably a restraining eye on the Statehouse. It is inspiring to know that this church has the age to guarantee sage philosophy and yet has a young and progressive spirit.*[17]

Addressing the congregation, Gladden predicted that the war would force religious denominations to drop their small differences and become more united by its end.

Church and State
Join Forces in World War I

*I*n time of war, people's need for spiritual nurture grows stronger. The gathering of more than 800 people at Trinity for prayer after the terrorist attacks in September of 2001 was not without precedent. After Congress declared war on Germany, a service was held at Trinity on the national day of prayer, April 11, 1917. At noon the chimes rang out with patriotic and spiritual music, including "My Country 'tis of thee" and "O God our help in ages past." The service affirmed the church's support of the state. Bishop Reese, flanked by an altar boy holding a cross and one holding an American flag, designated these as symbols of American principles. Standing between the cross and the flag, Governor Cox led the people in a solemn vow of allegiance to the United States and spoke of the importance of prayer: "Just as a flower turns its face to the sun, so humanity turns toward the Almighty God in times of stress." The choir led the large assembly in singing patriotic hymns.[18] It was at this time that the American flag became a fixture in the sanctuary of Episcopal churches, a practice sanctioned by Bishop Reese in his 1917 convention address.

"There is something very beautifully akin in the spirit of self-sacrifice of the Cross and in that of patriotism," he said.

Support for the Great War raised hopes of brotherhood among Christians as they worked to battle a common evil. Episcopalians held unity discussions with Lutherans and Presbyterians, and Bishop Vincent worked to bring his church into eventual communion with Congregationalists.[19] In Columbus, churches cooperated in an effort to make Christianity a force in people's lives. Trinity was one of 70 churches whose members went door-to-door on a city-wide campaign to increase church attendance. During the war years the congregation was urged to attend the Lenten union services. Held at noon on Mondays at the Grand Theatre, these were conducted by preachers from different congregations. The main floor was reserved for men, while women were seated in the balconies so they could attend unescorted. In a display of ecumenism tinged with competition, church basketball teams formed a city league. The victories and losses of Trinity's hoopsters were a staple of the monthly newsletter.

During the First World War, Trinity's parish house became a center for relief work. Louise Burr, whose husband Karl was a vestryman, supervised a branch of the Red Cross headquartered at Trinity. In the month of April, 1918, 220 women labored nearly 1000 hours on Red Cross work, knitting socks and hats for soldiers. Even small children were taught to make quilt squares for blankets.

The American Fund for the French Wounded also operated from the parish house, packaging goods for overseas shipment. Flora (Mrs. Samuel Prescott) Bush,

— To Plant Vegetables In Front Yard of East Broad Street Home —

In a patriotic move, vestryman Rutherford H. Platt plowed up the front yard of his East Broad Streeet mansion and planted a vegetable garden. This photo appeared in the *Columbus Citizen* on April 18, 1917.

the grandmother of President George W. Bush, organized this work while her husband, the president of Buckeye Steel Castings, assisted the war effort by coordinating industrial production. (The Bushes attended St. Paul's Episcopal Church, though Samuel Prescott Bush's funeral was held at Trinity after his death in 1948.) By February of 1918 women had shipped almost $13,000 worth of supplies, from bandages to baby caps, to soldiers and civilians in France.

All Americans were called to sacrifice both time and money. Members of Trinity were exhorted to keep up their attendance and their pledges, to contribute to the Episcopal Church's War Commission and the community's War Chest. Trinity's boy scouts won the prize for selling the most war savings stamps, and they went door-to-door offering liberty bonds. Parishioners invited soldiers from the barracks home to dinner and entertained them with social events at the parish house. The church encouraged its members to conserve fuel and food by preparing meatless and wheatless meals regularly. Prayer alone was insufficient and faith without action was deemed empty.

Supporting the war effort was consistent with the gospel of social justice, for the German government was depicted as the oppressor of free people and the enemy of democracy and self-determination. Even the Episcopal Church participated in this anti-German sentiment. In Columbus native Germans, who had numbered around 30 percent of the citizenry in Joel Buttles's day, accounted for only about two percent of the population.[20] Still, when America entered the war, Schiller Park and certain streets were renamed, German-language books were burned in bonfires, and Germans became targets of hatred.[21]

Trinity's Veterans and Volunteers

Several of Trinity's World War I veterans belonged to a family with a long history at Trinity. Rutherford H. Platt Jr. and Robert Smith Platt joined the service; they were sons of vestryman Rutherford H. Platt and nephews of the Civil War general John G. Mitchell. Their cousin Rutherford Fullerton, son of Fanny Platt and Erskine Fullerton, served as a field artillery captain. Another cousin, Edward Barry Wall, was the only known casualty from Trinity. He lived with the family of his uncle, vestryman Nicholas Monsarrat, since his own parents had died while he was an infant. A flight instructor, Wall died in an airplane accident at Mather Field in California on December 5, 1918.

Lucile Atcherson, one of several Trinity parishioners
who was a relief worker in France during World War I.

In all, at least 35 men of Trinity served in the war, many of them in the trenches and fields of France. Two were wounded in action, one severely. A former Trinity boy with the grand name of Desmond de la Peer Villiers Stuart, whose family had since returned to Ireland, was killed in action in France in 1917. Perin Monypeny, youngest son of William and Maria Monypeny, was promoted to captain but discharged for inefficiency. Kenneth B. Norton, who was with the ambulance service, and James Fullington, who participated in the Somme offensive, were awarded the French Croix de Guerre.[22] Fullington's father was on the vestry. Floyd van Keuren and his wife served with the Red Cross and directed relief and reconstruction work in the Somme. In 1922 he became the associate rector at Trinity.

A number of women followed their brothers to the fields of war. Emily C. Benham served overseas in a muddy camp as a canteen worker with the YMCA, while her brother enlisted as a soldier. Edith Tallant, a high-school teacher, and her younger brother Robert both served in France. Edith worked in a canteen in France and remained after the war as a Red Cross medical worker in a veteran's hospital. Even after she returned to Columbus, she continued caring for disabled servicemen. Ruth Casparis directed a fleet of motor cars making deliveries for the American Fund for French Wounded and the Red Cross.[23] Her brother William was a soldier. At home her mother collected funds for a four-year-old French boy, adopted in the name of Trinity Church.[24] Lucile Atcherson, baptized and confirmed at Trinity, was a paid worker with the American Fund for the French Wounded. She spent four years in France as a civilian relief worker, receiving medals of honor from the French government. She helped to care for hundreds of war orphans whose mothers entrusted them to the Americans to keep them from falling into German hands.[25] When she returned to Columbus, she battled gender bias to become the first woman diplomat in the foreign services, but she retired in 1928 when she married Dr. George Curtis.[26]

Conclusion

*W*orld War I, like the Civil War before it, revealed a host of moral and spiritual shortcomings in the American people. The words of the bishop of London were shared with Trinity's members as a Lenten reflection. The war, the bishop said, has revealed "our lack of preparation for an emergency, an amateurishness in dealing with great problems…the culpable lightness with which we have taken our imperial responsibilities, our engrossment with material interests…our inadequate support of foreign missions, the vagueness of our religion and our dislike of spiritual effort."[27] The national examination of conscience after the terrorist attacks in September of 2001 revealed a similar understanding of the faults that antagonized America's enemies.

The Rev. Egisto Chauncey, Trinity's rector during World War I, hated war and preferred to emphasize peace. His 1917 Christmas message to the congregation imagined the battlefield not only as a place of death, but also of birth:

> *This is the travail hour of the nations, yet God is working His purpose out. . . This must be the dawn of a new era of good will because selfishness is being cleansed by sacrifice and the brotherhood of mankind is drawing near. . . .[we] feel the promise of victory, the prophecy of peace.*[28]

After the war, however, the hopes of religious unity among Protestants seemed dimmer than before. Many churches, regretting their hearty pro-war stance, pledged themselves to pacifism. Americans in general became disillusioned, abandoning Progressivism and renewing their desire for isolation. But the progressive spirit still hovered over the realm of religion, inspiring important reforms, including greater participation for women. The advent of international warfare expanded the focus of the social gospel from its primarily domestic objectives. The worldwide mission of the church was given new emphasis, and even those in the pews at Trinity would feel their horizons broaden.

Notes

[1] According to the American Institute for Economic Research (www.aier.org), $1000 in 1913 would be equivalent to just over $18,000 in 2002.

[2] From a letter dated November 3 (1910), courtesy of Bill and Nancy Platt.

[3] Ahlstrom, *Religious History*, 763-84 (on liberal theology); 785-804 (on social gospel); Holmes, *Brief History*, 116-131.

[4] Jacob H. Dorn, *Washington Gladden: Prophet of the Social Gospel* (Columbus: Ohio State University Press, 1966), 93.

[5] Dorn, 86-7, 90-91.

[6] Knepper, *Ohio*, 329.

[7] Roseboom, *History of Ohio*, 315.

[8] *Centennial Celebration: St Paul's Episcopal Church, Columbus, Ohio* (Columbus, 1942), n.p.

[9] Address of Mr. E. O. Randall, *The Golden Jubilee of the First Congregational Church, Columbus, Ohio 1852-1902.* n.d., 116.

[10] John M. Krumm, *Flowing Like a River* (Cincinnati: Forward Movement, 1989), 55-79 (on Bishop Vincent).

[11] Sermon printed in *Trinity Record*, April, 1900 and June, 1900.

[12] *Trinity Record*, January, 1896.

[13] Atwood, "Ten Years in Trinity Church," 7-8 (emphasis added).

[14] *The Messenger of the Episcopal Church in the Diocese of Southern Ohio* (November, 1931) contains several memorials to Bishop Reese. Quotations are taken from p. 6, 5, 7, 13.

[15] Boyd Vincent, *Recollections of the Diocese of Southern Ohio* (Milwaukee, 1934), 82.

[16] See Art Kienzle and Bill Poinsett, "The Story of St. John's Episcopal Church, Columbus, Ohio" (1993), n.p.

[17] *Ohio State Journal*, May 12, 1917.

[18] *Ohio State Journal*, April 12, 1917; *Columbus Citizen*, April 12, 1917.

[19] On dreams of Christian unity, see Martin Marty, *Pilgrims in Their Own Land: 500 Years of Religion in America* (Boston: Little, Brown and Company, 1984), 338-55; Holmes, 124-6.

[20] Garrett, *Columbus*, 113.

[21] Harden, *Columbus Celebrates*, 94.

[22] *Official Roster of Ohio Soldiers, Sailors and Marines in the World War 1917-18*. 23 volumes. (Columbus: F. J. Heer Printing Co., 1926). Of the 35 names listed in the *Trinity Parish Calendar*, October 14, 1917, only 26 could be located in the official roster.

[23] White, *We Too Built Columbus*, 447, 404-406.

[24] *Trinity Church Calendar*, May 5, 1918.

[25] White, 409-10.

[26] "First Woman legation secretary," *Columbus Monthly*, v. 4, no. 3 (March, 1978), 69-70.

[27] *Trinity Church Calendar*, February 17, 1918. Details of parish life from 1916-1918 are culled from this publication.

[28] *Trinity Church Calendar*, December 23, 1917.

Chapter 8

SEEKING STABILITY
1918 – 1936

*I*n the 1920s progress in Columbus was evident in the new commercial buildings that dwarfed the city's churches. At 555 feet the American Insurance Union Citadel, now known as the Leveque Tower, was downtown's new spire. The Ohio and Palace Theatres, monuments to pleasure, vied with any church for magnificence. The *Dispatch* became Trinity's neighbor to the south and a new city hall was dedicated on West Broad Street. Trinity's congregation, located at the heart of this thriving downtown, was stable but forward-moving, embracing liberal theology and widening its missionary outreach.

When the bubble of prosperity burst and the Great Depression set in, Columbus did not suffer as severely as industrial cities such as Detroit or Cleveland because its economy was more diversified. Still by 1933 one-third of Columbus's work force was unemployed.[1] Trinity felt the blow as its income dwindled and leaders adopted severe cost-cutting measures. Its hardships reflected the economic diversity of the increasingly middle-class congregation, no longer comprised of wealthy Episcopalians.

Common wisdom has it that Americans turned inward following World War I, but at Trinity people's horizons widened. Women were active in the struggle for voting rights and in mission work. Through parish-based activities, men and women responded more deeply to the needs of others throughout the world and near to hand.

Stability of Leadership

*T*he stability of Trinity's leadership in the early decades of the twentieth century was an important factor in the continuity of church life. For 23 years encompassing the First World War and the worst years of the Depression, the

Rev. Egisto F. Chauncey served as rector of Trinity. Fritz Lichtenberg was Sunday school superintendent during those years, and Karl "Pop" Hoenig was organist and choirmaster from 1899–1941. The vestry was a virtual oligarchy with wardens and vestrymen re-elected year after year. Often elections were uncontested, and incumbent wardens and vestry were re-elected by acclaim. The issue of a rotating vestry was discussed several times in the early 1930s but shelved for lack of support. A 1938 "gentleman's agreement" that the senior two members of the vestry would voluntarily retire was soon abandoned, for it was argued that the congregation was always free to elect whom it pleased.

Among the longest-serving vestrymen were the banker William H. Albery, who served as treasurer for 33 years. George Hardy, a real-estate developer who was the grandson of Joel Buttles, served as vestryman or a warden for more than 30 years. Edward L. Hinman, first elected in 1870, had the distinction of being the oldest member of the vestry when he died in 1901 at the age of 74. A banker and manufacturer whose ancestors fought in the Revolutionary War, his name at the head of a church subscription campaign was said to guarantee its success. A.N. Whiting joined the vestry in 1871, left for a few years to organize St. Philip's, and then resumed his post until he died in 1904 at the age of 67.

Some families had a virtual monopoly on vestry positions. Henry P. Smythe, who first joined the vestry in 1856, was re-elected as senior warden until 1895 though he had not attended a vestry meeting for the last two years, probably

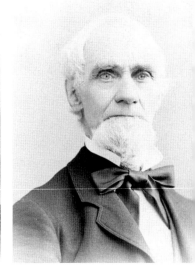

Between them, vestrymen Edward L. Hinman, George Hardy, and Henry P. Smythe had nearly 100 years' service to Trinity.

because of ill health. (He was 82.) Finally Arthur H. Smythe pleaded on his father's behalf, and the vestry permitted the elder Smythe to retire. For his part the younger Smythe served on the vestry until he moved to California in 1919. This family dynasty lasted 63 years, several of which father and son served simultaneously. When the elder Smythe retired, junior warden Charles E. Burr took over his post. By the time Burr died in 1902 he had served 24 years on the vestry. His son Karl E. Burr, was elected in 1904 and died in office in 1945, having served as junior warden for 22 years.

An even longer father-son dynasty was that of the Outhwaites. Congressman Joseph H. Outhwaite joined the vestry in 1878 and died in 1907, still a vestryman. That year his son was first elected; Singleton P. Outhwaite, a lawyer, served more than 50 years despite his increasing senility. (After he retired the parish by-laws were changed, with three-year terms for wardens and vestrymen.) Outhwaite's long years of service gave him a sense of ownership. Every Sunday during the singing of the Venite, he would walk down the middle aisle, consult his pocket watch, and adjust the temperature on the thermostat on the front pillar. This stewardship routine seldom varied.

Congressman Joseph H. Outhwaite (1841–1907) and his son, Singleton P. Outhwaite (1875–1963), a lawyer who was a warden of Trinity for 50 years. Professional vestries brought stable and conservative leadership.

Professional vestries contributed to institutional stability and continuity of vision. The men had a deep stake in the welfare of Trinity, and they brought business strategies to the management of its affairs.[2] The church was after all a corporation, and those best qualified to direct it were men of experience and success in the world of business, banking, and the law. Serving on Trinity's vestry made them esteemed in the community. In turn, their success meant that Trinity's reputation was enhanced.

On the other hand, stable vestries were resistant to change. Little value was placed on having fresh ideas or sharing governance among congregation members. This seemed to suit the congregation, which declined opportunities to make decisions. For example, in 1919 the vestry asked the congregation for a response to convey to the diocese regarding what it deemed an unreasonable assessment for the

Episcopal Church's Nationwide Campaign. The congregation passed a motion leaving "this very important matter…entirely in the judgment of the vestry." Most of the assigned sum was duly collected.

Church Fund-raising and Finances

*I*n 1921 it seemed for a moment that prosperity had finally come to Trinity. At the February 8 vestry meeting William Albery reported that all debts were paid, leaving a bank balance of $2,200. The stunning good news of a surplus prompted one member to propose raises for the rector and all the staff. In the discussion that followed, the men argued about how and indeed whether to spend the money. One member suggested that the $2,200 be distributed among the congregation, which sparked lawyer Outhwaite to object that it would have to be paid to every single donor of the church since its foundation, an obvious impossibility. Karl Burr, also a lawyer, reminded the vestry that the church was a not-for-profit corporation and could not legally distribute the funds. Someone else argued that the money could hardly be considered profit. At that moment there was a knock at the door, and the parish clerk handed in the complete financial report. In silence the vestry studied the report and realized the treasurer's mistake. The figure of $2,200 represented not the bank balance but the amount of the overdraft. The arguments ended, all motions were withdrawn, and the men resolved to use the Easter offering to make up the shortfall.[3]

After World War I Episcopalians were asked to dig deeper into their collective pockets to fund new programs inspired by Progressivism. One was the Church Pension Fund for retired Episcopal clergy, which was second only to the Red Cross as the largest charitable fund gathered in the United States for one purpose. It entailed a permanent new assessment on each congregation based on the ministers' salaries. Then the Episcopal Church instituted a Nationwide Campaign for all the church's programs, especially its missions. Trinity found its assessment to be unreasonable and was unable to meet its 1920 quota, but in the church as a whole, giving increased sharply. Congregation members were now expected to make two pledges: one for Trinity's general operating expenses and another for the Nationwide Fund.

Chauncey told his congregation they ought to give one-tenth of their income to charity, with 40 percent of that amount going to the church. In 1923 the parish canvass resulted in a total of 467 pledges for the general fund and 320 pledges for the

Nationwide Campaign. These numbers represented an overall increase of almost one-third in pledge units and about 16 percent in revenue. Adjusting for the changing value of the dollar, however, the average pledge amount differed little from 1900 figures. Either members did not as a whole experience the greater prosperity of the times, or their prosperity did not affect their level of giving. At St. Paul's in 1920 per-person pledging outpaced Trinity by a factor of two to one, suggesting that the city's wealthiest Episcopalians went to St. Paul's while Trinity's congregation was more middle-class.

In the 1920s the parish had close to 1,000 communicants and needed a full-time assistant clergyman. Despite growth and the good economy, Trinity still struggled to increase pledging and ease the deficit which ran for most of the decade. A new heating and ventilation system was installed at a cost of $10,000, a substantial expense on an annual budget of $25,000.

It must have been tempting when the Chamber of Commerce in 1923 offered to buy Trinity's property for a state office building. Property values in downtown were rising, tempting struggling churches to sell out and rebuild in an outlying area of the city. But the vestry unanimously rejected the offer, stating that Trinity's usefulness and effectiveness "depend so largely upon its central location and the historic associations connected with its present church edifice." First Congregational Church made a different choice. In 1928, hoping to sell their Capitol Square property for $700,000, the congregation moved to a new building at ninth and Broad Streets. Then came the stock market crash and the Depression, and the property did not sell until 1946 when it fetched a mere $225,000.

1921 view of Statehouse and buildings along South Third and East State Streets. Trinity is located at the far left.

Women's Changing Roles
at Trinity

While men publicly led the church, its business came to rely on women who worked behind the scenes as employees. The first paid office worker at Trinity was Bessie Smythe, hired as a bookkeeper in March of 1900. Later Edith Albery held the position of finance secretary with the authority to sign checks. Her salary was $20 per month. She was promoted to executive secretary in 1918. Both Edith and Bessie were daughters of long-term vestrymen. Throughout the 1920s Mildred Stouffer was the parish secretary at a salary of $1,040 per year. (By comparison the choirmaster received $1,500 and the rector $6,000.) As the Depression was lifting in 1935, the parish hoped to hire a young man to work as secretary. The small salary, however, attracted few men, and this work fell to women.

During Chauncey's tenure, Mrs. James E. Bauman served as his personal secretary for 18 years without pay. The Baumans had lost their three-year-old son in 1917, and perhaps to assuage her grief Mrs. Bauman devoted herself to volunteer work at the church. The marble floor of the sanctuary was given by the Sunday school as a memorial to the child. With Chauncey's departure in 1936 the church also lost the services of Mrs. Bauman.

Trinity had a progressive record on the issue of voting rights for women. Decades before the Nineteenth Amendment enfranchised women and well before most Episcopal dioceses allowed women to vote in parish affairs, women at Trinity were qualified voters in parish meetings.[4] The practice may have originated when the congregation was small, services were less formal, and there were fewer adult men. In 1878 the by-laws codified the practice, specifying that all pew holders of legal age (a category that included women) who had signed the articles of association were eligible voters. An undated list of voters from around 1870–1880 includes the names of women, and vestry minutes offer evidence that they were present, spoke, and collected ballots at the annual meetings. While they were not elected to the vestry, they chaired organizations and advised the rector. For most women this level of political participation was satisfactory. For some it increased their desire for full suffrage in the civic realm.

World War I furthered the cause of women's suffrage. Doing war work for pay and organizing relief efforts gave women leadership experience as they fought for full citizenship rights. Proponents of suffrage argued that it was hypocritical to battle autocratic governments abroad while denying the benefits of democracy to half the American population. Ohio's Governor Cox declared it unthinkable to deny a

Elizabeth Greer Coit

Elizabeth Greer Coit (1820-1901), one of Columbus's earliest advocates for women's suffrage, was a member of Trinity. Born around 1820, she was the daughter of a Worthington couple with close ties to Philander Chase. She was educated at the Female Seminary in Worthington and married Harvey Coit, a merchant. She spoke widely in Columbus and neighboring towns on the issue of women's suffrage. Her daughter Isabella married Frank Kelton and continued her mother's suffrage work. She was one of the first women admitted to the Ohio State University.

voice in government to "mothers who give their sons and their all" to the cause of human liberty.[5]

Several Trinity women actively worked for the cause of women's suffrage. Lucile Atcherson was in the forefront in the battle for municipal suffrage, then in the national suffrage movement. Annie Maud (Mrs. John Gordon) Battelle, a leader in the National Women's Party, picketed the 1920 Republican National Convention in support of women's right to vote. Mrs. William T. Wells was president of the National League of Women Voters before her death in 1925. Also active in the movement was Mary Horton, wife of William Neil King, who donated the memorial window above Trinity's altar.

In 1920, the year that the Nineteenth Amendment was ratified, the Episcopal Church also took up the issue of women's suffrage. That year a House of Church Women was established, meeting at the same time as the diocesan convention. From the eight Trinity women nominated, the wives of the rector, the bishop, and a vestryman were selected as representatives. The women wasted no time in presenting a suffrage amendment to the diocesan convention. Bishop Reese was supportive and looked for the day when women would be given equal rights with men on vestries and at the conventions. "The Church cannot be less just or democratic than the state," he told the 1920 convention.

Bishop Vincent was not a proponent of change. But in 1928 he welcomed women as full-fledged convention delegates. He was aware that the issue of women's ordination would arise in the near future, and he urged the church to act with "fairest justice" and "wise conservatism," two values that would seem to ensure different outcomes in the matter. He favored reliance on a male priesthood, though he granted that exceptional women could be prophets, evangelists, and teachers as in the early church.[6]

The rule allowing women to be delegates to the diocesan convention brought a bold and enthusiastic response from Trinity. At the 1927 annual meeting, in an historic move, six women were nominated for the vestry along with the usual nine men. None of the women were elected to the vestry, if the ballot-counters can be trusted, though the top vote-getters for the position of diocesan delegates were women. Almost 40 years later Helen Riley was chosen by the vestry to fill a vacancy, making her one of the first women in the diocese to serve in that capacity.[7] Not until 1970, however, were women seated as delegates at the General Convention.

In the years immediately after World War I, however, the Progressive movement lost momentum and conventional ideals of womanhood regained ground. As women retreated into domesticity the scope of their religious work also shrank. Government agencies and professional social workers took over much of the work formerly done on a volunteer basis by church women.[8] A reawakening of men's interest in religion also crowded women out of their active roles. The senior warden of a New York Episcopal congregation was quoted in *The New York Times* and in the *Trinity Church Calendar* as saying that "fostering the life of the parishes, and… spreading the religion of Christ…is a man's job."[9] In addition much of the work done by women in the Episcopal Church was overseen and controlled by the male hierarchy. Even the Woman's Auxiliary was a supporting organization governed by the Board of Missions, which had no women representatives before 1919. Despite their gains in the civic realm, many women were content with their subordinate roles and regarded service, not leadership, as their calling.

The Missionary Spirit and Parish Life

A characteristic of parish life in the years following World War I was the increase in mission activity, especially by women's groups. Because of the war and the Nationwide Campaign, people in the pews were more aware of the worldwide needs of humanity and their own duty to support the church's work both locally and abroad. Few joined the ranks of intrepid missionaries who took Christianity to dark corners of the earth, but many joined the women's groups that undertook the supportive work and focused on local initiatives. Educating people, rather than converting them, and improving their living and working conditions became priorities.

The primary missionary arm of Trinity and other Episcopal churches was the Woman's Auxiliary, and it involved more women than any other church organization. In 1922 Trinity's auxiliary boasted 255 members, most of whom also belonged to subgroups representing Alaska, the Philippines, Cuba, China, Appalachia, Africa, and Japan. At meetings in members' homes, women collected money, listened to speakers, prayed, and prepared boxes of clothing and supplies for shipment to missions. While the auxiliary was considered pre-eminent among parish organizations, one opinion held that it was "set in its ways and appeals only to a certain type of woman."[10] This "type" was the distinguished matron of the parish, exemplified by Laura Platt Mitchell, who was president for more than 25 years. Wives of the rector, the bishop, and vestrymen were its leaders, women who found common ground with the church's male hierarchy.

Another women's group with a less stodgy reputation was the Girls' Friendly Society, composed mostly of single working women. Its light-hearted name belied its success as an outreach organization. Members met weekly in the parish house for dinners, night classes or lectures, parties, and religious services. All were welcome regardless of church affiliation. The society was founded to protect the virtue of unattached women, but beyond that it offered a supportive community for independent single women and a wide variety of role models.

Many members were no doubt pleased to graduate to the ranks of marriage, motherhood, and the Woman's Auxiliary, but many single women maintained their lifelong association with the society. One was Mary Hutchinson, a granddaughter of William B. Hubbard who mentored working girls. Louise Kelton directed the society from 1906–1921. Others postponed marriage for careers or other adventures. Lucile Atcherson, a charter member in 1906, returned after she was appointed a diplomat to Switzerland to talk about her war experiences. Lucile Grapes was president of a local nursing association and continued her career and her travels even after her marriage. In 1925 Cecile Cowey was admitted to the bar, the first lawyer among the ranks of the Girls' Friendly Society in Columbus. Participation in the society broadened the women's horizons. They listened with amazement as a Bexley teacher, Miss Thelma Hammon, recounted her trip to the South Seas, where she paddled alone in a canoe between the islands, was marooned, and rescued by natives.

The activities of the Girls' Friendly Society also supported Episcopal missions.

Edith Tallant wrote to her fellow members of her mission work in Labrador, where she traveled the bleak coast of Newfoundland gathering hooked mats made by the native women. These were shipped to the United States for sale to supplement the villagers' meager income from fishing. Blanche Harris served almost four years as a nurse at a women's hospital in Shanghai, where she traveled and learned the language. Her missives for the newsletter take the readers on a vicarious trip through the region, its culture and religion.

A memorable service at the Girls' Friendly Society convention in Cincinnati in 1925 illustrates how the missionary spirit infused this organization. There were speeches by women missionaries to Japan and Mexico and a Chinese girl studying to be a deaconess in order to return to her village as a missionary. The choir sang "Send out Thy light and Thy truth, let them lead me…to Thy Holy Hill" while a figure representing America ascended the sanctuary steps holding a candle. After her candle was lit by the rector, she in turn lit the candles of other girls arrayed in a semicircle around her representing all the nations. The flame was then passed to every girl in the assembly. America then led the recessional followed by the nations and all the girls. The message was clear—that America's superiority entailed a clear spiritual duty to the rest of the world.

During the 1930s membership in Trinity's society waned as fewer young associates joined. Times had changed and the organization focused more on modest self-improvement and on relieving local and national needs. Celebrating women's independence was no longer a high priority. The group's meetings, educational talks, and bridge parties took on a humdrum nature more characteristic of the staid Woman's Auxiliary.

Church School and Mission

The mission theme that drove women's organizations extended to the church school curriculum. In January of 1920 the students performed an allegorical pageant on the theme of "building the City of God." Its purpose was to encourage support for the Nationwide Campaign and its missionary goals. In 1923 church school classes competed in an intercontinental race by plane, train, and steamer, accumulating points (mileage) for attendance and achievement. The biggest gains were earned for bringing in new members to the church school. Teachers marked the progress of the class on huge maps, and students sent postcards from the exotic destinations they learned about. Awareness of the wider world was also promoted in the 1930 curriculum, "Our World at Work." As the Depression gripped America,

In the 1930s the five Kelton sisters (clockwise from left) Laura, Grace, Ella, Louise, and Lucy pose before a picture of themselves as children.

Trinity's Kelton family illustrates the changing position of women in society. Edwin Kelton and Laura Brace Kelton lived in the house at 586 East Town Street where Edwin's parents had hidden fugitive slaves. Laura was the mainstay of Trinity's altar guild for many years. Edwin was a wholesale lumber merchant with investments in zinc and lead mines in the West. Though proud of his aristocratic Scottish heritage, he nonetheless raised his daughters to earn their own living. Their independence became a necessity as Edwin's business troubles mounted. When he died in 1914 his family was occupied for years sorting out a tangled legacy.

Well-educated and enterprising, the Kelton sisters straddled the fence that divided the leisured elite and the working classes. Grace, born in 1881 and baptized at Trinity, was a respected art teacher, antique dealer, and decorator. Grace was pious, and all her life she kept among her personal effects a book of Bible readings compiled by Bishop Reese and brochures from a 1925 class taught by Trinity's rector, Egisto Chauncey.[11] She died in 1975.

Louise Kelton (1880–1955), a graduate of Smith College, found her calling as a mentor to other single women. In 1913 Bishop Reese established St. Hilda's Hall as a residence for women attending Ohio State University. He asked Louise Kelton, who was already a national leader of the Girls' Friendly Society, to become the director. The pay was $800 for ten months, women's wages for women's work rather than a living salary. Louise wrote to her brother-in-law that the house was off to a good start and mentioned "the incidental pleasure of getting $80 a month, which gives me a feeling of pleasure that I have never known before."[12] Though circumstances made it necessary for her to work, she delighted in earning an income and gaining a measure of independence. She served as housemother and administrator of St. Hilda's, overseeing three houses and up to 40 women, until it closed in 1952.

Her commitment to women's education is reflected at Trinity Church, where a memorial window depicts St. Hilda, the learned abbess of Whitby in England. Louise and others gave the window in honor of their former teacher Lucretia Phelps, who with others of her staff attended Trinity and taught many girls in the congregation at her English and Classical School.

children learned about working conditions in light of Christian teaching. They presented stories about children who labored in the Philippines, Africa, China, and Japan. They also assembled boxes of clothing and other items for needy children in other states.

Church school was highly structured with homework, report cards, tests, and many competitions. In 1925 classes vied to earn points to "furnish" the church from the reredos and carpets down to each light and pew. The exercise taught them about stewardship. Competition extended to recreation as well. At the annual church school picnic in June of 1920, a full slate of 30 track and field events were offered for boys and girls in all age categories. The rector's son, Henry Chauncey, was a star, as were the Thornhill boys, who also excelled on the basketball team.

With modern life offering new Sunday pastimes such as Sunday driving and amusement parks, churches had to compete with their own enticements. Many incentives aimed to increase church school participation. The coveted St. Andrews cup went to the class with the best attendance record. Children received pins for perfect attendance. By 1932 Miss Norris earned a diamond pin for eight years of perfect attendance. A few years later Don McCullough topped Norris' record, winning a pin with three diamonds for his eleven years of perfect attendance. The purchase of a moving picture machine in 1920 enlivened Sunday School presentations, but attendance lagged again once the novelty wore off.

Prizes and incentives ntly worked to e Sunday school ance, especially among In 1928–29 the atten- rate for boys was lly greater than the for girls. More boys men were also being firmed, suggesting t the view of religion women's domain was anging. Perhaps some

1919 flyer promoting a church school contest to raise awareness of international missions.

ATTENTION!

An Audacious and Adventurous Ascent Across Atlantic

Daring, Dazzling, Death Defying Demons Devouring Distance

Trinity's Trans-Atlantic Trip *1919*

June 1st to 29th

Fifteen aeroplanes representing the Classes of Trinity Church School will take off for the Azores, Lisbon and Plymouth at 9:15 A. M., Sunday, June 1.

Your ship will need it's full crew if it's to make a successful trip, therefore, Be Present, ON TIME.

new recruits for this trip.

of the credit goes to Fritz Lichtenberg, who was superintendent of the Sunday school from 1914–1938.

Despite this success, the size of the Sunday school relative to the congregation had been shrinking. In 1895 there were 310 pupils in a congregation of 600 communicants. In 1920 the parish had about 1,000 communicants and 200 registered pupils, three-fourths of whom attended class regularly. It was becoming clear that the traditional way of attracting new members through Sunday school, which led to confirmation and admission to the ranks of communicants, was no longer most effective. The greater potential for growth was in newcomers to the city and other adults who were unattached to a church.

Chauncey's Liberal Theology

In the early twentieth century mainline Protestantism was becoming ascendant, expressing the values of middle- to upper-middle-class Americans. Religious fundamentalism held on in some quarters; in Tennessee John Scopes was convicted of teaching evolution in the infamous 1925 "monkey trial." That same year at Trinity Chauncey led a class that sought to reconcile science and history with Biblical truth. What men and women need, he said, is a "rational interpretation of the truth in the gospels" and to be brought into intimate relationship with God. To that end he offered a "scientific and devotional study" of the Gospel of Mark.[13] Such comparative and historical study of the four Gospels, which has now become orthodox, then marked Chauncey as a theological liberal. Under Chauncey Trinity exemplified broad churchmanship: socially conscious, receptive to modern thought, but still rejecting ritualism.

Egisto F. Chauncey, pictured with his daughter Edith, served as Trinity's rector for 23 years, longer than any other rector in its history. Chauncey exemplified liberal theology and institutional stability.

Chauncey himself originally believed in the divine inspiration of Scripture, but the study of modern scholarship changed his perspective. In Columbus he joined an informal group of liberal Protestant ministers who called themselves

CLOSE-UPS of COLUMBUS MINISTERS

HIS EARLY AMBITION WAS TO BE A CIVIL ENGINEER—

BUT HE WENT INTO BUSINESS IN NEW YORK INSTEAD—

EDUCATED AT GROTON SCHOOL, MASS., SPENT 5 YRS. AT HARVARD THEOLOGICAL SCHOOL; ELEVEN YEARS IN N.Y. PULPITS, AND FOR THE PAST 13 YEARS, RECTOR AT TRINITY CHURCH—

HIS ONE HOBBY IS ATHLETICS OF ALL KINDS IN GENERAL, AND TENNIS IN PARTICULAR

BORN IN PARIS, AND SPENT HIS BOYHOOD DAYS IN N.Y. CITY—

REV. E.F. CHAUNCEY, RECTOR OF TRINITY CHURCH

GREETINGS FROM SONNY JIM

JANUARY 1, 1927

This cartoon by "Sonny Jim" Baughman shows Trinity's rector as a well-known public figure in Columbus.

"The Theological Seventeen." Together they published *The Faith of a Modern Christian* in 1922, a work based on the premise "that science is not in conflict with religion, and... religion has a social as well as an individual message."[14]

Chauncey put his beliefs into action and was a recognized and beloved community leader. Known as Bill rather than by his unusual first name, he befriended government officials, business leaders, and ordinary people. A slight man only five feet eight inches tall, he had a scholarly mien. He seldom wore his clerical collar, preferring to be considered "one of the boys." He was seen regularly at Rotary Club luncheons and was the organization's president for a year. Its members all came to Trinity for the noon meditation on Good Friday. Said his successor, the Rev. Anson P. Stokes, "Protestants, Catholics and Jews, and unbelievers too, responded to his leadership."[15] Chauncey consorted with the Kit Kat Club, an elite group of university professors, newspapermen and authors, bankers and lawyers interested in literature, art, and the humanities.

Like his predecessor Theodore Irving Reese, Chauncey served the community. For eight years he was president of the Family Service Bureau, today known as Crittenton Family Services, and he served on various other social service and relief agencies. Perhaps his greatest contribution was chairing the first United Way fund drive, then known as the Community Fund Campaign. He was able to persuade the city's many charitable organizations to pool their separate fund-raising efforts. The 1923 campaign was successful beyond anyone's expectations, raising more than

$600,000 and involving nearly 30,000 contributors. At the opening of the following year's campaign, Chauncey's leadership was celebrated and he was given a gold watch. Karl Hoenig, Trinity's choirmaster, leapt onto his chair to toast Chauncey and lead the crowd of 600 in an improvised song.[16] The leadership of its rector also affirmed Trinity's preeminence among the city's churches on issues of social justice.

For all his social and civic activities, Chauncey was considered an unworldly man. He never discussed his salary with the vestry, determined to live on whatever amount they fixed. When Nicholas D. Monsarrat raised the issue at a vestry meeting Chauncey was quite displeased. Monsarrat later wrote a letter of apology, citing his shame at the tiny salary paid to the rector.[17] The Chauncey family did manage to live in some comfort in Trinity's spacious rectory with a servant, vacations, and private schooling for the children. The family attended motion pictures on the minister's complimentary pass and enjoyed plays and football games. Some luxuries, it is true, they could not afford. In 1922 Mrs. John G. Battelle gave her rector a blue Pierce-Arrow touring car that had belonged to her son, but Chauncey kept it for only a year as its upkeep was beyond the family's means.[18]

The Ministry of Karl "Pop" Hoenig

Even longer than Chauncey's 23-year tenure was that of Karl "Pop" Hoenig, who was choirmaster for more than 40 years. Under Hoenig Trinity's choir became a civic institution. In 1926 the choir consisted of 42 boys and eight men, many of whom were not members of Trinity. An active choir club consisting of hundreds of alumni held annual reunions. As the story went, every fourth man in the city could claim that in his childhood he had been a treble in Trinity's choir.[19] The choir's high reputation brought in new members via the choir stalls and the pews. One was Bill Anderson, a Presbyterian who sang in the choir as a boy, returned to Trinity as an adult, and was married there. Fifty-five years later his widow Clara was still an active member.

Hoenig had succeeded Julius G. Bierck, who established Trinity's professional-quality choir of men and boys. Like most choirmasters, Bierck needed to

Choirmaster for over 40 years, Karl "Pop" Hoenig made Trinity's choir a civic institution.

supplement his income by giving lessons, and he resigned from Trinity to take a position that would enable him to focus entirely on liturgical music. Hoenig, unlike Bierck, embraced secular music and used it as a form of outreach. He ran the music programs at Ohio State University and the Columbus School for Girls and the Republican Glee Club. During World War I he led community singing and organized bands, orchestras, and choirs to aid in fund raising campaigns. In 1935 his years of service to the community were honored with a song fest attended by 1,500 people and featuring the choirs of several churches and organizations. His name was a household word in Columbus, and many in the community referred to Trinity as "Pop Hoenig's church."

In 1940 Hoenig collapsed on the corner of Third and Broad Streets, and his illness forced him to retire the following year. John Deinhardt, formerly a member of his choir, stepped to the console and served as interim organist. Thrust into the limelight with virtually no experience, Deinhardt gamely played the organ and directed the choir in the Hallelujah chorus, its strains amplified by speakers on Broad Street.

Stern and affectionate, Hoenig referred to all his young choristers as "sonny boy." Boys were paid $1.50 per month, men about $10, and Hoenig's salary was $125. Being a choir boy was a privilege as well as an opportunity for adventure. In those days the choir room was in the basement next to the coal room and furnaces. A track surrounded by piles of dirt ran underneath the length of the church to the chute where coal was delivered on Third Street. The boys rode the trolley back and forth through the dark and coal-blackened bowels of Trinity. By contrast they shined like angels when they sang. Choir mothers fitted collars, tied bows, and tried to send the boys down the aisle with a semblance of order and dignity. At Christmas they caroled through the downtown business district, marching up Broad Street to sing at the Huntington Bank.

Hoenig also played the chimes for religious festivals and civic events, making people feel that the bells belonged to the city, not just to Trinity. On one occasion a parade of suffragists found comfort and welcome in the chimes. As one of the marchers recalled, "we were both cheered and jeered. Then when we were tense with suppressed feeling we turned into Broad Street toward Third and there rang out to greet us the beautiful chimes of the Episcopal Church. They were manipulated by "Pop" Hoenig, the great organist. I doubt if even the music of heaven will sound quite so wonderful."[20]

Suffering the Depression

Trinity never retired its debts during the decade of economic expansion, so when the Depression hit it was already weakened. Income from pledges fell by about 30 percent, and the vestry was forced to adopt a rigid economy. Conservation measures shaved 40 percent from the expense of church upkeep. Cheaper Ohio coal was substituted. The choir was asked to sing without pay, cutting the music budget in half. The secretary took a pay cut, the publication of the bulletin was suspended, and the rector managed without an assistant. Minor repairs extended the life of the organ, which was in need of major overhaul. By these measures Trinity managed to scrape by without adding to its deficit.

Trinity fared worse than her more affluent Episcopal neighbors. Throughout the 1930s members of St. Alban's in Bexley (founded in 1921) pledged twice as much per person as Trinity. St. Paul's had the second highest rate. On the other hand, the all-black congregation of St. Philip's pledged less than half of what Trinity's members were capable of. St. John's in Franklinton was also hard hit.[21] Despite the depressed economy, the annual every member canvass continued with the rector, vestry, and a team of parishioners visiting all parishioners. The aim was to promote fellowship, encourage attendance, and maintain interest in Trinity during difficult times. The question of financial support was secondary. Those who were known to be unable to pledge were not asked, while some members of the congregation were approached as emergency donors.

At the deepest point of the Depression Trinity's budget woes were quite serious. At the end of 1934 the cumulative debt was $4,600 (on annual expenses of $15,000). The endowment had lost about 25 percent of its value. A newly-established finance committee, acting as the fiscal agent of Trinity, sold some funds and reinvested others. The rector took a pay cut, and the vestry took out a loan of $1,500 to help meet expenses. But providence came to Trinity's aid; a parishioner died, leaving her property to the church. Though the family contested the will, Trinity finally received $2,500. Then A. N. Whiting died, leaving a bequest that was applied directly to the debt, and the bequests of Mary E. Hutchinson, granddaughter of William B. Hubbard, and Dr. Charles Hutchinson swelled the endowment. By 1936 the endowment was repaid, the loan was retired, and income ran just ahead of expenses. Because its finances were looking up, the vestry could contemplate hiring an assistant minister and a secretary for religious education.

At this point Chauncey announced his resignation. A sense of duty bound him to stay with the parish through the Depression, but now that prospects appeared brighter he felt it wise to leave. In his resignation letter of June 23, 1936, he wrote,

"This age calls for new leadership. Trinity needs an awakening and a quickening and has the right to expect it." Though he was exhausted from running Trinity single-handedly, leaving was painful to him: "It makes me feel lonely. I dread the hour of separation." The prospect of being rector of a small church in Florence, Italy, appealed to him despite the tense political situation in Europe.[22] Trinity bade farewell to its longest-serving rector and to an era, little knowing the great changes that loomed over the nearby horizon.

Notes

[1] Garrett, 119-20. Those interviewed for this chapter were Eloise Allison, Clara Anderson, John Deinhardt, and Rev. Gordon Price.

[2] This is the theme of Rima Schultz's treatment of St. James from 1895-1928.

[3] This hand-written account of the meeting was slipped between pages of the vestry minutes; it is not part of the official record.

[4] Information on women as voters on the parish level is difficult to come by. The 1890 parish bylaws specify that lawful voters can be male or female but speak only of vestrymen, evading the question of whether any lawful voter, male or female, can be elected to the vestry. See Donovan, p. 210, n. 38 for a survey of what is known about women voting and serving on vestries and as delegates. If Gunderson is right that between 1890 and 1920 many dioceses granted women the right to vote in parish meetings ("Women and the Parallel Church," 118-19), then Trinity was at the forefront, even ahead of the game.

[5] *Ohio State Journal*, May 14, 1917.

[6] Krumm, 96-7, summarizing Vincent's *The Pastoral Epistles for Today* (Milwaukee: Morehouse Publishing Co., 1931), 24-5.

[7] In 1966 two women were elected to the vestry of Cincinnati's Christ Church, a parish that prided itself on its liberal and progressive traditions. A few years after that, Christ Church in Dayton followed suit. Krumm, 101 n. 12.

[8] This general trend is borne out by the studies of Rima Lunin Schultz, "Woman's Work and Woman's Calling in the Episcopal Church: Chicago, 1880-1989," in Prelinger, *Episcopal Women*, 45-52; Donovan, 140-45, 157-66.

[9] *Trinity Church Calendar*, December 12, 1926.

[10] *Girls' Friendly Scout*, April 1925. Miscellaneous copies of this newsletter in Trinity archives are the source of information on this organization from 1906-1932. A chapter had been started in the early 1890s but was apparently disbanded at some point prior to 1906.

[11] I am grateful to Georgeanne Reuter, Director of the Kelton House Museum and Garden, a service of the Junior League of Columbus, for allowing me access to the personal papers and files of the Kelton family and for providing photographs.

[12] Louise Kelton to William Pierson, October, 1914. Kelton House Museum, Collection 3: Kelton Family Personal, folder #1.

[13] *Trinity Parish Calendar*, January 13, 1918.

[14] Cited by Henry Chauncey, *A Life of Faith in God and Service to His Fellow Men: Egisto Fabbri Chauncey 1874-1963* (Ithaca, NY: Grapevine Press, 1991), 72.

[15] From a letter of Anson Stokes, cited by Chauncey, 68.

[16] Chauncey, 57-61.

[17] From a letter by Nicholas D. Monsarrat, July 29, 1918, cited by Chauncey, 53-54.

[18] Chauncey, 42.

[19] *The Columbus Sunday Dispatch*, August 9, 1942.

[20] Cited in "The Chimes," n.d. (1943).

[21] Using diocesan records, a "pledging index" was obtained by dividing pledge receipts by number of communicants. Results in 1931: St. Albans = 38.8; St. Paul's = 23.7; Trinity = 17.5; St. Philip's = 8.15. Roughly the same proportions held in 1936 as well.

[22] The threat of war was like a serpent in this paradise, however, and the Chaunceys returned to the U.S. just as Mussolini declared war on France and England (Chauncey, 101-109).

Chapter 9

TRINITY *in* HER PRIME: WORLD WAR II TO 1960

orld War II was a contemporary watershed. It turned America into a superpower with a host of new responsibilities toward the world. It cured the economy, restoring full employment and economic prosperity that finally ended the Depression. The middle class expanded and more people were fulfilling the American dream of obtaining an education, a home, two cars, and a television. The post-war birth rate boomed and congregations took a corresponding leap in size. Some anxiety, however, accompanied this hope. The atomic age brought new fears that the world could be destroyed by nuclear weapons, and the specter of aggressive Communism threatened American's most basic values. To combat those fears during the Cold War, Americans wore their religion like a spiritual armor.

In 1954 Lenten worshippers at Trinity heard visiting Episcopal clergyman Thomas V. Barrett reflect on the need for faith in a changed world. He said, "We put more faith in man's capacity to control human problems than in God's." But the Depression, World War II, the Holocaust, and the advent of atomic weapons taught Americans the futility of human solutions to problems and the inadequacy of science to explain the world. Spiritually empty, people longed for a return to faith.[1] A revival of religion occurred in America, fed by hope for a better world. The Episcopal Church and other mainline Protestant denominations provided national moral leadership and support for democratic institutions.

In the years from World War II to the 1960s Trinity was a stable refuge from the uncertainties of the modern world. It maintained traditional forms of worship and structured its members' lives from youth through adulthood. As the family of the time looked to its father, the congregation looked to its rector for leadership. In the next generation ideals of family life would be shaken by the sexual revolution and the women's movement. During these interim years, however, Trinity remained a pillar church conscious of its premier place in the city, a landmark and lodestone that drew people from throughout the spreading metropolis.[2] Its public aspect conveyed moral leadership as the church faced issues of global import in a changed world.

The War Years at Trinity

Emerging from the Depression and looking for new leadership after Chauncey's 23-year tenure, Trinity called the Rev. Anson Phelps Stokes Jr. to be their rector. He was only 32, a well-pedigreed young priest, the scion of a family of wealthy eastern industrialists. In his education and career choice he followed the footsteps of his father, Dr. Anson Phelps Stokes, then canon of the National Cathedral in Washington, D.C. Both father and son, like Chauncey and the Rt. Rev. Henry Wise Hobson, bishop of Southern Ohio, were graduates of the Episcopal Theological School at Cambridge, Massachusetts, known for training clergy in a liberal and broad church tradition. Theologically speaking Trinity's leaders were drawn from a similar gene pool. Stokes was also friends with Julius Atwood and Theodore Irving Reese, bishops who were former rectors of Trinity. Within ten years of leaving Trinity, Stokes himself became a bishop, serving in Massachusetts until 1970.

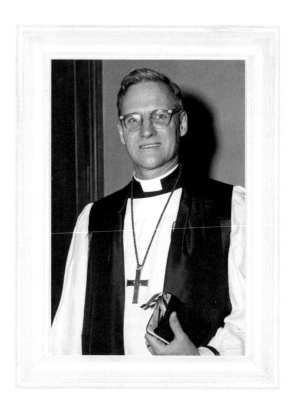

The Rev. Anson Phelps Stokes, rector of Trinity from 1937–1945 and later bishop of Massachusetts.

When he came to Trinity in 1937 Stokes was still a bachelor. He was a delightful guest who frequently dined at the homes of vestrymen and parishioners. They were sometimes joined by Bishop Hobson, a fellow Yale graduate, and a jolly camaraderie prevailed at these gatherings. In 1943 Stokes married Hope Procter, a member of the family that founded Procter and Gamble and endowed the bishopric of Southern Ohio. Stokes and his wife returned to Columbus to live until 1945, when he became rector of of St. Andrew's Cathedral in Honolulu. Stokes awed the young Joan Evans with his swift recitation of the liturgy, and she preferred to listen to him rather than to attend Sunday school with the other children. Some, however, found Stokes more ambitious than pastoral. He always had "the air of a bishop," one congregation member noted.[3]

Stokes also had a playful side. Officiating at his first wedding at Trinity, he found his role went beyond that of minister. When the friend who was to drive newlyweds Julia Davisson and Gordon Randall to their honeymoon destination did not show up, Stokes offered to smuggle the couple away in his own car. A chase ensued with up to 30 cars honking and careening through alleys and streets. Stokes turned into an empty garage and the crowd tore past. Back on the road again he ran out of gas, and the pursuers turned up, throwing rice. Defeated, the couple returned to the bride's home where they had started from. The next morning the bride's sister phoned Stokes to say that in all the rush and excitement, he had forgotten to sign the marriage license.[4]

Whether prompted by Stokes' leadership or by the human need for spiritual comfort or a combination of both, church attendance increased during World War II. Easter services drew crowds of over 800 people, many of whom stood in the vestibule and strained to hear the preacher. In 1943 Stokes noted that the average attendance at the 11 a.m. Sunday service had grown to 302, even with the addition of an evensong liturgy. Measured by the diocesan standard of numbers of communicants, the congregation grew 27 percent between 1938 and 1945. Stokes affirmed Trinity's role as a downtown church, calling it a spiritual oasis in the midst of the city. It was during Stokes' tenure that Lenten services featuring prominent guest preachers became a regular offering that drew hundreds to the corner of Third and Broad.

The increase in the congregation was accompanied by a financial recovery as well. As industries retooled for war production, the country bounced back from economic depression. Employment rose and people were again able to meet their pledges. In 1939 the vestry took steps to rebuild the endowment, which had lost one-third of its value during the prior decade, estimating that in ten to 15 years the endowment would be restored. In only seven years the value of the endowment had

The choir in 1944.

fully recovered. Stewardship goals were exceeded in 1943, 1946, and 1947. The years of plenty were underway.

The needs of the aging building, neglected throughout the lean years of the thirties, could no longer be ignored. Inside, new lights, fresh paint, and new carpet brightened the nave. New memorial windows were commissioned for the south transept gallery. The designer, Wilbur H. Burnham of Boston, sought to recapture the spirit of medieval stained glass. Part of the glass in these windows was twice torpedoed and rescued when being shipped from England early in the war. Outside Trinity received a facelift when a vestibule was added to the front of the church. Designed by architect Norman R. Sturges, the porch cost $7,700 and was made to blend neatly with the existing façade. It was even artificially smudged to give it the same aged look as the rest of the church. The gift commemorated Mary Elizabeth Jones Deshler, the wife of William G. Deshler and granddaughter of James Kilbourne. Deshler was baptized, confirmed, married, and buried at Trinity Church, and for most of her married life she lived on the northwest corner of Third and Broad Streets, where she could see the church from her windows.

In 1940 a porch was added to the front of the church. It was a gift in memory of the wife of William G. Deshler, a granddaughter of James Kilbourne.

Once America entered the war, spending for the physical needs of the church was put on hold. Work stalled on the memorial windows, for the Burnham company was denied authority to manufacture stained glass windows. The parish house needed new lighting, but no neon lights could be obtained. More bells were needed to complete the chimes, but none were being manufactured. At pre-war prices the estimate was $6,500, more than the rector's annual salary. New cabinets and office equipment also had to wait as industry produced materiel for war. But staff and clergy salaries rose and gifts and bonuses made working life more pleasant after so many lean years. When choirmaster Karl Hoenig retired due to infirmity, Robert Schmidt was hired without question though his salary demand necessitated a 25 percent increase in the music budget.

Wartime shortages also curtailed parish activities. Because of food rationing the 1943 annual meeting proceeded without the customary dinner. Gasoline rationing made it difficult for people to attend meetings and events, and clergy were unable to make their usual calls. Yet attendance at all services was increasing, and the Woman's Auxiliary maintained its meeting and work schedule. People planted victory gardens at home, and sextons and volunteers gathered spare bits of metal from the church grounds for the scrap metal drive.

The transept chapel in the church became a place to pray for peace and for the safety of Trinity's enlisted men. Consecrated in 1942 in memory of Bishop Reese, it remained sparsely furnished because of war shortages. But a parish honor roll listing all those in the armed services was hung near the small altar. In 1942 vestrymen George Kaufmann and Wilson Bradford entered the army. Kaufmann was in officer's candidate school, while Bradford was a lieutenant with the Army Corps of Engineers in Tennessee. Roger Wooten served two years as a pilot in the Air Force. George Gifford saw combat in the South Pacific as a member of the Marine Corps. Both Wooten and Gifford were ordained to the ministry in 1952. Arleigh Dygert Richardson III, descendent of George F. Wheeler, was wounded during the Normandy invasion when his ship sank. He was plucked from the water and recovered fully.

The war affected the entire congregation. Nearly everyone had a friend or close relative in the armed services. Eight men from the congregation lost their lives. So many men were in the service that the ranks of the Bishop Reese Club were decimated of college-age boys. The men who remained were needed in the labor market. Choirmaster Robert Schmidt took an essential war job in order to avoid being drafted. Like thousands of others, including women, he sought work at the local Curtiss-Wright plant, manufacturer of military airplanes, which became North American Aviation after the war.

As it had been during the First World War, the parish house again became a community center. Women met for Red Cross work, including sewing and winding bandages, and Mary Adams, an Englishwoman, operated a relief organization from the basement of her home on Mohawk Street. Special services and collections were dedicated for British relief as the Battle of Britain wore on. Trinity held a class to train air raid wardens to protect the church as Americans everywhere took similar precautions. During 1942-43 more than 2,300 servicemen attended the dances at the parish house. A new organization, the Business Girls' Club, also met there. Immediately to the south of the church was a USO outpost that caused some friction. Trinity agreed to share a strip of its property and reluctantly permitted the erection of an electric sign and an iron post. While they considered it a detraction, patriotism demanded a measure of cooperation.

Wartime as usual tested the separation of church and state. People everywhere debated engagement versus isolationism, and clergy and churchgoers were no exception. Bishop Hobson favored engagement, a view that Trinity's clergy echoed cautiously. In a 1942 sermon Stokes acknowledged that Christianity was a "fundamental pillar of our national life." While the church works by persuasion, the state may use force to restrain and protect. We must be loyal to the state, but we owe our supreme loyalty to God, he said.[5]

Stokes was assisted by the Rev. Richard S. Zeisler, a young priest of Jewish background who had converted to Christianity and left Harvard University to study at Virginia Theological Seminary. Zeisler advocated a strong Gospel that embraced suffering but opposed evil. When Stokes departed in 1945 Zeisler also resigned, which was customary, ending his short stint as an attractive, intelligent bachelor clergyman at Trinity. After serving as the rector of the American Cathedral in Paris, he eventually left the priesthood and the Episcopal Church, reverted to Judaism, and took a seat in a New York synagogue. An inheritance enabled him to become a stock dealer and art collector.[6] Surely the unfolding horror of the Holocaust profoundly affected this man who lived deeply within both Jewish and Christian religious culture.

On V-E Day spontaneous celebrations erupted throughout the city. People flocked to the churches to pray. At Trinity the din of car horns and street celebrations competed with the pealing organ. A long line of people waited in the narthex to sign the church register. The following day there were three services held at Trinity. At no time from morning to evening was the church empty.

Postwar Growth at Trinity

*I*n the weeks following the Allied victory on the western front, a new rector, the Rev. Robert Wolcott Fay, arrived at Trinity. He embraced the historic importance of the moment and the place. He spoke of being in the presence of a "cloud of witnesses, great and noble men and women who ventured much in obedience to the call of Christ, and for whom the trumpets have sounded on the other side."[7] The reference included Trinity's recent war casualties and its past members, including Robert Fay's ancestor Cyrus Fay, a founder of Trinity.

As a descendant of one of Trinity's own founders and staunchest lay leaders, Robert Fay must have been delighted at the call to become rector of Trinity. A graduate of the Episcopal Theological School in Cambridge, he had been a classmate of Stokes and the two remained close friends. Fay came to Trinity in 1945 from a

Mary Adams

Mary Adams met her husband, Richard Adams, while both were serving in Italy during World War I. She drove an ambulance and he was an American doctor. They married in England after the war, but not before recommendation letters, including one from Columbus mayor George Karb, satisfied the bride's family that the doctor was a man of good character. When they came to Columbus Mary immediately became active at Trinity. The Adamses saw two of their children leave for military service, daughter Beatrice enlisting as an army nurse in England after World War II and son Leslie serving in Korea.[8]

Mrs. Adams was director of the altar guild "in perpetuity," says one who remembers her well. Often the altar of Trinity was resplendent with flowers from Mary's garden. When she could no longer do the work herself, she had her husband drive her to church and assist her to the door, where she would preside over others in the task of laying the altar. "Ask St. Mary; she will know what to do," the rector would say in deference to her authority.

Mary Adams of the altar guild and Betty Magruder, longtime director of religious education, make wreaths to decorate the church at Christmas.

parish in Warren, Ohio, where he had a strong record of community service that fitted him for the rectorship of a downtown parish. He brought his wife, Helen Sargent, and children Robert and Susan, aged 11 and 7. Robert sang in Trinity's boy choir, and Susan was one of the first young ladies inducted into the junior altar guild.

Fay was an able administrator and an authoritarian. In the corporation model that Trinity embraced, the rector was like a CEO and the vestry its board of directors. Though the vestry and wardens were elected by the congregation, Fay decided who was allowed to be nominated and he ultimately controlled the vestry. This situation was accepted, according to Bill Davidson, the first senior warden to succeed Singleton P. Outhwaite after four-year terms for wardens were instituted. Fay's habit of control extended to parishioners' lives, and while some found

The Rev. Robert W. Fay and his assistant, the Rev. Gordon Price, with Bishop Hobson around 1950. Trinity's twentieth-century ministers were trained in a broad church tradition emphasizing theological liberalism and social ministry.

him a benevolent paterfamilias and spiritual guide, others rejected his authoritarian style. Among the former his charm and spiritual charisma are still legendary, and he helped inspire several men of the parish to join the priesthood. Robert Fay presided as patriarch over a multiplying congregation and set forth the public face of a downtown church in its glory years.

Trinity's growth during the postwar period reflected the changing landscape of the city. Before World War II St. Paul's had thrived because of its premier neighborhood and wealthy members, while Trinity's more varied congregation had fallen on hard times. Throughout the 1930s and 1940s, however, Trinity recovered its pre-eminence. It claimed about 25 percent of the city's Episcopalians, and its growth and level of giving eventually outpaced St. Paul's.

The decline of the city's core was paralleled by growth at its edges. In the half-century after 1945 the city would grow fivefold from its pre-war size of forty square miles.[9] The high cost of doing business in the city, with its aging buildings and factories, encouraged movement away from the crowded city as did the network of new freeways and housing developments. Increasingly the city center housed—and isolated—the less fortunate. Churches were also being squeezed out. Where more than 40 churches once occupied the core of the city, by the end of the 1990s fewer than 20 would remain.

Development in the suburbs had a dual impact on Trinity. By 1953 congregations in Upper Arlington, Clintonville, and Bexley claimed a third of the city's Episcopalians, and by 1960 that number climbed to 41 percent. Trinity's share shrank to 15 percent, though it was still the largest (barely) among the city's eight Episcopal congregations. Trinity continued to grow, drawing members from all corners of the metropolitan area as it had since the advent of streetcars and the automobile. Many families chose to leave their homogeneous suburbs purposely to worship in a more diverse congregation in an urban setting.[10] Trinity attracted members who were well-educated, cosmopolitan, and committed to supporting their downtown church. It was the wealthiest Episcopal church in the city with property and endowments totalling $613,000.[11] Its pledge rate was second only to St. Mark's in Upper Arlington.

For Trinity the high-water mark was the year 1955 when 54 infants were baptized, 68 youths confirmed, and the congregation topped 1,000 communicants. On an average October Sunday well over 400 worshippers attended the 11 a.m. service. Within ten years, however, those numbers declined. The congregation dropped to 700 communicants, and infant baptisms fell from an average of 30.6 for the years 1950–55 to 23.4 for 1960–65. Attendance at all services began a slow but steady decline. Nationally the birthrate slowed, but in addition the Episcopal Church found it difficult to retain its members. In the 1960s Trinity's prime passed as new social forces challenged the authority and primacy of mainline Protestant religion.

Education, Worship, and Parish Life

*W*hen the post-war boom began, Trinity was poised to absorb its impact, in part because Stokes had recognized the importance of education programs to equip the parish for growth. Hiring an assistant was a top priority for Stokes, and once the Rev. Almus Thorp arrived, he was given special responsibility for church school and young people's work. In 1940 the church school was reorganized and professionalized, and attendance soon doubled. When Thorp left in 1940 to become rector of St. Stephen's near the OSU campus, the Rev. Richard Zeisler assumed his duties. Supervising religious education was essential to the training of newly-ordained or aspiring priests, who by virtue of their youth were deemed most suitable for working with younger parishioners.

Donn and Bobbie Schneider, dedicated church school teachers, lead children in a lesson.

Education was a cornerstone of parish life. On Sunday mornings older children and adults met before the second morning service for an hour of education. Adult education focused on the needs of parents, supporting them in the religious educa-tion of their children. The latest books on spirituality and Christian living filled the shelves of the parish library. While Betty Magruder served as director of religious education, Trinity helped develop a new young people's curriculum. Bill Baker, who was later ordained to the priesthood, remembers the long hours spent designing the sessions, taping them, and reviewing the tapes for the publishers.[12]

Children over ten years of age were expected to attend worship following the education hour, while the younger ones attended school during the service. (In the summers when there was no church school, children were led from the church during the sermon for an activity.) For a time there were even additional classes on Saturday mornings, focusing on the Bible and the mission of the church. In 1953, 45 children in grades 4–8 were enrolled in Saturday classes. After 1952 the Sunday school adopted an ecumenical curriculum developed by the National Council of Churches, perhaps to draw newcomers of different faiths. During the 1960s com-pletion of eight grades of Sunday school was compulsory for those entering Donn

Schneider's confirmation class. Schneider and his wife Bobbie guided hundreds of children in their years of teaching church school. At any one time, up to two dozen teachers, most of them parents, were needed to staff the school. The goal was to make Sunday worship a family affair that was inseparable from the education of children and their parents.

During Fay's years worship practices at Trinity continued largely unchanged. Morning prayer was the corporate worship service with Eucharist offered only on the first Sunday of the month. (It was celebrated every week at the 8:00 a.m. Sunday service.) Children did not take communion, and those already confirmed were expected to fast along with their parents. Stomachs growling, they endured church school and a lengthy liturgy. In 1946 communicants were directed to take the wafer from the paten held by server and dip it into the chalice offered by the rector as he spoke the words of administration. When there was another clergyman, he placed the wafers in the palms of communicants. In the mid-1950s there was a discussion of "family communion," allowing young children to accompany parents to the altar but not to take communion. Girls and women wore hats and were expected to remove their gloves to receive communion. Men wore suits even in the warmest weather. The clergyman wore a black cassock and white surplice. Ironically the garb that caused such a stir at Trinity in 1840 now bespoke Protestant plainness.

Though Trinity had a broad church orientation, some rituals were becoming an accepted part of worship. For instance, lighted candles, long condemned as popish, were in use. The choir processional that so outraged Bishop McIlvaine after the Civil War was now a firmly established part of the service. A significant change occurred when Wilbur Held was hired in 1948. Facing growing competition from the Columbus Boy Choir, Trinity disbanded its boy choir in favor of an adult choir of men and women. Held, who had little experience with boys' voices, welcomed the greater versatility of the adult choir and the opportunity to present a richer program of music. Another change was the advent of public baptism. Baptisms had always been private ceremonies conducted after the services. In December, 1952, six infants and two adults were baptized during the 11 a.m. service, beginning a practice that is now standard.

Public baptism celebrated the communal and familial aspect of congregational life. By the 1950s Trinity had more than a dozen organizations that served the needs of all members at all stages of their lives. Children began in the Sunday school then graduated to the Bishop Chase and Bishop Reese clubs for young people. Boys joined the acolyte's guild, progressing from apprenticeship to the rank of master acolyte. The solemn experience of acolyting became a path to ordained ministry for

Alice Fay Potter (1856–1953) was a loyal churchgoer who exemplified women's quiet and unremitting service. She could be found every Sunday in the second pew beneath the pulpit. Gordon Price reminisced about this tiny but daunting lady: "You'd start the sermon, and if she went like this, she wasn't fixing her petticoat, she was turning off her hearing aid and then you knew you were dead in the water. But she was a great lady." Bent over from the weight of her shopping bags, she took food to the hungry, flowers to the sick. Said Robert Fay after her funeral, she had been "burned out in service to Jesus Christ."[13] Potter was the great-granddaughter of James Kilbourne and Cynthia Goodale. Here Potter is shown with the portrait of Lincoln Goodale, brother of Cynthia and founder of Trinity, painted after his return from the War of 1812.

several young men. Girls were inducted into the junior altar guild, setting the table being as close as they could get to the mysteries of the altar. High schoolers could participate in an annual convention for young people. Young married couples met as the Cana Club.

Organizations for women included the venerable Woman's Auxiliary, the altar guild, the remnant of the Girls' Friendly Society, and the St. Barnabas Guild for nurses. For men there was an usher's guild, a men's club, and the informal Sinner's Club of downtown businessmen. It was standing-room-only in the parish house one night in November of 1952 when the women met on the third floor to learn about the Episcopal Church in Liberia, while the the men's club gathered on the second floor. People were not afraid to go downtown in the evenings, and the parish house became a second home for many people, especially youth. Said the Rev. Gordon Price, assistant rector from 1947–1950, "The congregation had the sense of being cared for."

In this age of the stay-at-home wife and mother, the Woman's Auxiliary flourished, claiming 300 members in 1958. The auxiliary sponsored a spring fair and a fall festival, themed affairs intended to raise money for charities such as Neighborhood House. The Alaska, Panama, Japan and other missionary groups sup-

Officers of the Woman's Auxiliary plan events over tea. From left are Mary Baltzell,
Marjorie Wendell, Betty Grover, Doris Whitaker, and Connie Clatworthy.

plied cookies, knitted and crocheted goods, aprons, plants and flowers. In 1953
hand-made monkeys stuffed with old nylons and smoking cigarettes were the novelty
item promoted as ideal playthings for children. The fall festival in 1957 featured a
talent show with the rector as master of ceremonies in a derby hat and striped
pants, twirling a cane. Four flappers and Frank Smith, the treasurer, sang "You've
Got To Have Something in the Bank, Frank." During Lent women of the parish
served their favorite dishes and homemade pies before and after the noonday speakers.
An average seating was 140 though sometimes as many as 200 lunches were served.

An important addition to this busy slate of parish events were the neighborhood
study groups organized in 1951 for fellowship and to support parents in the
Christian education of their children. They were also a vital way of unifying a large
congregation that was scattered throughout the city. Six groups were operating by
1952. Those who participated felt that the groups strengthened the parish and deepened their faith commitment. Helen Riley's group was engrossed by questions of
agnosticism and humanism, while a Bexley group examined the faith set forth in the
Creed. In the 1960s, when three clergymen served the parish, each group had a

clergy leader and usually pursued the same course of study.

From birth through adulthood the church claimed its members, offering a full slate of social and educational opportunities that aimed to build Christian character and create good citizens and stewards. The premier event was the annual meeting, which combined business, fellowship, and education in a visible celebration of the congregation's vitality and commitment to shared goals. These were festive affairs. In 1955 a record 277 people were served a classic fifties dinner featuring swiss steak and mashed potatoes. A vast long table seated the clergy, staff, speakers, vestrymen, and their wives. Rovena "Connie" Clatworthy, organizer of the dinner, recommended that six hours be allowed to arrange flowers with four to five women assisting.

Not all members of the congregation, however, embraced the parish program. The attendance at the 1955 annual meeting represented only a quarter of the 1,046 communicants claimed by the parish. Some current parishioners who were members at the time report not belonging to any neighborhood groups, seldom going to Sunday school, and attending services only occasionally, yet they treasure memories of family baptisms, confirmations, and marriages held at Trinity. They did not see Trinity as an extended family, nor did it serve as the basis for their friendships. Trinity was seen even by its own members as a church that was run by an elite group of parishioners, vestrymen, and those holding offices in parish organizations.

A new feature of parish life in the 1950s, the coffee hour, promised to bridge social discrepancies and make the church more welcoming. At the time a coffee hour was considered quite an innovation for churches. The idea that fostering fellowship was part of the purpose of worship was also new to Episcopalians, sometimes jokingly referred to as "God's frozen people." Trinity held its first coffee hour on November 16, 1952, after the plaster dust was swept from the assistant rector's office where a dumb waiter was installed to transport coffee from the third floor kitchen. Due to the large congregation and limited space in the parish house, attendance was by invitation only. It took several months to work alphabetically through the parish list. Newcomers, however, were always invited and vestrymen introduced them while their wives poured coffee. Helen Fay circulated with her camera, taking candid photographs.

An outdoor coffee hour, around 1958.

The effort to be more informal and welcoming was a success measured by increasing attendance at Sunday services, and coffee hours became an established part of the morning ritual. Remarked Fay, "The principal benefit is the widening of family relationships in the church."[14] The concept of the congregation as an extended family was appropriate in these baby boom years, but it implied an intimacy that was hard to sustain in a large congregation at a church that was viewed and governed as a corporation.

At the Shrove Tuesday pancake supper in 1953, 840 pancakes were served to over 200 people, including Harry Grant, Margie Delany (Kay), Barbara Hoyt, Avis and Frank Smith, Virginia Towers, and Esther Webster, standing at right.

Trinity's Public Leadership

Media coverage of services, special events, and clergy activities kept Trinity in the public eye from the days of Anson Stokes on.[15] Trinity had its own director of public relations, Mrs. Elizabeth Kight, a member of the congregation and co-owner of Kight Advertising. Robert Fay was pictured in the local press in June of 1950 next to James Thurber when both received honorary degrees from Kenyon College. Thereafter he was "Doctor Fay." In 1951 Ash Wednesday and Good Friday services were broadcast over the radio, and in November a service featuring the choir was televised. Fay's numerous television appearances included the women's program, "Open House," where he discussed the religious aspects of daily life and interviewed visiting clergymen. He also appeared on the program "Faith in Our Day." Choir performances, church improvements, and activities of the young peoples' groups garnered valuable publicity for the church. Members of the Woman's Auxiliary were featured on newspaper society pages arranging flowers or displaying wares for their annual bazaar.

Religion was news in those days. It was the era of Baptist evangelist Billy Graham and Catholic Bishop Fulton Sheen, when radio and television made national celebrities of religious leaders. In Columbus many local ministers and bishops, Protestant and Catholic, were featured on radio shows, but Trinity, being downtown, probably received more than its share of media attention. Eloise Allison recalls that while she was parish secretary the *Dispatch* religion reporter regularly called the church office to ask, "Is there anything going on over there that we ought to know about?"

Trinity regularly made the news with its slate of nationally-known Lenten preachers. People lined up along Third Street to hear Dr. Ralph Sockman, a Methodist minister from New York City whose National Radio Pulpit program had been broadcast since 1928. Speakers were set up outdoors and in the parish house for those whom the church could not accommodate. On another occasion a small furor erupted when Methodist Bishop Bromley Oxnam was engaged as a Lenten speaker. An anonymous writer to the *Ohio State Journal* cited Oxnam's ties to an American-Soviet friendship agency as proof of his un-American views. Defenders asserted he was both Christian and patriotic and cited his leadership of the World Council of Churches. No doubt the publicity increased the crowd for Oxnam's speeches. At a time when Episcopalians were still highly parochial, Trinity was bridging boundaries, inviting preachers of differing denominations to address the public from within its walls, often on topics of considerable controversy.

The size of the crowds who came to Trinity for special events testified to the public's great interest in religion. On Good Friday of 1956 more than 2,400 people passed through the church during the three hours of devotions. In 1950 an eight-day preaching mission conducted by the Rev. Bryan Green of Birmingham, England, brought 1,100 people to its opening session alone, where Bishop Hobson and Gordon Price led the singing of hymns. One of Green's topics was the need to oppose Communism by a "militant Christian democracy" that denounced witch hunts and all forms of social injustice. Preachers like Green reinforced the message that ardent prayer and religious observance were vital to the preservation of American democracy.

Trinity was also a leader in the fledgling post-war ecumenical movement. In 1948 the chimes tolled along with church bells across the United States as the World Council of Churches met in Amsterdam for a historic conference on Christian unity. In 1953 Fellowship Church, an interfaith and interracial group,

Crowds line up to attend Good Friday services. Trinity's program of
Lenten speakers drew people from the wider community.

began holding Sunday afternoon services at Trinity. That spring Charles Templeton conducted a two-week revival at the fairgrounds. The biggest evangelist since Billy Sunday, Templeton preached at Trinity's noonday services following an interfaith Bible study. The ordination of Gordon Price at Trinity in 1947 was highly unusual in that it involved clergy of the Greek Orthodox, Roman Catholic, and Protestant churches to symbolize his entrance into the universal church.[16]

Trinity's clergy worked with other Columbus clergymen on social issues affecting the community. Many churchmen spoke out against the tactics of those who threatened civil liberties in their eagerness to root out Communist sympathizers. At least a dozen Protestant and Jewish leaders formed an advisory board for the Planned Parenthood center in Columbus. Protestant clergy joined forces in 1958 to urge their congregations to vote in favor of a child welfare levy. As one minister reminded, "The church is the mother of most social welfare institutions."[17]

Parishes in the diocese followed the lead of their bishop, the Rev. Henry Wise Hobson, who served from 1930 to 1959. During the Depression it was Hobson who initiated the Forward Movement, which became a national effort to revitalize the Episcopal Church both financially and spiritually and to increase membership and observance. Hobson was ecumenical, favoring union with the Presbyterians. The Wayside Cathedral, a mobile church that distributed books and clothing and baptized people in mining camps, military outposts, and remote areas, was a joint venture with the Presbyterians. Hobson was also international in his outlook. Finding isolationism to be "morally indefensible," he supported U. S. intervention on behalf of the Allies even while most Americans preferred neutrality. He urged the nation to take an

Bishop Hobson's last Confirmation at Trinity in 1959, the year of his retirement.

active role in rebuilding the world shattered by war. Hobson spoke out in favor of civil rights for all Americans. He was a vigorous and visible bishop staking the claim of Protestantism to bring peace and build free nations.[18] In 1958 the Episcopal Church, acting on a resolution introduced by Trinity's own Robert Fay, gave a Tokyo university and hospital a nuclear reactor to be used for scientific and medical purposes. In Hobson and Fay, Ohio had Episcopal leaders of national stature.

The nation's secular leaders made openly religious statements, and churches in turn pushed patriotism. President Truman, speaking in 1946 before the Federal Council of Churches gathered in Columbus, called for a revival of religious faith.[19] President Eisenhower was an outspoken advocate of religion's relevance to public life. Many prominent political figures were members of the Episcopal church, including Franklin and Eleanor Roosevelt and Ohio's Taft family. Trinity's patriotic gestures included tolling the chimes on election day to remind Christians of their civic duty. Trinity's flurry of flags also supported the nation. An American flag and an Episcopal Church banner hung in the sanctuary. Unfurling from the rear gallery were the blue United Nations flag, another Episcopal flag, and the Ohio state flag. A third U.S. flag stood in the side chapel. On Sundays an additional U.S. flag and an Episcopal flag were displayed outside.[20]

In this era religion was an essential component of patriotism. A 1954 Act of Congress added the words "under God" to the Pledge of Allegiance. In 1959 Ohio adopted the now-contentious state motto, "With God all things are possible," expressing a hopeful vision that government inspired by religious values could defeat evil in the world.

Robert Fay's Downfall

*W*hile Robert Fay was rector, Trinity was a leading congregation in the city providing moral leadership on public issues. Fay was known and respected throughout Columbus. The parish was at its peak in terms of membership, drawing families throughout the city with its cradle-to-grave educational and social programs. Many future clergymen were raised from the congregation and ordinary laymen and women inspired to greater faith and service. The family's patriarch, however, was afflicted with a weakness ironic in a man of great faith—namely infidelity.

Fay resigned as rector abruptly in June of 1959 when his adulterous affair with a parishioner was discovered. The woman and her husband, parents of several children, were active and respected members of the parish and the community. Within hours of being confronted by the assistant rector and junior warden, Fay was facing Bishop Hobson, who was in the last days of his tenure. Hobson was outraged and saddened, for the matter involved a close and trusted clergy friend. Fay had even been considered as a candidate to succeed him. Hobson was known to be intolerant of sexual indiscretion and his usual practice

The Rev. Robert W. Fay in the pulpit. Fay served as rector from 1945–1959.

was to hasten the offending clergyman out of his post quickly and quietly. Within a matter of days Fay had moved from the rectory.

The congregation was bewildered; many people never knew the circumstances of Fay's departure and felt the parish had suffered a great loss. A discreet staff member told the press that the rector was retiring because of illness. Those who learned of the circumstances were shocked and devastated but, says one long-time member, fortunately they didn't hold it against the church. Every effort was made to smooth the transition to a new rector.

The excuse of illness was not far from the truth. Fay's health declined and he died of a heart attack in Florida in 1967. He had remarried following the death of Helen Fay four years earlier. To the end Fay maintained the respect of many of his colleagues in ministry. Bishop Stokes and Bishop Blanchard, Gordon Price, who had served as his assistant, and Roger Wooten and Murray Goodwin, two clergymen nurtured by Fay at Trinity, attended his funeral in Massachusetts. They were able to understand that Fay, like the Old Testament patriarchs, could be used as God's instrument for good despite his sins.

The circumstances of Fay's resignation and its quiet handling make an ironic contrast to an earlier episode in Trinity's history. Robert Fay's ancestor, Cyrus Fay, was chief among those in the congregation who ousted the rector, Charles Fox, in a series of boisterous and vocal confrontations in 1842. In comparison to Fay's betrayal, Fox's transgression was nothing worse than going back on his word not to wear a surplice during the service.

In the July 1959 edition of the *Chimes*, assistant rector Dick Wyatt rallied the congregation to carry on in the wake of Fay's resignation. Wyatt emphasized "a tremendous revolution occurring within the Church, the whole Church, in the last decade. This revolution centers around the realization that the Church is *all* the people and all the people are called, each in his own way, to carry on the ministry of the Church." It was a prophetic statement and a compelling call for the congregation to look forward rather than backward.

Conclusion

Ralph W. Sockman, one of Trinity's most popular Lenten preachers, had his finger firmly on the pulse of religion in America. Addressing 1,500 clergymen at the Ohio Pastor's convention in Columbus in 1954, he criticized the church for "trying to sell religion," shaping loyal consumers by offering an array of education, fellowship, and worship options. Instead he urged clergy to create spiritual leaders of laymen, whose actions and example in turn would transform government and society. "We must preach the hope of a better world. Our religion has uplifted the world and we can make some progress. I think we can preach that with all the fervor of the social gospel."[21]

Sockman articulated a major shift in religious attitude. First, the day was coming when laymen would take a greater role in bringing the church to the world. Second, the social gospel that sought to create a just society had been defeated by the harsh realities of international war and its aftermath. An old evangelical principle was re-emerging, namely the idea that individual redemption was the precondition for change in the world.[22] Churches shifted their focus inward, aiming to educate, redeem, and inspire those who filled their pews. Sockman advised that those who were weary and dispirited "should go into the shelter of their faith to get away from the world and find poise and calm. Then they are prepared for further exposure to life."[23] The idea of religion as a refuge and the growing focus on personal religion posed a challenge for churches like Trinity that had traditionally emphasized strengthening and serving the community.

Notes

1. "We Live In A Lost Generation, Minister Says," *The Columbus Citizen*, March 10, 1954.
2. The term "pillar church" is borrowed from Carl S. Dudley and Sally A. Johnson, *Energizing the Congregation: Images that Shape Your Church's Ministry* (Louisville, KY: Westminster/John Knox Press, 1993), 4. The concept of a family church is described by Penny Edgell Becker, *Congregations in Conflict: Cultural Models of Local Religious Life* (Cambridge University Press, 1999).
3. Those interviewed for this chapter include Molly Morris, Joan Evans Taylor, Eloise Allison, Rev. Gordon Price, John Deinhardt, Margy Kay, Wilbur Held, and Ellen Rose.
4. This anecdote is taken from an undated newspaper clipping in a scrapbook in Trinity's archives, like much of the information for this chapter. When publication information is available, the article has been cited.
5. *Trinity Church Calendar*, June 7, 1942.
6. This outline of Zeisler's career was conveyed to me by John Deinhardt who was a close friend. Though Zeisler declined to be interviewed, he confirmed the general information.
7. From a parish bulletin, June 7, 1945.
8. "Two Generations Celebrate Threefold Veterans Day," *Columbus Dispatch*, November 11, 1968.
9. See Henry Hunker, *Columbus, Ohio: A Personal Geography* (Columbus: Ohio State University Press, 2000), 28-35.
10. Ironically Trinity member Don Casto, a local developer, did much to further the suburbanization of the city when he opened the Town and Country shopping center around 1950. It became a prototype of the suburban strip mall.
11. St. Paul's was second, with a value of $599,000. By comparison, Christ Church in Cincinnati was valued at $4 million, courtesy of William Cooper Proctor and his family.
12. William A. Baker, letter to Richard Burnett, February 27, 1999.
13. Roger Wootten, Letter to Friends, April 10, 1967.
14. "After-Service Coffee Hours Help Congregations To Grow," *Columbus Citizen*, August 7, 1954.
15. In 1940 Stokes arranged for WCOL to broadcast the Lenten noonday services, the first record I have found of such media coverage.
16. " Episcopalians Ordain a Priest," *Columbus Sunday Dispatch Magazine*, August 31, 1947.

17 "Protestant Clergymen Join To Boost Child Welfare Levy," *Columbus Citizen*, October 28, 1958.

18 On Bishop Hobson, see Krumm, *Flowing*, 110 ff; *The Messenger of the Episcopal Church in the Diocese of Southern Ohio*, vol. 77, no. 4 (May, 1955).

19 Robert Wuthnow, *The Restructuring of American Religion: Society and Faith Since World War II* (Princeton: Princeton University Press, 1988), 66.

20 "Churches Take Pride in Old Glory," *Columbus Citizen* July 12, 1952.

21 "Pastors Hear Call for 'Boldness'", *Ohio State Journal*, Jan 26, 1954.

22 According to Robert Wuthnow, "The church's larger role in society was. . . conceived of primarily as influencing the society by influencing individuals" (*Restructuring*, 64).

23 Ralph W. Sockman, in "Pastor Urges Extra Courage in Atomic Age," *Columbus Citizen*, March 17, 1959.

The 1967 wedding of Robert and Janice Griffith in the newly renovated church.

IN MEMORY OF FRED S. AND FLORA M. COLEMAN,

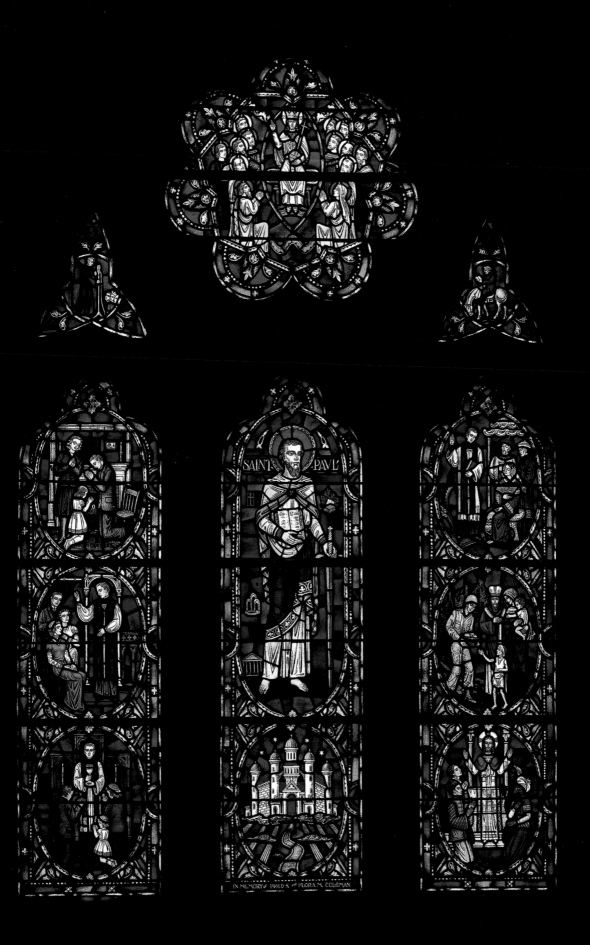

SAINT PAVL

IN MEMORY OF FRED S. AND FLORA M. COLEMAN

Trinity Episcopal Church on Capitol Square, built in 1869, was designed by architect Gordon W. Lloyd in the Gothic Revival style. The tower was completed in 1910 and the porch added in 1940. The church was named to the National Register of Historic Places in 1976. In 1993 the sandstone exterior was cleansed of over a century of urban grime, restoring its original brightness. Today skyscrapers dwarf the church but do not diminish its significance.

The red doors of Trinity's Third Street entrance are open daily, proclaiming its mission to the city and welcoming everyone. The inscription above the door comes from Isaiah 56:7, "My house shall be called an house of prayer for all people."

This magnificent window is the work of David Maitland Armstrong (1836–1918), who worked for Louis Tiffany before opening his own studio. The window features opalescent glass, made by mixing several colors on the same sheet, and uses multiple layers to give added richness and dimension. It was installed in 1910.

The central figures are the archangels Gabriel, Raphael, and Michael flanked by angels holding banners. Serene and watchful, the angels gaze in different directions. At the apex of the window Christ is depicted as King of Heaven, His hand raised in blessing. Above the angels' heads are the words of a prayer asking for deliverance of those who travel over land or water. The window commemorates Elizabeth Neil McMillen, the donor's mother, and the family of her son, Thomas Worthington King. King and his family were lost at sea.

The four windows in the north and south transept galleries were created by Wilbur Herbert Burnham of Boston, Massachusetts. By his use of small pieces of glass and medallions, Burnham sought to recapture the spirit of medieval stained glass. Read in sequence, the windows tell first the story of the Creation, then show how God aided mankind under the Old Covenant and the New Covenant, and finally depict the continuing work of Christians in the world.

The rose window depicts the seven days of Creation. The central figure in the window below is Adam, representing mankind. With his head among the angels and his feet mired in earth, he is both exalted and base. In the left lancet men seek through philosophy, natural religion, and science to know God. The right lancet depicts human acts of mercy and justice and democratic governance. But the expulsion of Adam and Eve from Paradise suggests that natural man is in need of redemption, for free will alone is not sufficient for salvation.

The theme of this window is the Old Covenant. In the rose window Moses is seen receiving the Commandments while the children of Israel worship the golden calf. The trefoils contain the symbols of the Law, the scroll and the Ark of the Covenant. The window's central figure is Isaiah, whose prophecies were fulfilled by the coming of Christ. Beneath him is John the Baptist, who prepared the way for Christ, seen approaching in the background. The left lancet depicts man's relationship with God under the Law. Details show Moses worshipping God in the burning bush and David praising God with psalms. The the right lancet shows human acts of mercy and righteousness according to the Law.

This window in the south transept gallery depicts Christ's life and death. The center lancet is a traditional nativity scene, while the rose window above depicts the Crucifixion. Below, an angel rests on the empty tomb following the Resurrection. The left lancet shows (from top to bottom) Christ as the symbolic vine, delivering the sermon on the Mount, and sharing the Last Supper. In the right lancet, Christ is represented healing the sick, forgiving the woman taken in adultery, and ridding the temple of moneychangers.

The theme of this window is the ongoing work of Christ's church in the world. The central figure is St. Paul the apostle. The left lancet shows the faithful in relationship with God through prayer, teaching, and the sacraments. In the right lancet can be seen images of the church serving the world. The rose window above celebrates Christ reigning in glory, guiding his earthly church. Below is depicted a vision of the New Jerusalem coming down from heaven.

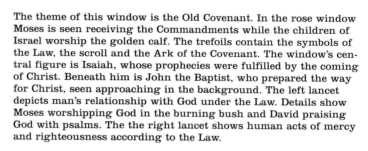

Dedicated in 1945, these windows reflect contemporary times. After World War II, many Americans shared the hope of enduring peace and a worldwide ecumenical communion. An American soldier is depicted giving bread to a starving child in war-ravaged Europe as an Eastern Orthodox bishop looks on. The next panel shows Christ uniting humans of differing races and religions in a spiritual fellowship, the church universal.

Chapter 10

CHANGING TIMES IN CHURCH and SOCIETY 1960–1980

While the years after World War II were a kind of golden age for Protestants, the 1960s brought turmoil to churches and society as a whole. Throughout America issues of social justice, poverty, racism, and war divided the old and the young, men and women, liberals and conservatives. In Columbus poverty and decline afflicted the city's core as businesses, residents, and churches moved away. Trinity, however, remained and undertook major building renovations. Demonstrating leadership, members of the congregation originated Capitol Square Ministries and the Open Church with programs for downtown workers and the homeless. After focusing on its own booming family in the postwar years, Trinity rediscovered its urban mission in the 1960s and 1970s.

Trinity's strong sense of identity helped it to weather the storms of change with minimal damage. Mainline Protestant churches were beginning to lose members as conflict over social issues broke down consensus and unity. At Trinity, too, attendance slackened. Some members left, finding church life too staid, too progressive, or simply irrelevant. At the same time, renewal and reform movements in the church showed evidence of a new spirit. Clergy leaders from the traditional yet forward-looking Roger Nichols to the pastoral and prophetic Walter Taylor articulated a clear vision that drew people together. For the most part the congregation accepted with good grace the revised Book of Common Prayer and the ordination of women. Many of them were becoming more involved in the growing lay movement. Despite controversies and difficult changes, a sense of energy and commitment characterized parish life in the 1960s and 1970s.

The Ministry of Roger Nichols

*I*n January of 1960 the Rev. Roger Bond Nichols became Trinity's new rector, beginning a period of healing following Fay's resignation. Nichols had been recommended by Gordon Price, rector of Christ Church in Dayton who had served at Trinity from 1947–50. The two became close friends while attending seminary together in Cambridge. Nichols almost didn't get the job though. When wardens Verle Baltzell and Bill Davidson visited Nichols at his parish in Greenfield, Massachusetts, they doubted he could be a candidate because of a speech impediment. Yet they were impressed with his wife Betty and saw a loving marriage. When Nichols preached at Trinity as a guest, the committee heard a dynamic and fluent preacher. Several parishioners today remember Nichols as the best preacher they have ever heard. He observed a strict limit of ten minutes and was called "St. Brevity" by his friends. "After the service was over, or the next day, everybody could tell you what the point of the sermon was," affirmed Bill Davidson.[1]

Besides preaching, teaching was Nichols's strength. His adult classes on Sunday mornings attracted sometimes as many as 180 people. They began with a discussion of "The Church in the News," which allowed people to voice their opinions and led to lively discussions on the issues of the day. Nichols's teaching on the experimental liturgies was instrumental in helping parishioners to accept the new Prayer Book in 1979. Trinity's offerings of good liturgy and music and cultural conversations were vital in getting people to bypass their suburban churches to come downtown.

The Rev. Roger B. and Betty Nichols (foreground) with parishioners Terry Henderson, Helen Anderson, and Anne and Bill Davidson at a parish annual meeting in the early 1960s. Nichols was rector of Trinity from 1960–1969.

The church in the world window was the vision of Roger Nichols, who wished to dramatize the church's ministry in society at a time when the relationship of church and society was growing more problematic. Designed by William G. Kielblock and funded by memorial donations, it was made by the Franklin Art Glass Company. The window was unique in its use of traditional Gothic lancets, rose medallions, and stained glass to depict contemporary, secular images. Flags of the United States, Ohio, and Columbus are centered in the rose windows. The five lancets feature such landmarks as the Statehouse, O'Shaughnessy Dam, city skyscrapers, Port Columbus airport, and Veteran's Memorial. Smaller details include a buckeye nut, John Glenn's spacecraft, an Interstate 71 sign, and symbols of science and technology. Reflecting Nichols's love of Buckeye football was an image of Ohio Stadium. (Nichols was known to celebrate an important football victory by including in Sunday worship a hymn sung to the tune of "Carmen Ohio.")

The resplendent window could be seen by the congregation exiting the church, reminding them that the world into which they emerged was to be redeemed and made holy. It could also be examined in detail from the gallery. Installed and consecrated in May of 1965, two years later it was illuminated from within for the benefit of passers-by outside. In 1970, however, the installation of a new organ in the gallery completely obscured the window from view. Those who disliked the window's modern design did not mind, while others simply accepted the tradeoff for a grand new organ.

With its modern, secular images rendered in stained glass in a Gothic Revival church, the window prompts questions about the scope of the sacred. Does the window glorify modern commerce, entertainment, and science? Does it suggest that the church too eagerly embraced the values of secular society, compromising its other-worldly sacredness? Or does the window boldly profess the all-encompassing nature of God and the church's hope of redeeming the world? Probably few people have given the question much thought, but if they did, some would criticize the church's openness to change and its worldly orientation. Others would be disappointed that the church does not do more to evangelize or to relieve suffering in the world. At issue are fundamental questions about the relationship of the secular and the sacred which affect churches like Trinity, located at the center of civic life. How well such congregations nourish their members while serving the needs of the wider community is crucial to their survival.

The modernistic Church in the World window, designed by William Kielblock and made by the Franklin Art Glass company, was dedicated in 1965.

On the pastoral front Nichols was the undisputed captain of a team of clergy that included the Rev. Dan Scovanner, a former Methodist minister who resembled Friar Tuck, and the Rev. David Dunning, who was noted for his projects involving youth and urban renewal. It was the clergy who initiated all programs, even leading the in-home study groups. While members of the congregation respected the clergy and expected them to lead, a few disliked the rector's dominating role. Nichols also took the lead with his vestry. He found church organizations too focused on fundraising, and he instituted the self-canvass, urging parishioners to give according to the "modern tithe" of five percent to charity and five percent to church. (Even at these figures pledge income was less than half of what he expected.) In financial matters Nichols was adept at cultivating relationships with local businessmen and wealthy parishioners. Vestry meetings, one former parishioner remembers, began with drinks and local financial gossip. Something of a patrician, Nichols identified with the establishment at a time when changes were beginning to loosen the prevailing hierarchical model of church leadership.

The church in the world window was an important symbol of Nichols's ministry in the city. Like his predecessor Robert Fay, Nichols continued in the visible role of a downtown rector. He was a great promoter of downtown renewal, and he would visit the construction site of the National City Bank across the street from Trinity proudly wearing his own hard hat. He was a leader among local clergy who founded the Metropolitan Area Church Board to address urban problems. Nichols was a deep admirer of the new bishop, the Rt. Rev. Roger W. Blanchard, who led the diocese with his prophetic ministry of social justice until the mid-1970s.

When Trinity celebrated its sesquicentennial in 1967, it had three urban renewal projects in the planning stages. One was a high rise apartment complex for seniors, an ecumenical project that failed for lack of federal funding. Another was a halfway house for newly-released prisoners. Alvis House opened at 971 Bryden Road early in 1968. The first center of its kind in central Ohio, it was the brainchild of Trinity's assistant minister, David Dunning, who was also a chaplain at the Ohio Penitentiary. Twenty months later, in danger of closing, it made an appeal to the community for funds. The third project was a parish house and community center, a dream ten years from its realization.[2] These initiatives were led by the clergy, and former parishioner Joel Gibson believes that the the congregation as a whole was slow to develop an "urban consciousness."

Trinity originated another form of urban ministry well in tune with the times. The Cracked Cup, the first and only church-sponsored coffee

Young adults gathered at Trinity's Cracked Cup coffee house, which opened in 1966, to listen to folk music and discuss issues of race and war.

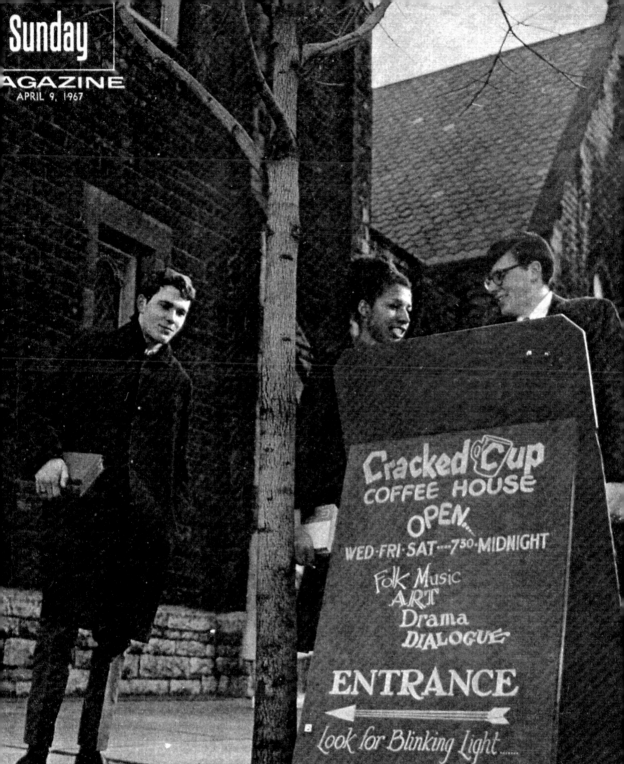

VITATION TO 'THE CRACKED CUP'
ch-Sponsored Coffee House
Popularity Among Youth ... SEE PAGE 45

house in the city, opened its doors in 1966. This too was Dunning's idea, and it involved a collaboration with St. Joseph's Cathedral and First Congregational Church. The Cracked Cup began as a ministry to young people of all religions and races studying or working downtown. Its alliterative name suggested the fracturing barriers of, religion, race, and education ("cracked") and the bond of unity that nonetheless holds people together ("cup").[3] It featured folk singers, an open mike, and discussions about the Vietnam War. Racial issues seldom raised within Trinity's congregation were aired in this forum. In 1973 the coffee house was still operating on Friday and Saturday nights at First Congregational Church.

The Episcopal Young Churchmen was another organization that prepared Trinity's youth for leadership. In 1963 their studies focused on the promises and problems of the city. Youth toured WBNS stations, the *Dispatch*, government buildings and banks, an art gallery, and the state hospital. They heard speakers from the county welfare office, Big Brothers, Alcoholics Anonymous, the Florence Crittenton Home, and the school for the deaf who raised their awareness of civic, moral, and social issues.

Church Renovation and 'Modernization'

Trinity participated in urban renewal in a concrete and visible way with the renovation of its own church, now nearly a century old. Nichols's hard hat came in handy as he oversaw construction. In the first phase beginning in 1961, workmen dug tons of rubble from beneath the church. What was formerly a dark tunnel between the coal chute on Third Street and the boilers and choir room became a finished space with several classrooms connected by a corridor that ran the length of the building. The Rev. Bob Hansel, Nichols's assistant at the time, recently described the excavation of the undercroft as a "physical symbol of the rebirth that helped pull Trinity out of the doldrums" following Fay's departure.

A philosophy of "out with the old, in with the new" governed much of the renovation project, for Nichols favored a modern style. Eliot Whitaker, a professor of architecture at Ohio State, was the final arbiter on all matters of design. With his assent the carved quatrefoils on the balcony woodwork were covered with a buff-colored substance known as Marlite. The effect was to horizontalize and simplify the high Victorian Gothic style. The ceiling between its dark crossbeams was paneled in dark wood. New pews were installed. Despite the sentimental value many attached to the old divided pews, they were given away to St. Paul's Baptist Church and the state hospital for use in their chapel. The church was painted, new carpet installed, wood floors refinished, and the parish house and rectory refurbished. A small but significant improvement was a new sound system, installed in 1962. Many people now could hear all the service for the first time. Nichols was amazed (and humbled) that so many many people had come to church for years unable to hear anything, including the vaunted sermons delivered by its preachers.

By the end of the decade Trinity had undergone $250,000 in capital improvements, including new lighting, the church in the world window, a new organ, and modifications to the chancel.

A girl peers at a conveyor belt set to remove tons of debris from beneath the church.

An impediment to the modernization project was one of Trinity's greatest treasures: the Maitland Armstrong window over the reredos. Roger Nichols disliked its pre-Raphaelite style and dark colors. On one occasion in 1962 the window barely escaped ruin. Workers installing a skylight between the church and the parish house accidentally ignited a smoky fire on the roof. Trinity's young cleric, Bob Hansel, who was in the habit of picnicking on the roof, dashed down the fire escape and into the office to summon the fire department. When firemen arrived Nichols, a former volunteer fireman in Massachusetts, urged them to break the window over the reredos for direct access to the flaming roof. Fortunately they chose a different strategy, and Nichols lost an opportunity to replace the classic window with one in the modern style he favored.

In the end there was moderate damage to the roof, the attic, and the third-floor dining room ceiling.

Eliot Whitaker also found that the window offended his aesthetic sensibilities. He argued that the figures in the window, being larger than those of the reredos, created a disharmony. Advocates of the modern style won a temporary victory when all light to the window was blocked by the addition of the fourth floor of the parish house in 1976. Twenty years later a campaign to light the window, led by donations from the Dargusch family, received overwhelming support from the congregation, though Whitaker threatened to leave if the window were lighted. When in 1996 the richly-colored figures of Christ and the archangels glowed once again above the reredos, Whitaker, true to his principles, left the congregation.

The Priesthood of All Believers

Although the congregation looked to its rector for leadership, a new movement was gaining momentum that would forever change church life. The lay movement deepened the involvement of men and women in worship, outreach, and governance. At the same time it posed a challenge to clergy authority as the "father knows best" era drew to a close. The process of decision-making grew more complex, and consensus was often elusive.

For many years the church had paid a kind of lip service to lay leadership. While he was rector, Anson Stokes declared, "It is through [laymen] that business, commerce, political life and international affairs can be redeemed." Clergy should encourage and inspire them, but laymen must lead forward.[4] Most people, however, felt that it was the job of clergymen to lead; a priest was a shepherd while they were but sheep. A 1956 pamphlet, "The Priesthood of the Laity," explained this unfamiliar concept to parishioners. In 1957 Fay commissioned several men of the parish as lay readers, among them J. Robert Park, who was still serving Trinity in that capacity more than 45 years later. Lay readers had long existed, but as long as there were plenty of priests they were not needed. Nor in those days could they administer communion.[5]

In 1958 Reginald Harvey, a captain in the Church Army, a movement for lay workers in the Church of England, joined Trinity's staff as an evangelist and urban missioner. He worked with children and youth of the parish. He also organized an interdenominational men's service on Thursdays at noon and led Bible study for a group at North American Aviation organized by Art Griffith, who was employed there as a commercial artist. These events modeled lay leadership that extended the mission of the church into the community.

The widely publicized Vatican II Council of the Roman Catholic Church (1962–65) put the issues of ecumenism and the role of the laity on every church's priority list. On the diocesan level, Bishop Blanchard was more amenable to shared decision-making that his predecessor Bishop Hobson had been. At the parish level, Trinity began long-range planning involving everyone in the parish in an attempt to define its mission and priorities. Newly-elected laywoman Helen Riley was chair of this commission.

Before the lay movement gained momentum, those who felt called to leadership had only one route open to them: that of ordained ministry. Here Trinity's own clergy were powerful role models. During the years of Anson Stokes, Robert Fay, and Roger Nichols, a dozen Trinity men were ordained or called to ordination. George R. Schoedinger Jr. sold his share in the family's funeral business to enter the ministry in 1952. In 1959 William A. Baker Jr. left his successful sales career, moved his family from their comfortable home and private schools, and he and his wife worked part time while he studied at Kenyon. His brother John entered the ministry a few years later. Trinity's clergymen were important influences for these men. Roger Wootton, for instance, claimed that his experience of acolyting for Anson Stokes led him to ordained ministry.[6]

Laypeople also influenced those who later became priests. When Joel Gibson attempted to sing in the children's choir while his voice was changing, Art Griffith, whose deep baritone anchored the adult choir, "bent down, put his hand on my shoulder, and said, 'Not bad; now you are beginning to sound like me.'"[7] Church school teachers in particular shaped the faith of young members. For Alex Seabrook, his Sunday School teacher John Graham was, along with his rector and bishop, a "model of what a man should be."

Even those who did not enter the ministry found fellow parishioners to be important models. Graham's daughter Marilyn Sesler, a lifelong Episcopalian active in social justice ministries, found in Betty Magruder, the longtime director of religious education, a model of a working woman who was a mother. Even before the concept of a priesthood of all believers was familiar to parishioners, they were actively teaching and leading each other.

Lay leadership in "the corporation" was opening up as wardens and vestry members were elected on a rotating basis. The volume of work made it necessary to spread the burden more evenly. Insurance company president and vestryman Verle Baltzell told a *Chimes* reporter that "the business of Trinity is much larger than that of most Columbus firms." More men were needed for this business. In 1962 Roger Nichols instituted the auxiliary vestry to give younger laymen experience in leadership and service. Eighteen men were elected on a rotating basis to this so-called "junior vestry," and many of them duly moved up to the regular vestry. Early in the 1960s vestry committees first included men and a few women of the parish in an advisory capacity. Nichols was tolerant if not enthusiastic about the participation of lay people in worship and governance.

The roles of women in the church changed as well. Some women found their opportunities shrinking during the Nichols years. When the all-male auxiliary vestry was charged with organizing the annual meeting and other parish events, women were displaced from some of their cherished jobs. The Woman's Auxiliary was renamed Episcopal Church Women, a seeming promotion from secondary status. But the local women's missionary groups were curtailed because Nichols disapproved of their focus on fund-raising and socializing. (The Panama group, however, continued to meet independently for many years, offering no apologies for its purely social purpose.) Instead Nichols channeled outreach efforts toward the community at large, hiring a director of volunteer services to match people and programs. In 1964 the women of Trinity listened to the chaplain of the Ohio State Penitentiary talk about prison reform. The concept of mission was being redefined, the focus shifting from far-off places like Japan and Cuba to the immediate urban environment.

Even as women were being directed to traditional forms of service, new leadership positions opened to them. In 1954 Mary (Mrs. Verle) Baltzell was the first women to co-chair the every member canvass. The event was worthy of a newspaper headline. In 1956 Helen Riley was elected president of the Woman's Auxiliary for the Diocese of Southern Ohio. Three years later she was on the committee that brought Roger Nichols to Trinity, the first woman to be formally involved in making such a decision. Riley was then a natural choice to become the first vestrywoman at

Trinity in 1966, when she was selected by vestry members to fill a vacancy.

Women also became professional church workers in the areas of education and administration. Betty Magruder, Florence Hoyt, and Bobbie Schnieder all worked as directors of religious education and shaped the experiences of a generation of children. The office staff, including Nellie Shelton, Eleanor Boardman, and Eloise Allison, handled all communications and public relations, serving as a direct link between the clergy, the congregation, and the wider public.

Even with a rotating vestry, most members of the congregation never served on the vestry. There was, however, a new appreciation for the ministry of ordinary people who were vital to the life of the congregation. One of these was Harry Grant, Trinity's unofficial greeter, whose weekday job was selling fire extinguishers. An avid Ohio State football fan, he would stand at the corner of the field yelling encouragement and swatting each player with a rolled-up newspaper as he trotted onto the turf. At Sunday services his welcome was only somewhat more gentle. Those who came in the door found their hands grasped with vigor as they were propelled into the church. Gordon Price recalled that one day a couple inquired where St. Joseph's Cathedral was and Grant replied

Lay leaders Helen Riley, William Anderson, George Eichenlaub, and Eleanor Boardman review pledges for the annual Every Member Canvass. Riley was the first woman to serve on Trinity's vestry.

with a wave of his hand, "'Oh, it's wa-a-a-y down there; why don't you come in here?' He was a great salesman." "When you were greeted by Harry, you stayed greeted," reflected the rector after Grant's death.

Myrtle Grady, a retired schoolteacher whose worn clothing suggested a penniless refugee, was not the kind of woman to lead a committee of church women. But when she came into the church office, money spilled from her tattered purse as she paid her pledge, left gifts for the clergy, or extra cash for one cause or another. Over the years her contributions provided for needs both great and small—organ repairs, lights for the parish house entrance, a new lectern Bible, and a top-of-the-line IBM typewriter and folding machine for the office. When she died she left most of her estate to Trinity.

Trinity Responds to
Racism and War

*W*hile the energies of lay people were being tapped for ministry within the church, their citizenship was being tested by events in society. Racism and war called people of faith to concrete action that was often divisive and controversial. In John Hines, presiding bishop from 1963–72, Episcopalians had a leader who committed vast sums to programs that assisted economic development among minorities and the poor. Some parishes and dioceses withheld their pledges from the national church to protest this perceived radicalism. Trinity was not among them, for Bishop Blanchard shared Hines's commitments to social justice, and Roger Nichols in turn deeply admired Blanchard.

Racial unrest seemed remote to many in the congregation. In the summer of 1967 the Watts and Harlem riots inflamed racial tensions across the nation. Though Columbus was not afflicted, David Dunning, following President Johnson's call, led the congregation in prayers appealing for divine guidance and calling for universal confession of guilt.[8] Racial equity became a larger issue in the late 1970s when forced busing was instituted to desegregate city schools. In 1977 Trinity's rector, backed by Bishop Krumm, spoke on behalf of church leaders who called for peaceful implementation of the federally-mandated desegragation order. It was carried out with very little trouble.

Trinity's rector, the Rev. Walter Taylor, leads local clergyman in supporting the peaceful integration of Columbus schools.

Trinity made an important public statement about racial injustice on Good Friday of 1972. Portraying Christ was Lou Sharp, who carried the cross around Capitol Square, followed by clergy and congregation members in prayer. Sharp noted how most people ignored him or looked away, not wanting to be involved. The Good Friday procession around Capitol Square has become a tradition at Trinity.

In theory Trinity favored racial equality. In the mid-1950s Benjamin Mays, president of Morehouse College in Atlanta and a scholar of black history, spoke at Trinity. A local Methodist minister preached a sermon "What is the Color of God?" In 1959 interim rector Richard Wyatt spoke out against exclusion based on race and was quoted in the local newspapers. But some racial prejudice was evident in the congregation. After the 1954 *Brown vs. Board of Education* decision that segregated schools were unconstitutional, Fay had to caution members of the vestry to be temperate in their comments on the issue. There were few if any black people in the congregation before 1950. The sexton Marion Starks and his wife Irene were the sole black members of the confirmation class of 1956, and the McCoy family was active during the 1950s. During the 1960s and 1970s the Gibsons, with their African, Creole, Native American, and Caucasian heritage, were the poster family for diversity at Trinity. St. Philip's Episcopal Church drew most of the Episcopalians who were black. (The expanding congregation built a new church in 1962.) By 2000 Trinity's claim to diversity was more genuine than in the past, for 10 percent of the congregation were identified as non-Caucasian.

A successful integration effort was the 1965 inclusion of the deaf worshippers into the regular Sunday morning congregation. The retirement of George Almo, minister of the All Saint's Mission since the 1940s, sparked the change. Arnold Daulton and Harry Scofield, who were deaf, signed the 11 a.m. service from the

Nellie Gillespie, Arnold Daulton, and Harry Scofield interpret the service for hearing-impaired members of the congregation in 1966.

Prayer Book while Nellie Gillespie, a hearing member whose parents were deaf, interpreted the sermons for many years. The clergy, staff, and some members of the congregation learned some sign language as well.[9] While he was rector, Walter Taylor made it a point to welcome the dozen or so deaf worshippers using sign language.

While racial issues scarcely disturbed the congregation, strong feelings about the the Vietnam War polarized young and old, clergy and lay people. Involvement in Vietnam (1964–1973) spurred the largest anti-war movement in American history. At first opposition was focused among intellectuals and the middle class, but it grew widespread. A watershed occurred in May of 1970 when Ohio National Guardsmen fired on a crowd of protesters at Kent State University, killing four students. In Columbus, Ohio State University was also rocked by demonstrations and rioting.

Episcopalians were divided in their response to the Vietnam War. At the 1967 General Convention 24 bishops signed a statement calling for an end to the conflict in Vietnam. Trinity's young clergymen vigorously opposed the war. One was the Rev. John Hines, son of the presiding bishop and an assistant at Trinity from 1970–72. With his red beard and his motorcycle Hines cut a figure that belied his fairly orthodox theology. At one Sunday morning adult forum on Vietnam organized by Hines and Steve White, tensions erupted as some older parishioners yelled "traitor" at the young men and called for Hines to resign.

In a 1972 plea for peace, then-rector Walter Taylor wrote to President Nixon and the Vietnamese premier to offer himself as a hostage in exchange for American prisoners of war. "I am aware of both the risks and the apparent naivete of this proposal, but perhaps both are needed at this particular juncture," he wrote.[10] He stunned the congregation with this offer, but several members of the general public offered to join him when the *Dispatch* publicized his campaign. Some parishioners left the congregation because they perceived an anti-war message in Taylor's sermons. Taylor remained philosophical, citing his obligation to preach on issues of peace and justice while avoiding strong political statements from the pulpit.

Increasingly Protestant clergy found themselves at odds with congregations, who tended to grow more conservative in response to rapid social changes. At Trinity the clergy and congregation avoided serious division, for Trinity had always drawn those who were progressive and sought out the downtown congregation precisely for its diverse views and engagement in social justice issues.

Urban Ministry in a Changing City

By the 1970s the face of downtown had changed dramatically from a generation before. Concrete and steel skyscrapers dwarfed the people who scurried in their shadows. Office buildings rose around the graying Gothic church, surrounding Trinity with commercial and banking activity. Trinity rejected a 1973 offer to buy its property for $2 million, taking pride in occupying such a valuable slice of real estate. Soon the church found itself surrounded by the new Ohio National Plaza with its six-tower office complex and the Galleria. The new building's travertine marble exterior was planned as a visual complement to the dark, rough sandstone of Trinity, its age-worn neighbor.[11]

But Trinity was to provide more than aesthetic relief in a commercial environment. A changed city called for new forms of downtown ministry. Attendance at the traditional Lenten speaker series was in sharp decline despite diverse speakers who reflected contemporary concerns. New forms of media and the fact of an increasingly secular society made Trinity's lecture series an obsolete form of urban ministry. Something new was needed.

In 1973 several members of Trinity met to consider the question of how to preserve the human element in the midst of an impersonal city. Attorney Carlton Dargusch Jr. envisioned a program similar to one operating at Trinity in lower Manhattan. He estimated that soon as many as 50,000 people would work

Scaffolding enfolds Trinity's exterior as construction begins on the parish house addition in 1975.

within a two-block area of Trinity. Dargusch conducted a survey of downtown Columbus employers that revealed a need for an affordable restaurant. In October of 1973 The Place to Be opened on the third floor of the parish house as a noonday ministry. It offered entertainment and lunches at break-even prices in a venue called the Living Room. In its first year an estimated 25,700 people were exposed to its programs.

Because of concerns that people would resist perceived attempts to convert them, the Christian aspect of The Place to Be was at first subtle. Gradually more programs of a religious nature were added. People came to AA meetings, the Lawyers Christian Fellowship, Bible study, organ recitals, and a Faith at Work symposium. The Rev. Jim Bills offered counseling services on a sliding fee scale. Hired as director in 1975, Bills was known informally as "rector of downtown Columbus" as the borders of the parish opened up to thousands. In 1973 the Columbus Arts Festival, then held then on Capitol Square, offered an allegorical and absurdist drama depicting the problems of the homeless and hungry. It was enacted on the sidewalk in front of Trinity.

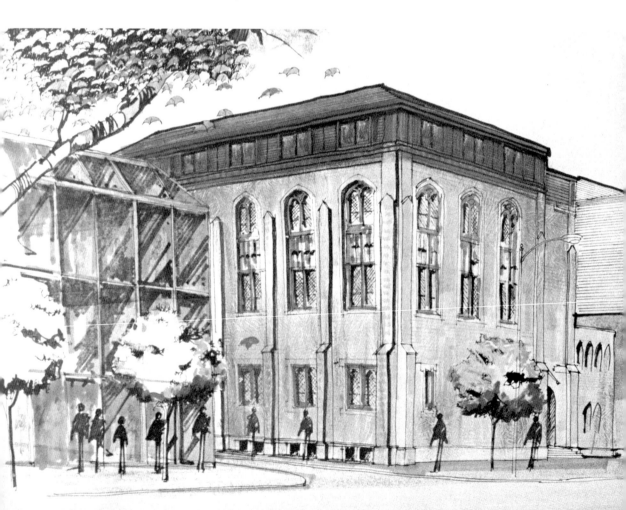

The congregation supported this outreach ministry. Dozens of women volunteered their services in the kitchen, which kept costs down. A gift shop, the brainchild of Marge Batterson, operated during the lunch hour and on Sundays after services. His Shop sold handmade items, crafts, books, cards, and gifts. Because its workers were volunteers, the shop was able to raise decent sums for missionary adopt-a-child programs, the Open Church, and the Sunday school.

The success of the noonday ministries made the renovation of the parish house more urgent. The need for major work had been discussed since the 1940s. The building had no elevator and did not meet fire and safety codes. Now the restaurant had displaced several church school rooms. In 1974 the congregation undertook the monumental task of raising the funds to renovate and expand the parish house. Steady membership numbers, despite a changing downtown, gave them confidence. The projected budget was just over $1 million, with the parish expected to supply half through a capital campaign and endowment funds. Corporate and community donors contributed $200,000 and a loan from the diocese provided $100,000, leaving unmet expenses totalling $247,000—the goal of the "second mile" campaign following the renovation. In 1978 the Episcopal Church Fund and the diocese pared that figure to $42,000.

The congregation suffered a blow in January of 1975 when Dargusch was killed in a plane crash enroute to Washington, D.C. Also killed in the crash were *Dispatch* publisher Edgar T. Wolfe and Frederick W. LeVeque, a real-estate executive. Dargusch's death propelled Trinity's renovation project forward as hundreds of people in the congregation and community donated to a memorial fund that was used to renovate the undercroft. The Wolfe and LeVeque families were among the contributors. Community leader Hal Field stepped into Dargusch's shoes, working to create partnerships with business. At the end of 1975 Capitol Square Ministries became a non-profit organization in order to encourage funding from corporations and individuals who were not in a position to fund church activities.

Architect's drawing of the parish house with the fourth floor addition.

The Place to Be opened in 1976 in the newly-renovated undercroft. To the right can be seen wares in the windows of His Shop, the gift shop operated by Trinity volunteers.

In November of 1975, nearly a decade after the renovation was proposed at the parish sesquicentennial, work finally began. For many months the staff and congregation suffered the dust and fog of construction. The parish office temporarily relocated to space provided by the Catholic Diocese on Gay Street. The choir rehearsed in the organ loft surrounded by boxes of music and vestments. Scaffolding rose in the nave as the church interior was painted. A heating system was installed, but the decision was made not to air condition the sanctuary given the current energy crisis. For a tenth of the cost a fan system would serve. A fourth floor was added to the parish house with an elevator. The second floor was equipped for a planned day-care center, and new classrooms were built on the second and third floors. The undercroft was expanded to accommodate a modern food service facility. The renovated Place to Be reopened in October of 1976, and the following May the Trinity Downtown Center was dedicated to Dargusch's memory.

Open Church

If The Place to Be catered to daytime workers and shoppers, the Open Church served a different clientele: the homeless, the hungry, runaways, and poor families. Clergy and staff had always assisted these visitors with food and money for shelter, and the church was open during the day to all the denizens of downtown. Then as well as now, most downtown churches were locked even during the day. Trinity also recognized the need to help people during the evening hours.

The Open Church, an ecumenical ministry, began operating in October of 1973. Each night the church was staffed by a clergyman and volunteer from one of the participating congregations. At first the church was open all night, but soon the hours were limited to 8 p.m. to 1 a.m., the time of greatest need. Those who stopped in were assisted in finding lodging at Faith Mission or the Volunteers of America shelter. Families received vouchers for lodging at the Norwich Hotel on Fourth and State Streets. Meal vouchers and bus fare were provided. Police brought vagrants to Trinity rather than taking them to prison. Volunteers listened, prayed with people, or referred them to daytime community services. About 1,000 people a year found assistance through Trinity's Open Church, and up to 32 congregations were involved.

There was some opposition to this new ministry. Some in the congregation feared the church would be vandalized or the volunteers endangered. It was

A weary visitor rests on a pew beneath a banner proclaiming Trinity's commitment to urban ministry. The Open Church operated at Trinity for almost 20 years.

sometimes hard to enlist helpers, as people were fearful or felt they lacked the ability to deal with clients' problems. Many people saw only a gulf between "the holiness of church and the profanity of the world at its door," explained Elizabeth Lilly, who was Trinity's on-call staff person for the Open Church. The rector was also among those who championed the effort. "The church should be a sanctuary," Taylor insisted.

Renewal and Reform
in the 1970s

A t Trinity one could say that the sixties didn't really happen until the seventies, when the sheer tide of social change finally swept churchgoers along with it. People sensed the beginning of a new era with the arrival of the Rev. Walter Taylor in 1969. Roger Nichols had left Trinity to assume a position on the diocesan staff in Cincinnati. Compared to Nichols, a senior priest with establishment credentials, Taylor was something of a maverick and a youngster. But Bishop Blanchard told the vestry that youth and inexperience were not valid reasons for Trinity not to hire Taylor. A native of Cincinnati, Taylor studied at Virginia Theological Seminary where parish ministry was emphasized. He served Holy Trinity parish in Oxford, Ohio, before coming to Trinity. He and his wife Mary had two sons and also cared for a foster child. Members of the congregation were surprised and delighted when he sat down on the floor with the Sunday school children and told them a story. They had never before seen a rector do this.

Taylor embraced change, believing the church had to adapt to a changed society. He had a vision of Trinity as a civic leader, and he was able to inspire the congregation to develop and support a downtown ministry. He saw clergy as servants of the servants, their role being to enable lay leadership. To that end the Community of the Lay Apostolate was organized in 1975, and Taylor commissioned five lay people to visit the sick and make calls. He was comfortable with a collaborative style of parish governance rather than the top-down model of administration favored by his predecessors. For example, though he was in favor of Anne Stoddard's request that girls be allowed to become acolytes, he referred the matter to the vestry, which gave its consent.

Taylor also emphasized a vigorous parish life. He restored women's voluntary organizations, harnessing the energies of female parishioners to assist with everything from serving food at The Place to Be to organizing weddings. Many women put their efforts into running the gift boutique, His Shop. Active membership in St. Margaret's Guild, a ministry to the sick and shut-ins, was up to 54. Year-round opportunities for fellowship included the Christmas breakfast, a children's Christmas party, newcomers' dinners, the Shrove Tuesday pancake supper, the Easter breakfast, a Pentecost reception, and parish picnics. Adult education on Sunday mornings sometimes offered three or four

Rector Walter Taylor and his assistants, the Rev. Donald Wilkinson and the Rev. John Hines, pose in their psychedelic robes in 1973. Most parishioners were receptive to the changes in liturgy and welcomed their dynamic young clergymen.

different classes, many led by members of the congregation.

John Hines, Taylor's assistant from 1970–72, called Taylor a good "pastor and prophet," one who was deeply attentive to his parishioners' needs while calling them forward on a timetable too slow for the radicals, too swift for the traditionalists. For his part Taylor appreciated the congregation's openness to new ideas. He saw a fervor, an eagerness to take risks and to lead the community. He also realized, however, that many people in the pews were less ready for change than the clergy and bishops, and he was grieved to see some of his parishioners unable to accept the changes.

A new spirit moved through Christian churches in these years as people reacted against the church's social activism and the empty promises of secular society, turning inward to fill a spiritual void.[12] The charismatic phenomenon, associated with speaking in tongues and healing, made its way into mainline churches as a renewal movement promising a deeper spiritual life. In 1973 Trinity hosted a teaching mission on charismatic ministry that drew more than 150 people. Spiritual renewal was also the purpose of Cursillo, a short course in Christianity that was founded by lay Catholics. The Rev. Don Wilkinson, Taylor's assistant, persuaded a priest at St. Joseph's Cathedral to allow Episcopalians to attend a retreat. Word spread and soon many Trinity members attended Cursillo weekends. The event was an initiation experience that produced a strong spiritual impact and equipped participants for leadership among other laypeople. Catholics and Episcopalians celebrated the Eucharist together until the Roman Catholic bishop put a stop to the practice. Eventually Episcopalians had their own Cursillos, though the retreats never appealed to more traditional church members.

A related lay-led movement founded in 1970 was Faith Alive, which focused on parish renewal. Trinity held its Faith Alive weekend in March of 1973. Participants John and Barbara Stoddard experienced some discomfort when the leaders, who were "very much of the 'Praise the Lord and Hallelujah' variety," encountered the relatively staid and unemotional people of Trinity. Many had come out of curiosity and were put off. Those who remained for the weekend found it rewarding, and it resulted in the formation of a youth group. That same year Taylor took a new approach to stewardship with Emmaus groups—small, informal, "encounter" groups that aimed to deepen people's spiritual commitment to Trinity.

Changes in Worship and Liturgy

*P*erhaps the most contentious issue of the era for many Episcopalians was the revision of the 1928 Book of Common Prayer. This process threw many congregations into complete turmoil. One such congregation was St. Paul's, which had become a refuge for conservatives. Its rector, the Rev. G. Wayne Craig, opposed the ordination of women and the new Prayer Book and attempted to take the parish and its property out of the diocese, but to no avail.[13] But in 1978 a cohort of 49 traditionalists left St. Paul's to form Christ Church Anglican, and soon an Anglo-Catholic branch broke from that group and eventually affiliated with the Reformed Episcopal Church.[14] The events at St. Paul's prompted Fred and Joan Taylor to return to Trinity, where Joan's family had worshipped since pre-Civil War times.

Though Trinity was more progressive than many Episcopal congregations, many people were loth to give up the rich Elizabethan language of the 1928 Prayer Book. Even so, Prayer Book revision was less divisive at Trinity in part because the clergy took great pains to instruct the congregation about the changes. The process began with the 1967 trial liturgy, the first step in returning to a form of worship resembling that of the early church. In January of 1973 the Green Book liturgy was used on a trial basis at Trinity. Many people chuckled over the letter a disgruntled Episcopalian wrote to Presiding Bishop John Hines: "If Jesus Christ knew what you are doing to our Book of Common Prayer with your devilish Green Book—He would turn over in his grave."[15]

While the wording of the liturgy was being modernized, the accoutrements of worship also changed to reflect the times. In 1971 Taylor, Hines, and Wilkinson, who sported long hair and sideburns, decked themselves in modern vestments of purple and chartreuse. Psychedelic appliques of flowers and butterflies symbolized the Easter season. At the time chasubles were still uncommon among Episcopalian priests, especially in Columbus. For Hines, a confessed "flower child," the colorful vestments represented a reaction against the dulness and lack of color in the service, an effort to shake up the staid church. Following the vogue, acolytes wore tie-dyed robes.

Changes in worship were presented as a return to the practices of the early church before the accumulation of tradition. The revised Rite II liturgy provided for more congregational involvement and response. The clergy vestments, too, were modeled after the Hebrew aba, a loose-fitting cloak worn by Jesus and his disciples.[16] Despite their updated garb, however, the clergy still faced the limitations of the worship space at Trinity, and they sometimes stood at an angle to the altar to avoid facing completely away from the congregation. Hanging in the chancel, bright banners made by the women of the parish combined contemporary symbolism with an earlier tradition of pageantry. With Bishop Krumm, Taylor introduced the practice of foot-washing at the Maundy Thursday service. Home liturgies also attempted to recover the spirit of the early church. These were conducted using the new trial Prayer Book and spontaneous prayers. The hosts provided bread and wine, and all sang to the accompaniment of a guitar.

To an extent unthinkable in earlier years, Taylor encouraged feedback from the pews regarding changes in worship. An open forum in the *Chimes* revealed that many people felt uncomfortable with the practice of the congregation voicing petitions, and only two women regularly spoke. Some had no interest in greeting each other at the Peace, especially strangers they were likely never to see again. Others took the opportunity to criticize their too-liberal clergy. One writer felt that "the church service is no place for expounding controversial political beliefs."[17] It was an era, however, when secular politics—views about racism and war—and matters of religion could not easily be held apart.

Liturgical dancers perform in the chancel.

Another contested area was music. Trinity's pride was its rich repertoire of sacred music sung by a choir of about 30 men and women. Under Wilbur Held the choir performed many ambitious choral works, some with orchestra. In 1966 it recorded Mendelssohn's oratio, *Elijah*, featuring Metropolitan opera baritone Calvin Marsh. In 1968 the choir presented the mystical and contemplative *Missa Brevis* of Hungarian composer Zoltan Kodaly. To Held's dismay the young people called for music that was more relevant to the times. Taylor supported a measure of musical innovation, and thus Trinity participated in the nationwide trend of guitar-toting teenagers, folk singing, and the occasional liturgical dance.

Trinity's downtown location and its community programs had an impact on its worship. In 1971 the Lenten speaker series, suffering from declining attendance, was

Organist and choirmaster Wilbur Held with Donald and Gloria Chapman, donors of the new organ. Dedicated in 1970, the 64-rank organ, made by Casavant Freres of St. Hyacinthe, Quebec, contains more that 3,600 pipes. The new organ obscured the church in the world window. Lighting was then installed so the window could be viewed from the outside by passers-by at night.

paired with a festival that explored ways to incorporate the arts into worship. The Columbus Civic Ballet performed Carl Orff's *Carmina Burana* in the sanctuary. The songs of medieval students and monks celebrating drinking and lovemaking were more profane than sacred but perhaps appropriate to the unconventional times. A chancel drama culminated the series. The Jubilee Singers of Fisk University, a black college in Nashville, performed spirituals and Renaissance motets, a Baroque cantata and music by twentieth-century black composers. The balladeer John Jacob Niles, inspired by Christianity, Zen Buddhism, and Woodstock, sang folk music and carols at morning prayer on December 26, 1971. In the same Advent season Wilbur Held led the choir in his own musical compositions based on "O come, O come, Emmanuel" and traditional liturgical music. Though conservative parishioners winced at the innovations, the variety of traditional and contemporary music kept liturgy from ever growing stale.

The forces of tradition gained permanent ground, however, with the installation in 1969 of a new 64-rank organ made by the Casavant Company in Quebec. The balcony was expanded to accommodate the $100,000 organ, a gift of Donald

Chapman, president of insurance provider Gates McDonald, and his wife Gloria, in memory of her late parents. The organ was dedicated on May 31, 1970, in thanksgiving for the ministry of Wilbur Held, who had served as organist and choirmaster since 1949. It was quite a tribute for a slight man who was considered by many to be himself an instrument of grace to the congregation. The dedication day featured services both traditional and contemporary. The 11 a.m. service was an experimental liturgy featuring a media sermon, entitled "Prayer Song," a dialog between Walter Taylor and folk singer Susan Bruce. The traditionalists no doubt preferred the afternoon service, a choral evensong featuring organ works by Brahms and a new anthem commissioned by the Chapmans to celebrate the organ's dedication.

Installation of the new organ involved other changes to the worship space. Music-making now occurred in the rear gallery out of the congregation's sight. The organ console and ten-foot-long choir pews were removed from the chancel, which was shortened, adding about 15 feet to the length of the nave. Front pew-sitters were closer to the altar than before, and wider steps led to the communion railing, promoting a more immediate experience of liturgy. A firm line, however, still separated the nave from the sanctuary and the congregation from the clergy, stating Trinity's allegiance to traditional forms of worship and authority.

The Ordination of Women

*L*ike the civil rights and anti-war movements, the women's movement was a secular development that had a great impact on the Episcopal Church. Progress towards women's ordination had been steady but too slow for the proponents of change and undoubtedly too rapid for its opponents. In 1958 the Episcopal Theological School, alma mater of Trinity's rectors, voted to admit women as candidates for the degree of bachelor of divinity. In 1970 southern Ohio elected a bishop, the Rt. Rev. John Krumm, who supported the ordination of women. Former rector Roger Nichols was defeated in that election in part because of his conservative views. That same year the General Convention voted in favor of ordaining women to the diaconate, but clergy in the House of Deputies defeated a motion to ordain women to the priesthood. (The measure passed among laity in the House of Deputies; the Episcopal Church Women overwhelmingly supported it.)

At the 1973 General Convention the measure was defeated by a technicality. Moreover, the newly-elected presiding bishop of the Episcopal Church, the Rt. Rev. John Allin, was an opponent of women's ordination. Allin's election represented a retreat from the church's liberalism, but the momentum gained by proponents of women's ordination could not be stopped. In 1974, 11 women were ordained by three retired bishops in Philadelphia. A furor arose about whether the irregular ordinations were valid. Trinity's former assistant, John Hines, expressed his support of the women by putting a moratorium on his own priestly duties until the women were allowed to serve as priests. In 1976 the Episcopal Church finally approved the resolution admitting women to the priesthood and the episcopate.[18]

At Trinity the conflict over women's ordination was defused through the quiet presence and diligent service of the Rev. Deacon Elizabeth Lilly. Lilly and her husband Carter had been confirmed at Trinity shortly after their wedding, before they undertook the itinerant life necessitated by Carter's career in the Air Force. Back in Columbus a serious illness and a soul-searching Cursillo retreat moved Lilly to seek ordination as a deacon. Unable to overcome the hostility of her rector at St. James in Clintonville, she approached Walter Taylor, who offered his full support. Lilly joined Trinity's staff in 1974 while she was attending theology school. For six years she coordinated the Open Church and various other social services. Soon after being ordained a deacon in 1976, she felt called to ordained priesthood. She was not

Current and former clergy who served Trinity gather at the 1977 dedication of the renovated parish house. From left are Reginald Harvey, Rev. Gordon Price, Rev. Almus Thorp, Rt. Rev. Anson P. Stokes, Rev. Roger Nichols, Rt. Rev. John Krumm, Rev. Jim Bills, and Rev. Walter Taylor. In front is Rev. Deacon Elizabeth Lilly.

militant but simply determined to heed a call to ministry she felt since her youth. Finally in 1984 Lilly was ordained to the priesthood.

The presence of a female deacon on the staff and assisting in the services prepared the congregation to accept women priests. There were those who made disparaging remarks or crossed the aisle at communion to avoid taking the Eucharist from a woman's hand. But most grew to accept the change. For the staunch and high church Harry Kay, who did not believe women should be ordained, knowing Betty Lilly and seeing her in action changed his mind, according to his daughter. Once after Lilly had led the congregation in morning prayer, an elderly female parishioner embraced her, weeping and proclaiming that her opposition to women priests had been overcome. On another occasion Bishop Krumm, finding the doors of St. Paul's locked against his scheduled visit, walked down the street to Trinity and entered to find Deacon Lilly reading the Gospel to the congregation.

Though Trinity took women's ordination in good stride, accepted the new Prayer Book, and showed leadership in its ministry to the downtown community, the picture was not all rosy. From 1960 to 1980 Trinity maintained its membership and a consistent slice (17 percent) of the city's Episcopalians. Yet total annual attendance at services declined by almost half during these years. This decline slowed, however, and even reversed slightly during the period from 1970-1975, reflecting the energy and commitment generated by The Place to Be and the renovation project.

Trinity's successful urban ministry was copied by downtown churches in other cities, and the rector was eyed with envy by other congregations. In 1977, having brought the renovation project to completion, Taylor accepted a post at a suburban church in Darien, Connecticut, ending his eight-year tenure at Trinity. By 1980 Sunday attendance was down by one-third from its 1975 highs. In the next four years, from 1980 to 1984, the number of communicants declined from 766 to 602, a 20 percent decline. This may have been a response to the change in clergy leadership, but surely it reflects some disenchantment with broader changes in the church. During those same years, the nine Columbus parishes lost 16 percent of their members. A few joined Anglican congregations led by male clergy using the 1928 Prayer Book, and others switched to other Protestant churches, but some departed from institutional religion altogether.[19]

Conclusion

The American religious scene was changed by the tumultuous decade of the 1960s, when traditional values and habits came under question, a new sexual morality emerged, and demands for racial and gender equality were sounded. To some it seemed that religion was in decline, soon to be engulfed by the rising tide of secularism. Others such as Robert Wuthnow emphasized the "restructuring" of religion as educated and socially mobile Americans faced (or created) more choices in the area of religion. Their loyalties shifted from one congregation or denomination to another. In making choices, people increasingly sought spiritual experiences that were relevant to their personal lives.

This trend towards private religion was difficult for churches like Trinity to address. Leader congregations historically emphasize outreach and public mission. They do not tend to make a priority of meeting their members' individual spiritual and emotional needs, pointing them instead towards an ethic of Christian service.[20] In the 1970s Trinity's congregation was challenged to minister in new ways to the changing downtown community, from those who worked on the top floors of banking buildings to those who slept on the streets below. At the same time parishioners were offered opportunities for inward spiritual renewal and fellowship, equipping them for ministry and leadership in the world. Trinity never ceased to emphasize dynamic corporate worship, a traditional strength and source of spiritual nourishment, nor did it overlook its historic role of being a servant church in the city.

Notes

1. Information about the Nichols years cited in this chapter comes from interviews (in person, by phone, or e-mail correspondence) with Bill Davidson, Elizabeth J. (Betty) Nichols, John and Barbara Stoddard, Eloise Allison, Bill Davidson, Joel Gibson, Robert Hansel, Gordon Price, Donn and Bobbie Schneider. Other cited or paraphrased are Marilyn Sesler, Bill Dargusch, Walter Taylor, Jim Bills, John Hines, Elizabeth Lilly, and Janetta Orris. The comments and insights of many others who were interviewed have been incorporated into my interpretations.

2. "What is a Sesqui-centennial for?" Sermon of Roger B. Nichols, May 7, 1967.

3. "The Cracked Cup," *The Columbus Dispatch Sunday Magazine*, April 9, 1967.

4. "Thoughts of Ministers," undated newspaper clipping (ca. 1937-40).

5. In 1967 the diocese considered allowing licensed lay persons to administer communion on a trial basis.

6. Letter to people of Trinity, February 27, 1999.

7. Letter from Joel A. Gibson to members of Trinity Episcopal Church, March 7, 1999.

8. "Clergy Responds To Call For Racial Peace Prayers," *Citizen-Journal*, July 31, 1967.

9. "Deaf Churchman Finds Much to Do," *Columbus Dispatch*, January 20, 1968.

10. "Second Letter Sent to Leaders," *Interchange*, July 1972.

11. Ohio National Plaza newsletter, July 1975.

12. See Booty, ibid., 78-83.

13. Krumm, *Flowing*, 169.

[14] That group now worships in Dublin, Ohio, using the 1928 Prayer Book and remaining opposed to the ordination of women, according to member Robert Halley.

[15] "Trinity Chimes," March 26-April 1, 1973.

[16] "Mod Vestments Brighten Service," *Columbus Dispatch*, April 11, 1971; "Colorful Banners Expressions of Faith," *Columbus Dispatch*, August 21, 1971.

[17] "Trinity Chimes," March 19-25, 1973.

[18] Susan Hill Linley, *"You Have Stept Out of Your Place,"* 315-16; Booty, *Crisis*, 65-72.

[19] According to Wade Clark Roof and William McKinney and other sociologists, the (surprising) trend among liberal Protestants is the loss of members not to conservative denominations, but to the ranks of unchurched and unaffiliated. See Roof and McKinney, *American Mainline Religion: Its Changing Shape and Future* (New Brunswick: Rutgers University Press, 1987), 4-5.

[20] This summary is indebted to Becker's summary of the scholarship on congregational issues since the 1960s (*Congregations in Conflict*, 211-232.) See also Robert Wuthnow, *The Restructuring of American Religion: Society and Faith Since World War II* (Princeton: Princeton University Press, 1988), 142-70; Howard Zinn, *A People's History of the United States* (New York: Harper and Row, 1980), 435-528 gives a good sense of the Zeitgeist of the period.

Teenagers participate in the 1973 Faith Alive weekend,
an event focused on parish renewal.

Chapter 11

BALANCING OUTREACH *and* INREACH 1980–2003

*I*n a vestry meeting in 1983 the rector described a shift in Trinity's focus. If the seventies were all about outreach, he noted, the eighties were becoming more about "inreach," about pastoral care and exploring ways to nurture the congregation. Trinity's shift was a sign of the changing religious climate nationally. Episcopalians knew they were no longer possessors of a civic religion, for most Americans no longer shared the values of mainline Protestantism. They were among the "sideline" faiths who watched as people flocked to conservative denominations and Roman Catholicism or left organized religion altogether.

Declining membership has been a harsh fact of life for most Episcopal congregations, including Trinity. Between 1980 and 1995 the Diocese of Southern Ohio lost about 20 percent of its members, according to the *Episcopal Church Annual*. Columbus parishes collectively lost twice that figure with the sharpest declines at St. Paul's and Trinity. Many of Columbus's downtown churches have lost half or more of their members since their heyday. Others have closed, merged with other congregations, or moved to the suburbs. Of the remaining downtown churches, Broad Street Presbyterian has remained a powerhouse and First Congregational has also been strong. Trinity, because of its prime location, its history, and its commitment to urban ministry, has remained more visible in the community than its congregational strength would suggest.[1] But declining membership has changed many aspects of parish life and challenged Trinity's lay and clerical leaders.

Like other Episcopalians, members of Trinity looked within for ways to reverse the exodus and refill their pews. When they came to church, which was less frequently than in the past, they expected their personal spiritual needs to be met. But the more religion becomes privatized, the less it serves the social function of binding people together in a community of shared belief.[2] Individualism can take a toll on congregational life. The challenge facing Trinity, which prizes its diversity, has been to build community among diverse individuals, foster stewardship in a time of diminishing resources, and define a mission for rapidly changing times. Never turning its back on the neighborhood, Trinity has striven to balance outreach and inreach, to hope, pray, and work for the transformation of individuals and culture through Christ.

Clergy Leadership in the 1980s

After Walter Taylor's departure in 1978, the congregation sought a spiritual leader who would provide excellent preaching and worship, which were deemed Trinity's greatest strengths. Providing community leadership was the lowest priority perhaps because 94 percent of the congregation already saw that as one of Trinity's strengths. All wanted the downtown ministry to continue, diversity to be maintained, and growth to occur. But there was a clear consensus that the next rector needed to focus on pastoral care, especially the education of children and youth.[3]

With this expectation, Trinity hired the Rev. William S. Brettmann, a native of Alabama. He and his wife Lelia and their two daughters took up residence in the church rectory at 44 Ardmore Road in Bexley. Brettmann had many years of experience in parish ministry, most recently in Grace Episcopal Church in a suburb of Jacksonville, Florida. While canon of Christ Cathedral in Louisville, Kentucky, he was instrumental in starting an inner city mission near the church. His strong credentials in both pastoral and

The Rev. William S. Brettmann, rector from 1978-1984, greets a family after Sunday services. Brettman aimed to increase lay involvement in parish governance.

urban ministry made him a desirable candidate for the rectorship of Trinity.

One of Brettmann's goals was to increase lay leadership in the parish. At the close of Walter Taylor's administration, Trinity had a parish structure that put it in the forefront among area churches. Seven parish commissions headed by laypeople comprised the areas of worship, education, fellowship, evangelism, service, stewardship, and planning and review. Each had a mission statement and objectives, lay volunteers, and a vestry or staff liaison. In addition the women's service board was comprised of chairs of all the volunteer groups. The altar guild under the leadership of Vesta Griffith had 29 members. A lay apostolate assisted the clergy with visitations. Parish administrator Charles Scherer, an insurance company executive, brought outstanding management skills to Trinity.

Despite this strong corps of lay workers, Brettmann still found Trinity an "excessively rector-centered parish." While the lay people looked to Brettmann for leadership, he encouraged them to take initiative and to work to revive parish life. He told the vestry that he considered them colleagues in ministry. He favored the image of the priest not as shepherd of the flock but as its sheep dog, barking, nipping, and nudging the flock in the direction where the shepherd, Christ, is leading.[4] To that end he encouraged the commission system that involved more laypeople in active roles within the parish. Commissions all met at the same time, with the rector circulating so as never to be in the position of chairing or controlling a group.

Brettmann gives instructions to lay Eucharistic ministers.

In 1980 the vestry commended Brettmann for his leadership in revitalizing Trinity and strengthening the community. But the relationship between Brettmann and his parishioners was not an intimate one. Brettmann felt hampered in his work by conflict with his associate, Jim Bills. Bills had been the interim rector before Brettmann's arrival, and his work with Capitol Square ministries made him a familiar presence to parishioners. He was outgoing and well-liked, and his dismissal six months after Brettmann's arrival upset some parishioners. For his part, Brettmann felt Bills was undermining his authority. This incident cast a pall over Brettmann's ministry at Trinity and made it difficult for him to gain the affection and trust of parishioners. Those who knew him well saw his warm and witty nature. Others found him an introvert who did not seem to relish visiting with his parishioners.

A boon to the congregation was the Rev. Peter Strimer, who joined the staff in 1980 as a newly-ordained deacon and two years later became the associate. Strimer was a jack-of-all-trades responsible for assisting Brettmann with pastoral care, urban ministry, and youth ministry. A mere youth of 26 bestriding a motorcycle, Strimer appealed to Trinity's teens. He led them on enviable camping, canoeing, and sailing trips. With a master's degree in social work, he was a professed activist who offset Brettmann's more reserved style of ministry. Strimer deeply admired his mentor in ministry for his wide-ranging scholarly interests and his deep commitments to social justice. He conceded, however, that Brettmann had "a professor's mind but not always the pastor's touch."

The Rev. Peter Strimer (front), known for his social activism, pictured with Trinity's youth group around 1981.

Indeed Brettmann's was an intellectual approach to ministry. A graduate of the University of Oxford with seminary training at Sewanee and Yale, he was considered an outstanding teacher of the adult forum and a good preacher. Brettmann's interest in Mayan archaeology led to his concern for the wars in Central America and a conference hosted by Trinity on the plight of Nicaragua and El Salvador.

In 1984 Brettmann accepted a position that suited his strengths: chaplain at North Carolina State University in Raleigh and director of continuing education for the Diocese of North Carolina. Peter Strimer also said his farewells and left Trinity to begin a Ph.D. program in telecommunications. Before his departure Strimer challenged the congregation to continue its community-based ministry while at the same time serving the needs of its members. The answers to Trinity's problems "will not come in the form of a white knight disguised as a new rector. The answers are to be found within our parish community."[5] This was a challenge to Trinity's lay leadership that Brettmann was intent on fostering.

Seeking a New Vision

Morale in the congregation was low in 1984 when interim rector Dean Malcolm Eckel supervised a parish self-study. A survey identical to one administered in 1978 revealed sharp declines in satisfaction in every area of Trinity's parish life. In the main, members expressed disappointment in the clergy and their relations with the congregation. In 1978 more than 9 out of 10 felt their clergy would assist them in need, while in 1985 barely two-thirds agreed. Less than half felt that communication was good, down from 84 percent. Perceptions of conflict had doubled, and shared understanding of parish goals had declined accordingly. Admittedly Walter Taylor was a hard act to follow, but people were also demoralized by changes in the church beyond any rector's control. The Rev. Robert Hansel, who had served Trinity under Roger Nichols, returned briefly in 1985 after Eckel's departure. He was shocked at the contrast with the booming church of the early 1960s. "It was like somebody had turned the lights out," he said.

On the positive side the survey showed optimism about growth, improvement in ministry to youth, and a growing sentiment for lay leadership. People still primarily valued pastoral strengths in their rector. Yet the search committee emphasized Trinity's dual and equal ministries as both an Episcopal parish and a downtown center for Christian outreach. In addition to strong preaching, educational, and administrative skills, Trinity called for an experienced rector with leadership ability who would interact with the business and political communities. The rector was also expected to foster lay participation, enable effective stewardship and, of course, demonstrate deep Christian commitments and values.

It was a tall order, and a tall man was engaged to fill it. Long-time parishioner Donn Schneider (a short man) joked that upon meeting the Rev. James S. Miner II, he stood on a chair to shake his hand. Miner arrived at Trinity in 1986 from Trinity Cathedral in Cleveland, where he was canon and executive assistant to the bishop of Ohio. Before that he had served 13 years in parish ministry with emphasis on pastoral care as well as the role of the church in the community. An excellent match to Trinity's needs, he had the unanimous support of the search committee.

Miner's initial assessment of Trinity was a positive one. He was impressed with Trinity's accomplishments, given its "narrow financial and human base." He recommended that Trinity choose what it does best rather than trying to "do it all." He felt it was time to formulate a new sense of purpose to replace an outdated mission that had guided the congregation since the 1970s. He wanted the vestry to concern itself more with the church's mission, not just its business. To that end he revived the parish commission system that put lay

The Rev. James S. Miner II with Bishop Black and parishioners Doris Graham and Margy Kay at a 1993 coffee hour. Miner, who was known as a skilled and caring pastor, served as rector from 1986–1995.

people who were not vestry members in leadership roles. His next priority was filling the pews. The vestry expressed a high degree of satisfaction with their new rector. By the end of 1987 pledge income was up 11 percent, though attendance had yet to rebound.

Despite a weak financial picture, Miner was committed to hiring an associate. Without one, he argued, Trinity was "staffed for decline." With the assistance of a congregation member, Trinity secured funding from the Reinberger Foundation to support the salary of an associate for three years. Miner selected for his assistant a long-time friend of his with 28 years of pastoral experience, the Rev. John Simons. Simons's duties at Trinity were somewhat circumscribed by his military commitments as chaplain of the National Guard, where he held the rank of colonel. When the Gulf War began in 1991 the congregation was relieved that he was not called to active duty. The compatible relationship of the two rectors greatly benefitted the congregation. Simons, his military rigor tempered by a friendly and engaging manner, recruited many newcomers and enlisted them in parish activities. He and his wife Nancy were much loved by parishioners.

After Simons's departure, Miner's partner in ministry was the Rev. Karen K. Burnard, who came to the Episcopal church after growing up in the Greek Orthodox tradition. Hired initially as a deacon intern, Burnard was promoted to assistant rector after her ordination at Trinity in June of 1992. Burnard had the distinction of being the first (and, to date, the only) woman to be ordained at Trinity.

The congregation welcomed her. The tall, fair rector and his short, dark assistant presented a striking visual contrast and a complementary team in ministry. Miner's sermons were more intellectual, while Burnard based hers on themes and images that were more earthy, often maternal. As the mother of a young son, Burnard gave close attention to the church school, which was nearing its goal of drawing 50 children regularly. In 1995 Burnard accepted a post as vicar of St. Andrew's, a new Episcopal parish in nearby Pickerington.

During Miner's years as rector, the congregation underwent a great deal of soul-searching. To define a new mission and future course for Trinity, task groups were organized in 1989. These explored fund-raising and proposed a capital funds drive to renovate the church. They considered ways to increase member involvement and pledging. Another goal was to increase tenant income; soon the Council for Ethics and Economics expanded to the third floor of the parish house. (Efforts to lease the second floor to the State of Ohio for a day care center had faltered in 1984.) Then in 1993, just as the church exterior was being cleansed of decades of city grime, the Vision 2000 focus groups met to foresee the next stages of Trinity's life. Education, communication, outreach, music, and growth were areas identified for work.

The Rev. Karen Burnard, the first woman ordained at Trinity, served as a deacon and then as the assistant under Jim Miner.

As part of this process, talks also began concerning a potential merger with St. Paul's, which had a mere handful of parishioners and a weak financial base. Trinity hoped that such a union would boost the congregation and that the churches' combined resources could strengthen their ministry to the central city. The congregations began a cautious and well-intentioned courtship. St. Paul's feared being absorbed by Trinity and wanted to reserve their financial resources for special projects. Trinity worried that its own endowment would not be protected. It was clear that not all St. Paul's parishioners would choose to attend Trinity. Finances, real estate issues, and questions surrounding staffing and leadership were sticking points. Moreover, the diocese did not lend its support. In November of 1993 merger talks were called off by the vestry of St. Paul's.

Finding a vision and acting upon it were proving to be problematic for Trinity. Some members of the vestry were growing frustrated with Miner's deliberative style, feeling Trinity needed more decisive and action-oriented leadership.

Management and communication skills were deemed in need of improvement. Miner took a sabbatical from June to October of 1994, and upon his return the vestry asked him to articulate a vision for Trinity. He did so in series of sermons based on the theme "a house of prayer for all people." The vestry was apparently not satisfied, and some members of the congregation felt the vision lacked particulars. Conflicts emerged once the vestry began to renegotiate the rector's contract at his request and to clarify the responsibilities of the clergy, wardens, and vestry. After weeks of meetings and negotiations, it became clear to the rector and to the vestry that their expectations about how to achieve certain goals at Trinity were widely divergent. Their working relationship had broken down. First the wardens, Sue Huffman and Sherm Everett, offered to resign. Then Miner, seeing that matters were at an impasse and himself unable and unwilling to meet the vestry's demands, tendered his resignation. Suffragan Bishop Kenneth Price was a party to some of the negotiations, and Bishop Herbert Thompson wrote a sympathetic letter commending those involved for their good intentions and the mutuality of their decisions.

These events occurred in March of 1995. On June 25 the congregation bade farewell to Miner, who preached a moving sermon urging members of the congregation to look for the Messiah in one another. At the coffee hour following the service, the congregation expressed their thanks. Many were in tears.

Congregational Leadership Issues

Because of the manner in which it came about, the separation was particularly painful for the congregation, especially for those who did not perceive any problem with Miner's style of leadership. The situation was worsened by a *Dispatch* headline that blazed "Trinity...wants rector to leave." In the view of many parishioners, it was a small group of malcontents working behind the scenes who had determined that the rector had to go. They were upset that the congregation as a whole was not consulted. In the aftermath of the decision, the vestry and wardens reviewed the events in letters to the congregation and in a parish meeting. They stressed they were committed to "move Trinity Church forward in health and in wholeness," but it was clear that the process had taken its emotional, physical, and spiritual toll on all involved. The depth of affection and support for Miner became more evident after his resignation as people recalled his compassionate pastoral care. In the view of the Rev. Sherm Everett, who was junior warden at the time, the vestry's sin was in suddenly taking away the spiritual leadership of the congregation.

The events surrounding Miner's resignation highlight the perennial issue of leadership in the Episcopal Church. Congregations typically have high, even unreasonable, expectations of their rector. A long-time member involved in a recent rector search observed that Jesus Christ himself couldn't do the job Trinity described for the ideal candidate. Disappointment is inevitable when the rector does not prove to be the outstanding preacher, counselor, administrator, and fund-raising expert the church needs. The personal nature of the pastoral relationship also affects the congregation. People are often fond of the rector despite his shortcomings.

The role of the vestry in parish leadership has been complex and sometimes contested. Under the model where non-vestry lay people chair parish commissions, vestry members can be uncertain about what their roles and responsibilities are. Many at Trinity feel that the vestry has not been particularly strong and visible in its leadership. Trinity has historically preferred strong rectors who set the tone and clearly delineate responsibilities. As a former senior warden stated, "the priest ought to be running the church, with the advise and consent of the vestry." On the other hand, dissatisfaction sets in when the vestry becomes a mere "rubber stamp committee." In the Miner case, perceiving a void in the clergy leadership, the vestry fully exercised the authority granted to it by canon law to act in the best interests of the congregation. Trinity has continued to wrestle with the rector-vestry relationship, says one former warden, who believes that "leadership has to be on two sides of the table."

The events surrounding Miner's resignation recall an incident in Trinity's more remote past. In 1842 the congregation called a parish meeting and demanded the vestry take action to dismiss an unpopular rector, Charles Fox. In so doing they bypassed the canons of the church, leading one observer to remark in horror that their behavior was more Congregational than Episcopal. Fox's departure was divisive, with some members leaving Trinity to join the newly formed St. Paul's. At that time the congregation was comprised of many wealthy and prominent members who felt entitled to take matters into their own hands. Priests then were minimally trained, poorly paid, and easily manipulable. By the late twentieth century the congregation, a product of the recent lay movement, had grown to expect a voice in parish governance. The clergy, though better trained and more professional than in the nineteenth century, still found themselves answerable to the vestries that hired them and could, with good reason or ill, end the pastoral relationship.

Outreach in the Changing City

*I*n downtown Columbus, the process of development and reclamation begun in the 1970s continued. While old landmarks were torn down, organizations such as Capitol South bought derelict properties for redevelopment. In 1984 the Hyatt on Capitol Square and the Huntington Center opened. That fall Trinity celebrated 150 years on Capitol Square, while the city marked its own sesquicentennial. Downtown was looking up. Two years later One Columbus was built on the site of the former Deshler Hotel, and in 1989 the City Center Mall opened as an upscale shopping mecca.

Countering this downtown renewal was the pull towards the suburbs. Development along Columbus's outerbelt, I-270, surged in the 1990s, and fewer people chose to shop and work downtown. In 1998 Banc One merged with First Chicago and moved its headquarters from downtown Columbus. At the turn of the century vacant office space downtown was at a high of 20 percent. Nearby hotels and conference centers brought temporary visitors, not residents, to the city's core and to churches like Trinity. The new Nationwide Arena and the Brewery districts brought vital nightlife to areas adjacent to downtown. A renovated Statehouse with glorious lawns, however, drew visitors to the center of the city. Still, on a daily basis, fewer people thronged the corner of Third and Broad Streets than at midcentury.

Changes in the urban environment, coupled with diminishing resources, reduced Trinity's outreach programs since the 1980s. A case in point is the demise of Capitol Square Ministries, the organization that provided outreach to the downtown community through The Place to Be restaurant and programs. After Jim Bills's departure in 1979, the energy of Trinity's urban ministry waned. The organization was pulled in two directions, for it sought support from the community and local businesses, but it required a close relationship to Trinity to ensure its tax-exempt status. Though its finances were separate, it owed money to Trinity's endowment, so Trinity had a stake in its success and the clergy and vestry offered guidance.

When The Place to Be began to lose money, Trinity acted to protect its own financial stake. Business had declined sharply since Bank One opened its own cafeteria for employees, and in August of 1987 the vestry decided to close The Place to Be. Phone calls from surprised and saddened patrons and members of the congregation flooded the office. The closing saddled Trinity with $10,000 of unexpected bills, swelling the deficit for that year and necessitating a loan from the endowment. With its primary purpose gone, Capitol Square Ministries effectively fizzled. (Within a year, however, The Place to Be reopened as a private restaurant.)

The other centerpiece of Trinity's urban outreach program, the Open Church, continued to serve the needy from Trinity's office and sanctuary. In the 1980s

"Reaganomics" adversely affected those Americans already living on the edge. According to Peter Strimer, "the face of homelessness changed from single men to families and children." The city was also becoming less hospitable for the needy. In 1983 the Open Shelter was forced out of downtown and into Franklinton by development of the City Center Mall. Trinity's was the last open door for people in need at night. Ann Gilbert spent hours in the church office by day, meeting with clients referred by evening volunteers. She administered the Open Church for 16 years.

There were those in the congregation who favored moving Open Church out of Trinity's sanctuary, citing instances of damage and vandalism. The vestry under senior warden Fred Taylor was vigorously pro-outreach and held firm to the current practice. Brettmann maintained that Trinity suffered less vandalism than other churches precisely because it befriended street people. Trinity's neighbors were not pleased with the ministry either. When the Galleria opened its outdoor eating area adjacent to the church property in 1990, it struck a bargain with Trinity to reroute Open Church clients away from the café in exchange for access to the parking garage on Sunday. Trinity accepted the deal, for the lack of accessible parking had long been a perceived obstacle to growth. During renovations to the nave in 1993, scaffolding made it unsafe to host the Open Church. It was relocated to the Faith Family Center on East Long Street, the beginning of a collaboration with other homeless agencies. The symbolic value of having Open Church at Trinity's building had been significant, but the new collaboration promised to improve services to the homeless.

At a time when social activism was on the wane at Trinity, Peter Strimer kept the flame burning. He saw his clerical duties in the larger context of being a community organizer. Strimer was the administrator of the Diocesan Hunger Network and a strong advocate for the Open Church. He organized a demonstration that resulted in Gov. Richard Celeste restoring welfare benefits during Christmas week of 1983. He was proud that the Council for the Study of Ethics and Economics began under Brettmann's initiative, as did the diocesan Peace Initiatives Network.

Smaller lay-led outreach programs also date from this time. In 1981 the service commission began setting a food basket in the narthex on Sunday morning and presenting it at the offertory, a visual reminder of the congregation's duty to feed the hungry in their midst. In 1983 the congregation volunteered to cook and serve dinner once a month at His Place, located at St. John's in Franklinton. This revived a relationship with the former mission congregation. A ministry that brought clothing, sundries, and prayer services to prison inmates was undertaken by Nick Sanborn and carried on by Dick Green. It eventually foundered because prison officials were uncooperative.

Sarita and Sidra Dhiraprasiddhi join Peggy Short and Cynthia Callaghan in serving dinner at St. John's Episcopal Church on Town Street.

Though Jim Miner affirmed Trinity's identity as an urban parish, he was not a social activist. For instance, in 1986 he favored a quiet, prayerful response to the evils of apartheid in South Africa, while others on the vestry called for a more public manifestation such as a march. He had little desire to be a visible public leader like many of Trinity's past rectors, though he was respected by those in the downtown community, especially other religious leaders. He felt that Capitol Square Ministries and the Open Church had served a good purpose and run their natural course. Miner was mindful of Trinity's wider obligations, but he was also responsive to the new emphasis on the parish's internal life, the need to recharge its spiritual resources.

The Changing Parish

The downtown location that calls Trinity to urban ministry proves a challenge when it comes to building a community out of the diverse and far-flung members of the Sunday congregation. People have always had to be highly motivated even to attend Sunday worship at Trinity. Moreover, busy family schedules, parking issues, and the perception that downtown is unsafe have made midweek events at Trinity very sparsely attended. One attempt to unify the congregation was the creation of a neighborhood network in the early 1980s. The city was divided into six neighborhoods with a chair and callers in each area responsible for visiting newcomers or members in need. Under Peggy Short's leadership the system operated effectively for several years. Personal contact, especially with the minister, was recognized as a key to drawing and keeping members, so calling on newcomers was made a priority. "Congregational development" was a buzzword of the 1980s.

Social changes in the last 30 years have had a marked impact on parish life. Women's increasing participation in the paid workforce reduced their ability to provide the supportive work in the church. In 1978 Bobbie Schneider resigned after 14 years as director of Christian education, becoming one of an increasing number of women entering the work force full-time. Marge Schultz, who succeeded Schneider as director, left in 1981 to pursue seminary training, an option not open to women a decade earlier. Trinity came to rely increasingly on lay volunteers to administer the church school. The education budget shrank when cost-cutting became necessary. A small Sunday school program in turn discouraged the attendance of families at worship. In 1982, in order to increase Sunday school attendance, children in grades 1-6 began meeting during the 10:30 service, joining the congregation for Communion. The immediate result was a two-to-threefold increase in attendance. At the time of Miner's arrival in 1986, there were fewer than 40 children between the ages of three and 17. Of the four high-schoolers, only two were active. The adult class was the most viable element of Trinity's educational program.

Church school children present a Christmas pageant in the late 1980s.
The Rev. John Simons, associate rector, observes at right.

Volunteer efforts continued though on an ever-smaller scale. A committed group of volunteers assisted with The Place to Be restaurant and the window shop until the latter closed in 1988. Women (and some men) continued to serve on the altar guild, work which could be performed on Sunday mornings. St. Margaret's Guild also continued its quiet ministry but, as one member pointed out recently, there was less to do, for the elderly tended to me more healthy and independent than in the past. Ministry to the deaf community resumed with a monthly service led by Deacon Sherm Everett at the residential facility in Westerville.

The role of clergy wives also changed. Betty Nichols was the last rector's wife to take on the job of supporting her husband's ministry in addition to homemaking and child-rearing. The wives of Walter Taylor (Mary) and Bill Brettmann (Lee) pursued careers as teachers in addition to raising families. Betsey Miner worked as a chemist while she and Jim raised two sons. These women supported their husbands' ministries to the extent that they were able, hosting parish gatherings at their homes. In 2003 the rector's wife, whose children are grown, has a career as a physician's assistant that limits the amount of time she spends in Columbus. The model of the rector's wife as the domestic center of the parish around whom women's ministries and volunteer work coalesce is as outdated as a 1950s fashion magazine.

The church is simply no longer at the center of its members' lives providing numerous occasions for worship, service, education, and fellowship. Groups such as the Brotherhood of St. Andrew, Foyers groups, and neighborhood potlucks have had brief lives in an effort to foster fellowship. The Shrove Tuesday potluck, the Maundy Thursday supper, and the Pentecost reception, traditions of 1950s parish life, continued through the 1980s. In 2003 parish social life centers around coffee hour and special events: luncheon or dinner for the annual meeting, Easter brunch, the church school picnic, a fall brunch, and newcomers potlucks. Trinity has become a Sunday-only parish where worship, education, and fellowship share the same morning slate.

Stewardship in a Time of Diminishing Resources

*D*espite efforts to revitalize the parish, expectations of growth were continually disappointed. Turn-out for many parish social events was low. Total annual attendance at services fell over 40 percent between 1975 and 1982. The number of communicants dropped from 922 in 1976 to 602 in 1984. Ten years later Trinity had upwards of 400 active communicants, a number that stabilized in the late 1990s.

Stewardship of increasingly scarce resources has been a major challenge to the congregation since 1980. The decline in membership made financial issues paramount, for fewer members were left to shoulder the burdens even as the needs of the aging building grew. Throughout the 1980s the parish operated on deficit budgets, and holding expenses down was a priority. A good year was when the deficit was lower than projected. On the other hand, a successful 1984 campaign finally retired the debt incurred for the 1970s renovations. For every dollar Trinity raised for its endowment, the diocese retired a dollar of Trinity's debt up to the balance of $50,000. By 1985 Trinity was out of debt.

Trinity's endowment has been a mixed blessing. It provides vital income but creates a perception that Trinity is rich, hindering efforts to increase pledging. (For that reason, in the past the clergy and vestry kept the congregation in a state of ignorance about the endowment.) In the 1980s the vestry began to draw regularly on the endowment to cover operating expenses, against the advice of many, including the rector and senior warden Rufus Short. Yet careful stewardship was not neglected. Helen Bierly, the new junior warden in 1981, urged the reinvestment of endowment income, much of which had been used to relieve operating deficits. Bierly also took it upon herself to instruct the congregation in methods of planned giving. In response to pressure to divest in companies that did business in South Africa or promoted tobacco addiction, the vestry formulated a policy for socially responsible investment. In 1995 the entire endowment was reinvested according to a policy of total return.

Even as Trinity struggled to meet its budget, gifts kept the endowment growing. In 1975 Carlton Dargusch Sr. gave Trinity 574 acres of land in Perry County. Unable to develop it as a religious retreat and nature preserve as Dargusch intended, Trinity sold the land in 1994 and placed the proceeds in the endowment. In 1993, boosted by a recent $100,000 gift from the Clyde Martin estate, the value of the endowment reached $1 million. By

A glazier with Franklin Art Glass repairs a leaded stained glass window. The needs of the aging church building placed a growing financial burden on the congregation.

the turn of the century, after a decade of unprecedented economic growth, its worth was $1.75 million. Gifts in memory of Helen Bierly Sandbo and Edna Krieger also enhanced its worth. In the late 1990s the rector reminded the vestry that the endowment was hardly vast, given Trinity's size and age and considering that there were some in the congregation whose net worth exceeded that of the church's endowment.

Income from the growing endowment helped Trinity meet its operating expenses even as pledge units declined from a high of 285 in 1977 to 154 in 1995. The percentage of pledge income to total income shrank from around 75 percent in the 1970s to between 40 and 50 percent in the 1990s. In the 1990s, thanks to a bullish stock market and judicious vestry leadership, Trinity maintained its good financial health. While pledge income declined, investment and rental income made up the difference. Still, programming and funding for a second clergy position depended on an increase in membership and pledging units.

Trinity and the Diocese

Trinity's relationship to the diocese has often hinged on financial issues. In 1985 interim Robert Hansel urged the congregation to propose Trinity as a pro-cathedral. The change in status would bring additional financial resources to Trinity while allowing it to maintain its autonomy. One compelling point was that Trinity already performed many of the functions of a pro-cathedral with its visible outreach programs. The Rt. Rev. William G. Black, then bishop of southern Ohio, considered the proposal but opted instead to establish a diocesan education center on the fourth floor of the parish house. Its purpose was to train lay leaders and those dealing with social issues of hunger and homelessness. Thus the proximity to the Statehouse was an asset. The terms of the lease agreement wiped clean the slate with regard to Trinity's diocesan assessments, which had been reduced as the parish struggled with indebtedness.

Gratitude and appreciation of the diocesan presence were not universal, however. Some vestry members wanted the diocese to pay top dollar for the space, not to be treated as a preferred tenant. They also questioned how the diocese calculated parish assessments and wanted the diocese to justify its budget to parishes. Those who wanted to take care of parish needs first disagreed with those who saw supporting the diocese as an important part of Trinity's wider mission. In 1990 the diocese adopted a new method of calculating a parish's mission share. Finding Trinity's assessment increased by 28 percent, the vestry filed an appeal and succeeded in negotiating the amount. The diocesan mission share has become one of the last financial obligations Trinity attends to, often grudgingly, during its fiscal year.

Trinity's feelings toward the diocese affected its response to the 1994 Vision Covenant, a diocesan campaign to fund congregational development, outreach, and improvements to Procter camp. The congregation had been wrung dry from its own recent capital funds drive for church renovations, with some pledges still outstanding. Trinity also found itself unable to fund a second clergy position. Miner urged participation in the diocesan campaign, pointing out how much Trinity had received in direct diocesan support. As many parishioners perceived Trinity to be wealthy because of its endowment, Trinity in turn perceived the diocese to be wealthy because of the William Cooper Procter Fund. In the end the vestry did not support the campaign.

In reality most members of the congregation were unaffected by the diocesan presence in the parish house. A survey conducted in 2000 revealed that half of the congregation did not consider Trinity's relation to the diocese and the bishop to be important or had no opinion on the matter. One former parishioner who grew up at Trinity and has been active at all levels in the Episcopal Church said that the diocese has been too quiet and not provided the kind of leadership people would recognize. In the view of a former rector, the bishops have not made the people feel that their contributions support actual field missionary work, not just the diocesan machinery.

Matters of finance and governance aside, most parishioners deeply respected their bishops. The Rt. Rev. Herbert Thompson Jr., elected bishop in 1988, brought a prophetic vision of reconciliation, liberation, healing, and service to the diocese. With the new millennium, he identified areas of strategic planning, including nurturing new congregations and ministry to youth. On his episcopal visits to Trinity, Thompson, raised in a high church tradition, brought ceremony and an aura of holiness while conveying prayerfulness and deep humility. The congregation also welcomed the genial presence of Suffragan Bishop Kenneth Price. Consecrated in October of 1994, Price maintained an office in the parish house and was a frequent visitor and preacher at Trinity.

Capital Fund Drive

*I*n 1990 a diligent *Dispatch* reporter noted a large crack on the south side of the church and called the city's building inspectors. Although the crack itself was not significant and Trinity was in no imminent danger of collapse, the state of

the building was becoming an embarrassment. An occasional chunk of mortar or piece of stonework fell to the pavement, endangering passers-by. The bell tower needed repairs and drainage problems were persistent. Decades of grime darkened Trinity's facade. Inside, water seeped through the plaster, leaving blisters and dark stains.

The time was auspicious for a capital funds drive for building renovations. Pledging was up to 196 units and the economy was good. A feasibility study showed that the community regarded Trinity's good works and historic presence highly and the congregation respected Miner as a unifying force. Then an assessment by the architectural firm Schooley Caldwell revealed the need for nearly $1 million worth of renovations. Jerry Sellman, who chaired the campaign, doubted at first whether Trinity could raise more than $350,000, a mere drop in the bucket. Pam Beck of Ward, Dreshman and Reinhardt worked with the steering committee to determine that a goal of $800,000 was possible. When the matter was put to the parish and they were told that their vote was considered a promise to pledge, the support was nearly unanimous.

The campaign kicked off in September of 1991, taking as its theme "Linked with the Past, Committed to the Future." The first phase involved raising pledges from the congregation, friends, and other supporters. By January, 202 pledges totaled $571,000. More than a third of that amount came from 12 pledges, showing that Trinity still had a small base of wealthy donors. The second phase, led by Dick Oman, targeted the community. The response was less hearty than expected, for corporate Columbus was hesitant as always to contribute to a religious organization. Still, contributions came from the Jeffrey Fund, Society Bank, the Huntington Bank, the Wolfe Fund, Harry C. Moores Foundation, and the Reinberger Foundation. By the end of 1994 the total contributions exceeded $900,000, surpassing all expectations. The Schooley Caldwell firm was selected to coordinate the renovations.

In fall of 1992 the exterior work began. Up to 85 percent of the mortar needed to be replaced. A dark gray crust of carbon, smoke, and dirt was gently cleaned with water pressure, restoring the light tan color of the original sandstone. Finials worn down by weather and pollution were replaced. Roof work, tuckpointing, and window repair brought the total for exterior projects to about $600,000. The interior was replastered and painted, the lighting improved, and a new hot-water heating system replaced the clanky steam heat. A building oversight committee under Bill Form coordinated all the work. Jim Bliek and Barbara Stoddard oversaw

A broken pinnacle atop the tower before the 1992-93 cleaning and restoration of the church exterior.

the planting of a new garden and landscaping. During renovations to the sanctuary the congregation worshipped in The Place to Be, where many found the informal, even cozy, atmosphere a boon to community. The congregation returned to the renovated sanctuary in time for Easter of 1994.

The processional enters the church for the 1994 service marking Trinity's 125th year at the corner of Third and Broad Streets and the completion of renovations.

That fall Trinity celebrated the completion of its renovations with a service that was a symbolic rededication of the church to the city. Honored were several public figures including Chief Justice Thomas Moyer of the Ohio Supreme Court, state and city council representatives, and Bishops Thompson, Price, and Black. This event continued Trinity's historic role as the "site for services of public proclamation and commemoration," Miner wrote.[6] Honoring his sabbatical, however, he did not attend the service. A reception in the Statehouse atrium followed the ceremony. The event also coincided with Trinity's 125th year on the corner of Broad and Third

Streets. A nostalgic backward look was provided to those who bought reprints of
A Book of Favorite Recipes Tried and True, a cookbook originally compiled by the ladies
of the parish in 1911.

Not all of the improvements suggested by Schooley Caldwell were implemented.
For example, not enough funds remained to illuminate the window over the reredos, a dark blur since the parish house addition blocked the light. In the fall of 1994
one panel was illuminated. This was enough to inspire the congregation. People dug
deeper into their pockets, contributing an additional $16,000 so that soon the
entire window glowed in all its pre-Raphaelite glory. Upon entering Trinity one's
eye was immediately drawn to the resplendent sanctuary. The importance of this
window to the congregation suggested not only pride in the historical fabric of the
building, but a priority placed on the site of sacramental worship.

Worship: What Trinity Does Best

*T*he last 25 years have seen Trinity's evolution in response to a multitude of
changes. Formerly a leader congregation, Trinity was at the forefront of the
community with its liturgy and its outreach and education programs. In recent
years, with fewer members and resources, Trinity began to capitalize on its major
strength, worship. The "house of worship" model best fit the congregation.[7] That is,
Trinity primarily provided the Sunday congregation with worship experiences and
helped them commemorate significant life events. Trinity's rectors facilitated this
shift. Jim Miner saw his primary job as "the ministry of Word and Sacrament," he
told the vestry shortly after his arrival. His strength was in liturgy that proclaimed
Trinity's values.

By the year 2000 public witness occurred primarily through Sunday liturgy and
special services, among them the celebration of Martin Luther King Day, the traditional Good Friday observances, and worship for participants in the annual
Columbus Marathon. A prime example of liturgy as public ministry was manifested
in the aftermath of the tragedy of September 11, 2001, when 800 people, few of
whom were congregation members or even Episcopalians, thronged the church on
the national day of prayer. On the first anniversary of the terrorist attacks, hundreds
visited the church throughout the day for prayer, and volunteers tolled the bells
with solemn regularity from morning until late afternoon.

As they have for generations, Trinity's members continued to value traditional
worship styles and music, a survey taken in 2000 revealed. After the period of liturgical innovation surrounding the introduction of the 1979 Prayer Book, people

Volunteers toll the chimes at ten-second intervals on the first anniversary of the September 11, 2001, terrorist attacks. Each toll of the bell symbolized one of the victims of the attacks.

became less willing to seek new ideas for worship. The early 1980s were still a time of transition with some members embracing the new Rite II liturgy and wanting Communion every week, while others favored morning prayer on three Sundays as in the past. To satisfy as many in the congregation as possible, it became standard practice to celebrate Rite II Eucharist on three Sundays, with morning prayer on the fourth Sunday. Rite I Eucharist was occasionally offered. This compromise and flexibility signalled Trinity's broad churchmanship, favoring neither Anglo-Catholic ritualism or low church forms of piety.

From the days of its boy choir and the unforgettable Karl "Pop" Hoenig, music has been central to worship and outreach at Trinity. In 1978 Wilbur Held retired from his position as Trinity's organist, which he had held since 1949. That fall William Haller was hired as organist and choirmaster. Replacing Wilbur Held was

The choir sings from the front of the nave during a 2003 service. Kevin Wines directs and Brad Blackham plays Trinity's new grand piano.

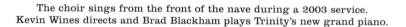

a daunting task even for this experienced church organist and Capital University professor. While Held had been able to rely on a number of volunteers, Haller found himself hiring more professional singers, and the music budget expanded accordingly. The choir under Haller offered Hayden's *Seven Last Words* on Good Friday and Poulenc's *Gloria* in May of 1979. The more modern liturgical offerings, however, were unpopular with some members of the congregation. In 1981 Haller accepted a faculty position in West Virginia, and though he wanted to continue to commute to Trinity, the vestry decided to open the position.

William Osborne, professor of music at Denison University, was hired to succeed Haller. The vestry liked his approach of encouraging more congregational participation in the singing. Yet shortly after being hired, he insisted on a 30 percent increase in the music budget in part to hire singers. The increase was implemented at a time when costs were being trimmed in every area. During Osborne's tenure many felt the music was the highlight of the liturgy. However, the choir felt unappreciated. AA meetings held in the choir room left residual smoke that affected the singers' voices. Osborne and Miner also clashed, and Osborne resigned in 1990. A number of singers also departed, forming a choir in exile at St. Paul's.

The period since 1980 saw the increasing professionalization of the choir, with more paid singers than congregation members. Barry Bowen, a native of Australia, was hired in 1994 with the hope that he would involve more parishioners in the choir and develop a children's choir. He was also eager to promote music as an outreach ministry to the city with concerts in the garden and organ recitals. After Bowen's departure Ron McCarty became organist and music director, and Kevin Wines, formerly interim choir director who had sung opera around the country, returned as choral conductor. This team produced consistently inspiring music for worship. Though the congregation favored traditional liturgical music, classical music, and hymns, the *Lift Every Voice and Sing* hymnal, featuring spirituals, was recently introduced to Sunday worshippers.

Music has always been Trinity's forte, and its prominence has been reflected in budgets. Nearly one-tenth of the annual budget is earmarked for the music program. Few have challenged the priority accorded to music, for it has not only filled a deep need within the congregation, but it has also enhanced Trinity's public reputation. The acquisition in 2000 of a grand piano, a gift in memory of long-time member Ruth Pyne, positioned Trinity to become a concert venue. Jazz concerts in the garden enlivened the downtown scene and brought crowds to the corner of Third and Broad. The congregation has agreed that excellence in music is essential to Trinity's continued vitality and growth.

Public Ministry in the Burnett Years

After the departure of Jim Miner, Trinity began the process of healing and a search for a new rector under the Rev. Canon Domenic Ciannella. Though participation declined, in the end only a few parishioners left Trinity permanently. Ciannella's great cheer, optimism, and faith consoled the congregation. Under his kind exterior, however, Ciannella was an authoritarian who took control of the vestry and the parish at a time when firmness was needed.

The interim period was also a trying time for the congregation, which chafed at the slowness of the search process. It began in the fall of 1996 with parishioners meeting in focus groups to define their needs. Not surprisingly the rector profile was partly a reaction to recent events in the parish. It called for a rector with "organizational and management skills" who was willing to be a "dynamic leader." Preaching and pastoral skills were important, but more emphasis was placed on articulating a vision for Trinity as a downtown parish and leading the parish to embrace it. The rector was also expected to be active in increasing membership and achieving financial stability. As usual it was a lot to ask for. While Bishop Black had not guided Trinity's choice of candidates in the 1985 search, this time Bishop Thompson took a firm hand in the process. After Trinity had screened hundreds of candidates and arrived at a short list, Thompson offered the name of the Rev. Richard Burnett, who soon became the the search committee's choice.

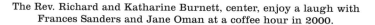

The Rev. Richard and Katharine Burnett, center, enjoy a laugh with
Frances Sanders and Jane Oman at a coffee hour in 2000.

Burnett, a graduate of Yale Divinity School who was ordained in 1983, came to Trinity from St. James in Suffolk County, Long Island, New York. He proved to be the dynamic rector Trinity had sought. Moral and spiritual fervor animated his sermons, which Burnett saw as occasions for instruction. He quickly came to know everyone in the congregation and was able to address them by name at Communion. Many newcomers admitted being drawn to Trinity by the rector's energy, intellect, and personable nature. He demonstrated the ability to tap the talents of congregation members, and he oversaw every area of parish activity. With the vestry he demonstrated an ability to take counsel, but to make his own decisions.

Burnett believed that worship, education, and service should exist in a harmonious and dynamic interrelation, like the Trinity itself. Worship, however, became the central and unifying event of the parish community. For the first time in Trinity's history the priest regularly faced the congregation, standing at a table in the chancel to celebrate the Eucharist. The baptistry was relocated to the center of the nave to emphasize the communal nature of the sacrament. These changes invited the congregation's participation, while other enhancements to the liturgy, such as dance, jazz ensembles, and musical soloists, placed them in the role of appreciative audience.

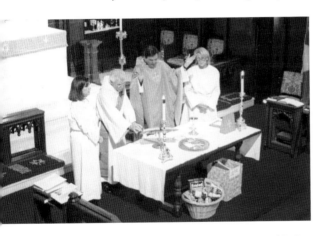

Burnett introduced the communion table to Sunday worship, facing the congregation during the Offertory and the celebration of the Eucharist.

While liturgy was the first outlet for Burnett's energy, outreach was a close second. Pastoral care and education were accorded lower priority. The hiring of the Rev. Mary P. Johnson, who served for two years as associate for Christian nurture, was a recognition of the need for a priest devoted to these concerns, even as scarce resources meant that Trinity was unable to fund a second clergy position in full. Under Burnett then, the emphasis at Trinity began to shift from "inreach" back to outreach.

Burnett saw Trinity as a church with a strong sense of place and deep roots in the downtown community. He embraced Trinity's historic commitment to urban outreach, and his passion for social justice became evident. His voice from the pulpit challenged the congregation to take a stand on issues such as capital punishment, gun control, and hate crimes. In the local media, his voice urged restraint in the

In all seasons, Trinity's red doors are still thrown open every weekday, all day, to the city.

government's relations with Iraq and morality in business and economics. In August of 1999 an ecumenical prayer service emphasizing reconciliation featured the Columbus Gay Men's Choir and the State of Praise gospel singers, representing two groups that have historically been oppressed and excluded. In 2000 Trinity was known not so much for its outreach programs as for the strong moral leadership provided by its clergy. Burnett admitted that the church was no longer a catalyst in society, but affirmed that it could still react and respond to the wider culture.

Unique among downtown churches, Trinity's sanctuary remains open for prayer and meditation. On a typical day in the parish office clergy and staff members handed out food, toiletries, bus tickets, clothing, and counseling to those in need. Jim Bliek, director of public ministries and communications, estimated that probably five times as many people as come to Trinity on Sunday were assisted by its various weekday programs. People headed to the second floor for meetings of Alcoholics Anonymous and AlAnon. At The Place to Be, downtown workers, street people, and Ohio Supreme Court justices rubbed shoulders, and the governor held a staff meetings in an alcove just off the main eating area. The Forum for Faith in the Workplace, an ecumenical group that addressed issues of faith, work, and ethics, held its meeting there. The Trinity Gallery shared the restaurant space. With exhibits of photography, paintings, and sculpture, the gallery affirmed art as an element of public outreach. Burnett circulated among the people as the pastor of all these diverse groups and individuals.

Sociologist Bill Form, surveying the downtown religious scene, concluded that among downtown churches, only Trinity is truly metropolitan. It has developed a separate "second congregation [that] depends on the formal one for its spiritual sustenance and nourishment, contributing little materially. Yet it plays an important role for the formal congregation in helping it realize its religious commitment of selfless giving," wrote Form.[8] Form provided a different standard—not pledge units or membership numbers—by which to measure Trinity's success.

The Congregation in 2000[9]

The Sunday congregation at Trinity in 2000 had at least one thing in common with those who chose Trinity a century earlier—they came from all areas of the city. In the twenty-first century, people come to Trinity no longer to rub shoulders with the well-to-do or because downtown is a prestigious place, but because they are committed to the values that Trinity represents. One of these is diversity. About a tenth of members are of non-European heritage. Several are gay. As a whole the congregation holds liberal views on issues from abortion to the ordination of gays and lesbians, though older members tend to be more conservative. Those who come to Trinity value its commitment to urban outreach, although less than half directly participate in community service. They also value the historical richness of Trinity reflected in its building and in its worship.

In contrast to the weekday congregation, Trinity's Sunday congregation is relatively privileged. According to a survey taken in 2000, 80 percent had at least a

Long-time members Deacon Sherm Everett, Jody and Bob Park, and Joan Everett at a recent outdoor luncheon.

bachelor's degree, and two in five had a post-graduate degree. A large number of professionals and white-collar workers make up the congregation. Socio-economically Trinity's congregation is middle-class to upper-middle-class. It is a graying group with half older than 55. In recent years, however, more people in their twenties and thirties have joined. Many of them are new to congregational life altogether. One long-time member described Trinity's congregation as transitional and highly mobile, mirroring the changing times and the shifting economic picture.

The feminization of church life was a concern to leaders in earlier generations. Women have continued to hold a slight majority in the congregation; in 2000, 89 percent were regular worshippers versus 77 percent of men. More unmarried women than unmarried men attended. More women than men reported strong spiritual and emotional responses to the worship service. While the great gap between men's and women's participation has narrowed to a fraction of what it was in the nineteenth century, still more women than men participated in worship and parish life. No longer behind the scenes, women have become visible with men in the public arena of church life as priests, acolytes, lay readers, ushers, and vestry members. Trinity has not, however, called a female rector.

Whether young or old, members of Trinity continued to cherish the traditional Anglican worship and music, although over half of the adults, the rector estimated in 2003, were not cradle Episcopalians. Individual choice, not habit or tradition,

Bishop Kenneth Price lays hands on a young confirmand. Worship and the sacramental life receive strong emphasis at Trinity.

Though receptive to new forms of music and worship, the congregation maintains the traditional practice of kneeling for Communion.

brought them to Trinity. For others, coming to Trinity has been a family tradition that dates back several generations. Bill Dargusch's parents and grandparents were leaders at Trinity. Some members have formed a strong attachment to Trinity but wonder whether their children will feel the same sense of connection. Marilyn Sesler was raised at Trinity, but she switched to a different Episcopal congregation while her mother, Doris Graham, remained active at Trinity. While still loving Trinity, Sesler confessed that she did not have her mother's loyalty to one particular parish.

Congregations can no longer count on a rich legacy built on generations of families. Changing habits of church attendance are in part responsible. A hundred and fifty years ago the rector castigated his parishioners for not coming to both Sunday services. In the twentieth century other leisure activities began to crowd out Sunday churchgoing. By 2000 about half of Trinity's members reported worshipping on a weekly basis.

There have always been those who came to Trinity because they did not want to be a part of neighborhood parish life, preferring to worship in relative anonymity. Sherm Everett and his wife Joan admitted to being among this group when they first came to Trinity in 1988. Gradually they were drawn deeply into parish life, Joan as an office volunteer and director of the altar guild, Sherm as a deacon. It was Trinity's clergy and laypeople who reached out to them, offering opportunities for fellowship and service.

Many people continue to feel strong ties to Trinity even though they have not attended in years. Jack Chester, a former state legislator and fourth-generation lawyer in his family's firm, identified himself a downtown person who was "raised at the corner of Broad and High." For him Trinity has always been an integral part of downtown, an important symbol. "I'm not a religious person, but I'm mindful of the value of churches in our culture," he stated.

The continued vitality of Trinity depends on the vitality of downtown as a place where people live and work, shop, and play. The push for downtown living gained a boost from the upscale apartment and condominium development, Miranova. Because of higher building costs in the center of the city, affordable residential housing has not been available. But in 2002 Mayor Michael Coleman called for a ten-year plan to revitalize downtown with 10,000 new housing units and improved recreational and retail spaces. Three center-city residential developments were soon underway, together with a plan to develop the site of the former Jeffrey Mining Company just north of downtown. These developments, which will enable people to live, work, and worship in the center city, will also provide opportunities for evangelism and growth at Trinity.

An Old Challenge
for the New Millennium

On March 7, 1999, a special service celebrated those whose ministry was nurtured at Trinity in the post-World War II years. The preacher was Gordon Price, Robert Fay's assistant from 1947–1950. Price took as his theme the ever-present tension of the church and the world. Christians, he said, must always remember that while "we are citizens of this planet by our birth…we are citizens of God's Kingdom by our baptism." Acknowledging the profound changes of the past half-century, Price admitted "we are minorities in a pagan world." On the threshold of a new century he called his listeners "to enter deeply into the beauty and wonder of worship and prayer and bring a sense of quietness and holiness (wholeness) back into the noise and confusion of this world."[10] Price articulated the ageless dynamic of congregational life: it nurtures the souls of people, strengthening them for work in the world. The balance remains essential to keep religion from being either private and self-satisfying or public witness of hollow men and women.

Rugged individualism and the commitment to community are the two traditions that shape American moral and civic life, according to Robert Bellah, author of *Habits of the Heart*. Today the religious congregation remains a place where people find traditional community and spiritual meaning in the midst of the secular world ruled by reason and the values of individualism and economic gain. An historically significant congregation like that of Trinity can serve as a community of memory, offering a rich language of tradition and commitment.[11] Seen another way, individualism and communalism are inseparable, for social attachments, which are made in places like religious congregations, form our identity as individuals.[12] Those who worship at Trinity have been profoundly shaped by their contact with the holy and their integration into a historic community of like believers. They have shared the promise of individual salvation and the hope of transforming the world into a communion of love.

The realization of Trinity's historic ministry should awaken long-time members, newcomers, and casual visitors to stronger faith, a new spirit of evangelism, and a renewed sense of community rooted in past generations and committed to future ones. For nearly two centuries the spirit of Trinity, embodied in her buildings and in her people, has hovered over downtown Columbus bearing the Gospel message. She has brooded in the bell tower, alighted on the Capitol and on downtown highrises, and circled the city's remotest neighborhoods. Trinity has long embraced the poor, the homeless, and the suffering within the sanctuary of her red doors flung wide and within the open hearts of her faithful. The continuation of this ministry of Word and Sacrament is the deep desire of all who worship there.

Notes

[1] Bill Form has undertaken exhaustive study, based on footwork, visitation, and phone calls to gauge the relative strength and characteristics of over twenty churches. I am much indebted to his work.
[2] This is one theme of Roof and McKinney, *American Mainline Religion*.
[3] From a congregational survey and parish profile, 1978. Information on this period is drawn from interviews with Bill Brettmann, Peter Strimer, Jim Bills, and includes quotations from vestry minutes. Others interviewed for this chapter include Jack Chester, Bob Hansel, Lori Dhiraprashiddhi, Marilyn Sesler, Sherm Everett, Jim Blick, Rufus and Peggy Short, Fred and Joan Taylor, Ann Gast, Richard A. Burnett, Bill Dargusch, Claudia Lauer, and Jim Miner.
[4] The Chimes, September 14 and 27, 1984.
[5] The Chimes, February 28, 1985.

[6] "Church to reaffirm Downtown service," *Columbus Dispatch*, September 17, 1994.

[7] Becker, "Congregations in Conflict."

[8] William Form, "The Central City Metropolitan Church: Ecological Opportunity and Outreach Response," unpublished essay, quoted with permission.

[9] In this section are summarized results of a survey administered to the congregation in 2000, together with material gathered in interviews.

[10] Gordon Price, Sermon delivered at Trinity Episcopal Church, March 7, 1999.

[11] Wade Clark Roof, 240-242. Roof follows Robert Bellah, *Habits of the Heart*, in seeing rugged individualism and the commitment to community as the two traditions that shape American moral and civic life.

[12] Nancy T. Ammerman, *Congregation and Community: A Study of Congregational Change* (New Brunswick: Rutgers University Press, 1997), 353.

**"Seeking Faith, Hope, Love here."
Worshippers exit Trinity on a
summer Sunday in 2003.**

Index

Photo Credits

Photographs were used by permission of the following organizations and individuals:

The Columbus Dispatch
    pages 126,193,195,235,242(top)
Columbus Metropolitan Library (Columbus Circulating Visuals Collection)
    pages 5,15,16,25,26,29,52-53,54,55,58,67,75,78,80,88,97,98,108-109,
    116-117,123,131,140,143,145,169
Grandview Heights Public Library (*Columbus Citizen Journal* Photo Collection)
    pages 2,161,206-207,221
The Kelton House Museum and Gardens
    page 149
The Ohio Historical Society
    Front cover and pages 37,40,106,115,135

****

James Bliek page 121
Ann Chauncey for the estate of Henry Chauncey pages 151,152
Robert Griffith page 180
Betsey Kausch pages 77,181
Sally Larrimer page 98
Count Alexander zu Lynar-Redern page 88
Molly Morris page 118
David Platt pages 71,89
Gordon Price page 165
Peter Strimer page 224

****

Color photographs on pages 183-188 by David Barker
Photograph by Jack Kausch (courtesy of Betsey Kausch)
    page 181
Photographs by Lisa Klein
    pages xxi,xxii,6,65,102,129,245,249,252
Photographs by Doug Rose
    pages xiv,248

****

All other pictures are from the archives of Trinity Episcopal Church

About the Author

Lisa M. Klein received her Ph.D. in literature from Indiana University. For nine years, she taught English literature and writing at the Ohio State University. She received several grants and awards for her scholarship, including a National Endowment for the Humanities fellowship in 1997–98.

Klein has published a book-length work of literary criticism and several articles on Renaissance poetry and early modern women's history and culture.

The opportunity to work on an unexplored topic of local history and thereby contribute something original to posterity led her to accept the offer to write Trinity's history. Her prior academic work concerned Protestant themes in literature and she has an undergraduate major in Theology from Marquette University. She has been a member of Trinity's congregation since 1989 and recently completed a 3-year term on the vestry.

Trinity's history project, under Klein's guidance, has received grants from the Ohio Humanities Council and the Historical Society of the Episcopal Church.

Klein lives with her husband and two sons in Columbus, Ohio. She is currently working on a Shakespeare-themed novel for young adult readers.

Signed April 5th 1869   Signed March 30.187_

M. G. Mitchell
W Dennison
Wm ~~A. H.~~ Herd (Dup)
Walston Failing
Wm. A. Platt
Robt S Smith
Walter C Brown
M. J. Gwynne
U. F. Jones
C. R. Lane
C. P. Matthews
Annie. E. Doddridge
Mrs J S Ridgeway
Wm Joel Buttles
J. A. Platt
N. J. McCann
Emily Creed
O. K. Jones
Francis Collins
John Hromack (Dup) (fee 1860)
Mrs J. Carter
Saml McClelland (Dup)

Signed. March 30. 1870.
~~Rev. ~~~~~~.~~
S. M. Smith
Hiro Comstock
A. Barringer.

J. E. Neil
Jno Hutcheson.
B. F. Wheeler
Geo W Gleason.
Arthur H. Smythe
John A. Rea
B. Gwynne
Sam'l Thompson
James L. Bates
Chas Wallcutt
W J Savage
Mrs J. C Broadrick
Rev. L. C. Howard
P. L. Andrews
E. L. Hinman

Eastes Monday. april 18. 1870
Mrs. W. B. Hubbard
Mrs Sarah K Geiger
Mrs Alfred Kelley
Mrs Lydia Griffith
Mrs Caroline C. Hulburd
S. A. Owen

Augustus N. Whiting   Nov. 18. 187_
Charles E. Burr Jr Apr 1st
Mrs. Mary W. Hutcheson
Wm W Rhoads